More Words from Spirit

HUNDREDS OF QUESTIONS ANSWERED DIRECTLY
BY A POWERFUL TEACHING SPIRIT ENTITY.

**Aleisha
&
Ishamcvan**

BALBOA.
PRESS

A DIVISION OF HAY HOUSE

Balboa Press books may be ordered through booksellers or by contacting:

Balboa Press
A Division of Hay House
1663 Liberty Drive
Bloomington, IN 47403
www.balboapress.com
1-(877) 407-4847

Because of the dynamic nature of the Internet, any web addresses or
links contained in this book may have changed since publication and
may no longer be valid. The views expressed in this work are solely those
of the author and do not necessarily reflect the views of the publisher,
and the publisher hereby disclaims any responsibility for them.

The author of this book does not dispense medical advice or prescribe the use
of any technique as a form of treatment for physical, emotional, or medical
problems without the advice of a physician, either directly or indirectly. The
intent of the author is only to offer information of a general nature to help
you in your quest for emotional and spiritual well-being. In the event you use
any of the information in this book for yourself, which is your constitutional
right, the author and the publisher assume no responsibility for your actions.

Printed in the United States of America

ISBN: 978-1-4525-6977-2 (sc)
ISBN: 978-1-4525-6978-9 (e)

Balboa Press rev. date: 05/08/2013

Index

Introduction

I knew it was extremely hot. Not a hot day like we are used to in our summers here, but more an extreme sultry hotness that touched everything around me, at the same time bringing with it a slight breeze which wafted the room with an unexpected lightness of feel as it touched my face. But the heat didn't seem to make me feel uncomfortable or in any way disturb me. I was at peace like nothing I know now. I felt surreal to my surroundings and totally comfortable with everything I encompassed.

The room itself seemed to be made of large unadorned blocks of pinkish yellow sandstone which rose upwards to a high intricately painted ceiling. It was quite large in size with openings along the L- shaped exterior walls. Not windows but more like narrow open view points through the thick, yellow walls. The floor was shiny, maybe marble or travertine. I could see clearly that there was only one actual interior wall and the solitary doorway to the room was covered in a thick fabric drape in what I know now to be a traditional Persian pattern in red, blue and turquoise colours. I knew that the doorway led to the top of a spiral staircase and that our room was the entire top floor space of some type of square tower. But it was the remaining wall of the room that was of the most brilliant of design and magnificent architectural splendour. Although this wall had a surround of more yellow sandstone the centre of this wall was constructed of finely carved open wooden panels in the minaret style which made an open screen. I realised it was from this screen that I felt the breeze.

I lay propped up with very large pillows on what I can only describe as a very wide and long day bed which had its head to this fascinating viewpoint. I seemed mesmerised at looking through the screen, but I was lazy and without purpose. The room I was in was very high up, and there must have been many rooms one on top of another beneath ours. Through the screen I could look down and saw what could only be described as an oversized internal courtyard, or so it appeared. I could see that the actual room I was in was at the top of its wall elevation and widened out immediately below us. Although large in size, the whole structure took up the short width of the rectangle and the other sides had tall, single walls with no windows but did have arches to the outside gardens, I presumed. I wasn't sure if these other walls were the façade of other rooms or attached buildings although I had the impression that the building was one large castle or fortress-like structure which was built around a central courtyard. I could see far below me the vision was what I can only describe as an enormous bathing pool, rectangular in shape, and I guessed it was not at all deep because I could see way down below me that there were ladies who were standing in the vivid blue water which came no higher than their knees. Most wore long gossamer type robes which became wet and clung to their legs like an extension of their beautiful bodies. Other men and women sat around the edge talking and laughing, with some gently playing their feet in the water so that they made ripples which I found quite entrancing. Other people walked around the wide perimeter where there were trees and plants in huge urns and pots on the paved floor. I cannot say that this very large bathing area was inside or outside the main building because it had no roof, but it did have walls with many arched open doorways which seemed to lead to other courtyards. The scale of everything was so vast and although the room I was in appeared to be several stories high from the ground, some of the walls of this pool area extended much higher than where I was lying on the bed. These walls shaded the room I was in so that it was cooler without having any direct sunlight.

My sense of peace and calm was extraordinary. I would have difficultly in describing the fact that I had no fear, no apprehension, and I only felt what I suppose must have been pure contentment and exquisite love.

Across the room the man stood beside one of the small window openings in the wall which looked outwards from the building. He was dressed in long pale robes which reached to his feet. He had nothing on his head but I knew that the long white scarf which fell softly around his shoulders was meant to be an easy sunscreen or disguise should he wish to quickly wrap it around his face to completely cover his black curly hair, leaving only small slits for his eyes. He also had a full black beard which I guessed was part of his culture, and as he turned to watch me from time to time I knew that without words we were one with each other and that each was a greater part of the other. Sometimes he slowly paced the room as if in thought or waiting for something or someone. At other times he returned to the window.

Eventually I rose from the bed and felt the floor cool against my bare feet, my long robe ethereally flowing behind me as I walked slowly across the room to his side. Without any exchange of words he gently stoked my hair as I too looked out of the window to the scene far below and beyond. A beautiful wide river was not too far away and there was a slight bend to the right which went around the building and blocked our view. But to the left I could see that it disappeared way into the distance. The landscape was flat and the only signs of vegetation were high green plants which grew out of the water and along the banks which reminded me of bamboo, although these were much more lush and dark green in comparison. Further off beyond the vegetation on the far side of the river I could see dessert. It was as if this place had been cultivated and beyond there was nothing. The room we were in was high up of course, and the thick walls meant we could see far into the distance without the glare of the sun.

As far as I could tell we were looking at the wide shallow steps which led from the building down to the water. These looked similar in appearance to the sandstone walls of our room but were very weathered blocks, smoothed from the constant kiss of fine sand which had fashioned them into more irregular shapes and sizes. At the bottom of these steps a large open boat with a canopy held up with four corner sticks like poles, bobbed with the ebb and flow of the water as if waiting for us to board. Several men tidied the boat and others waited on the landing platform. They were waiting for something, but I knew not what.

We waited for some time and neither of us spoke at all. He made endearing clicking sounds with his tongue though, which I knew meant nothing more than a loving form of communication. Whatever we were waiting for it was not a threat or frightening in any way. I knew we were soon to depart to somewhere else although it was not yet time.

My life with this man was always changing, going somewhere new and at a moments notice. He showed me many places where we went to together. It seemed as if we were destined to travel endlessly but definitely it seemed I did not crave to be in any place without him. He seemed somewhat older than me, but he was strong and agile and if the age difference meant anything, it was not that he was weaker or very old, but perhaps I was very young and that was all.

Later when we boarded the boat with a full entourage of soldiers and servants I realised that this man was someone very important, a commander of men, a prince, a king. But my relationship with this man intrigued me when I reviewed this scene. Was I a wife, a daughter, a concubine? I doubted any of these descriptions would be accurate. I was definitely a lover because the sensuous feeling, like electricity that passed between us, could not have derived from any platonic relationship.

Apart from this scene it was some time later that I saw this man again. This time I awoke to a vision of endless sand. I appeared to have opened my eyes when I was lying down at ground level and all I could see was dessert with endless sand and many undulating dunes in the distance. However I soon realised that I was in fact in the shelter of a large crude tent- like structure and was lying on soft knotted rugs in reds and blues of traditional eastern designs, with many tapestry-like pillows. I had in fact pulled aside the tent flap with my left hand and was shading my eyes with my right hand across my head as I tried to focus through the swirling sand to a distant movement on the horizon. I had heard the sound before I saw the apparition advancing towards me. At first I was confused by the speed the rider was making and wondered what type of horse could go that fast across such a sandy plane. But quickly through the haze the vision materialised as it came closer and I saw it was a camel, not a horse that was galloping towards me. The rider who appeared moulded to the animal had to be a man from his size, but from my viewpoint he was totally unrecognisable, being covered from head to toes in swathes of fabric which flew out behind him like a series of flags blowing in the wind. As he neared the tent I stood and went outside. The camel appeared not to slow to halt too dramatically but galloped and then trotted ungainly in an arch in front of the tent close to where I was standing. The rider lowered himself completely over one side nearly touching the ground, grabbed me by my waist and swung me up onto the saddle, then holding me tightly to him he pulled his robes around me until I too was totally wrapped in them like a baby in its mother's swaddling blanket. Even though it all happened so quickly it did not seem strange to me at all, so I guessed I had experienced it many times before. I knew it was the same man, not by seeing him or feeling him but by a spiritual sense of awareness that is beyond description. He eased the camel to a leisurely trot and went in a continuous large circle around the encampment of tents, horses and men for some time, each of us clinging to the relief and ecstatic contentment of being with together after what appeared to be some sort of miracle of escape.

When I talked to him many years later and asked about our connection he told me that I travelled with his royal caravan and we were together most of the time. I was his mistress, he said, if I could understand the terminology. He had wives but he and I were the souls that were intertwined. We were the ultimate of all love affairs.

I cannot date these experiences and neither do I know exactly the location. I am told that we travelled in Turkey, but I have to say that it was thousands of years BC and definitely everything occurred in the Middle East somewhere. My immediate reaction was that it was Egypt but I know now that the architecture was not correct for that region. However, many aspects of the palace, for that is what I presume it was, were similar and the river could have been the Nile. I believe it was more to the west, maybe Morocco or Mesopotamia, wherever they may be.

My name was Ali-a'esha and that was what the man called me then and what Ishamcvan calls me now. And the man and the spirit entity who calls himself Ishamcvan I know and recognise as one and the same.

It is strange however, that my early sessions of regression meditation way back in the 1970's, but never erased from my memory, should have rekindled themselves in the mid 1990's with the sudden appearance of this same spirit entity informing me that we should work together, him as my spiritual teacher and me as his scribe. I know I wasn't prepared or ready and it has taken time and a long road of understanding to have progressed to where we are today. Our work, he told me, was to teach the simplicity of understanding about the world of spirituality and how it affects our lives on earth. I wondered then and I do so still today, why there was such a long gap in my early visions of a seemingly past life regression to a connection some twenty years later, with what appears to be the same spirit entity asking me to work with him. He appeared to be a stranger to me. How can that be? If we were one through many lives on earth, as he says we were, would I not automatically recognise him as being one half of my whole? I had many questions. He had many answers. The dialogue began and over time gradually also encompassed many hundreds of other people who asked through me to him a multitude of different questions. They didn't understand many things, so they asked and received the answer direct from this spiritual source.

In our first book, Words from Spirit, the start of our journey together with this work was unveiled and many unedited questions and replies were recorded in separate categories. This, the second book, expands the range of subject matter with a whole new set of criteria and answers.

Ishamcvan says that we should never stop questioning and never stop learning because that is the essence of life; the water of knowledge; the stream of our understanding.

Synopsis of the First Book

Words from Spirit

My teaching guide Ishamcvan first made contact with me in 1998 and through him I have taken a kind of dictation of his words. He told me at the time that I was chosen to do this work because of his belief that I would record and transmit his message with exact clarity and without any changes whatsoever, because it is essential that only true spiritual messages are given to people in our world.

Even though his words were coming fast and furious, and I was writing about 200,000 words a year, it took me a long time to come to terms with the fact that spirit was speaking to me and it was not a fantasy of my own imagination. I asked him one day, why me, and he simply said, "Why not?"

The following is Ishamcvan's summary of basic spirituality as discussed in the first book in answer to various questions presented to him. He said:

I will explain to you first about spirit entities and spirituality. Spirit is nothing more than an essence. It has no form and only takes on a physical body in order for it to pass through your world on earth, on your progression to learn. I will talk later about the lessons. Can we imagine then an essence that has no physical body, yet comes and goes from our spiritual world, our home world, to the next, your world, and back with ease and simplicity that is beyond definition?

Your spirit or soul as it is sometimes called, is you. You are not your body or your mind. You could be a genius in this life and a simpleton in the next, but your spirit is the same. Try to learn to know your spirituality, which is you, not your body or your mind.

A spirit is on its own path yet is part of the essence of spirituality as a whole. But I have said that spirit has no form so how can it be part of a whole? As a molecule of a cloud is in itself alone yet part of the cloud which is a whole.

So let us look at one spirit entity as part of a whole spirit entity and see what we have and what is its purpose.

It is said that God, which we will call the highest spirit, was alone. In order to make observations of itself it had to become more than it was. It had to see itself, which it could not do, as a one. a high cluster of one. So it made hundreds of thousands of spirits as little versions of itself so that these spirits could see spirituality and the high spirit for what it was and what it represented. These tiny spirit entities, which were made at various times, had the irresistible urge to purify and make themselves as good as the highest spirit entity. So each was put on a journey and during its path of discovery it was presented with many tests and challenges which it had to pass to be able to call itself more spiritual and have the full understanding of spirituality itself.

The path of spiritual progression therefore has come from nothing to us as we are today and on and on ad infinitum, way beyond our line of visions, to get to the ultimate, the highest spirit. They are a bit like turtles that are born on a beach a great distance from the water. Their instinct tells them that to survive and grow they have to get to the water. They climb obstacles and go on a very twisted route if necessary, all to get to their goal.

I am not saying at all that we are conscious of the purpose

of our spiritual journey, but we have to understand it in order to progress in a more smooth and accelerated rate.

So, back to you as spirit entities that are at present occupying a body on earth in order to learn lessons, experience many things, and use your own spiritual understanding to tackle problems and deal with people and situations as and when they arise. I will say to you that love is the only key to open your understanding. For if you are without pure love you are without true spirituality. Love should be given unquestionably and without expecting anything in return. If you have true love for all things, including animals and humans then you are, by giving love, connecting with them spirit-to-spirit and not body-to-body. There is a big difference. Your progression as a spirit entity has started from nothing yet is a one in the world of spirituality, which we will call the next plane of existence, or home. That is where we live and we only return to earth to learn or help others to learn if we are chosen to spend a life on earth assisting someone else. For helping others we learn too.

Your spirit has journeyed through bodies such as an amoeba to a shrimp to a bird, a fish, a dolphin, a tiger, an elephant, which is one of the highest levels of spirit in an animal body. From there you progressed to a human. Although you had some spiritual knowledge by then, you were naïve and had to learn. From the next plane of existence, your home and resting place between lives, you can see all things spiritual. You know your path to the higher spirits, what you have already learnt and what you need to learn in order to progress. So from there you chose to have several things to experience in a life on earth. Maybe suffering; maybe humility; maybe jealousy. You also chose your guide, another spirit entity, to be with you throughout that life to give you support and help you, if you ask him, whenever necessary. You are then ready to go to earth. You chose your parents for the lessons they could teach you, or for what you could teach them, and then you are born. Once back on earth you have your spiritual memory taken away from you, although your karma has been set and cannot be altered. Karma is something like a database. It is personal to you and contains all the necessary files about your existence as a spirit entity. Once you have successfully experienced something you get a check mark so to speak, and are therefore richer in your spirituality. You will go through your life, jumping or crawling over the hurdles not realising that these in themselves are making you richer than if you had had a wonderful idyllic life with no problems and no lessons. This theory in itself explains misery and suffering and the strength that some people have in overcoming these in a saintly way. Because of this you must realise that everyone on earth is at different stages of progression, although in their bodies they all look the same. Can you see their spiritual advancement? No, but you can know it instinctively or by progressing in your awareness.

Now let us look at these spirits in bodies in your world who are at different stages of development. How about the people who ride relentlessly over people in general? Dictators? Persecutors? Bullies? Are they spiritually advanced? No, because they do not give love unconditionally to all others. They do not, by their own observation, see things from the other person's perspective. They are new spirits learning or not learning. Then let us take the more spiritually advanced entity who by instinct knows the true understanding of spirituality and projects this in their lives to a high degree. They can be paupers in the gutter or kings on their thrones, it makes no difference who they are, it is their Karma which is important, their spiritual experience. In-between comes everyone else at varying degrees of advancement.

Those of us, still in varying degrees, who know or feel or are being spiritual, want to learn and experience that which is required by spirit. We want to get more points in this test of life, but more so we want to love unconditionally and be spirit more than a body.

For the progression of our spirit and our spiritual record, our karma, there are rules which our higher spirits and their higher spirits set down and these cannot be changed. However, we have free will on earth and can choose whatever we desire.

There is no right or wrong from the spiritual perspective whilst we are living in a body because we have free will, but when we return home, we can see from the spiritual plane that the spiritual laws are necessary. Although we are not penalized for not obeying them, we know we will have to keep experiencing that test from a different angle until we understand the law and behave in a way that we believe is right, not because it is a law. There is a difference.

Along your path through life you meet many people. Some upset you and many give you pure joy. How do you deal with them, you have asked many times, but the answer is always the same, with love. Love thy enemy. Stand back and observe. Say nothing. Do nothing, but understand the spirit of the person and you will understand the position of advancement of that spirit within that person, whether it is learning or failing its test. You must give love to this spirit and not anger. However you may defend your life, for to kill any living thing, including a human or animal, is the most terrible of all things, unless unprovoked they try to kill you.

The world of spirituality is pure and simple. It can be understood by a small child. It is not complicated and if anyone gives it to you under the guise of falseness or power, then this is not to be tolerated.

Let us look at mediums as being ordained by spirit as a link between the spirit world and the world of matter. A true medium is a very advanced spirit. They can connect to the spirit world, easily and without any tools or rituals. They open themselves up and spirit talks through them or gives them a message to pass on. It is easy for them. They have the belief and experience to make it happen, so it does. It is the same with a true healer. They open up and spirit heals. Whether from the other side of the bed, the room or the world, it makes no difference. They do not need to stand on one leg with a crystal pointing to heaven or such like, that would be futile. They open up and spirit comes through. Always only one guide with whom they work for that purpose. A medium will connect to any spirit entity that is powerful enough to get the message through. These are high spirits as people, working at connecting to spirit.

In between the person who flays around being unspiritual and the one who is advanced, there are many other people who are in varying degrees of advancement. The more advanced they are the more they instinctively want to work with spirit. But to want to be more spiritually advanced is not the same as actually being so. For this reason you have on earth many, many people who want to work with spirit and try desperately to make it happen. In order to gain creditability in their chosen subject, they invent things, make complicated what is not and generally are dramatic and outgoing with what they then truly believe to be the truth. It is a fine line to know whether a person is genuine or not as many have the right intentions but not the actual spiritual advancement to make it real. A medium is ordained by spirit to work with spirit. A false medium is not, yet may to the uninitiated seem the same. You have to understand that if anyone tries to tell you a complicated web of intrigue and you become confused or question their words, then this is false. Trust your own instincts. And what of tools, are they necessary? I am always asked this question. Yes in the beginning when you are learning, but no when you have advanced enough to know how to easily connect to spirit, which comes as a really natural thing. Whether connected for words or healing it is the same. You open up to spirit and spirit comes through. Why would you need more? But in the early days I know Aleisha used the Tarot cards as her tool. Spirit turned the cards so she could see with her own eyes what was being said, not mistrusting her own instincts.

There is much to learn. It is easy to understand. I tell you a child of 5 would grasp the concept. Why not test this and know it to be true, for to have faith is the essence of your connection to spirit? With faith we can move mountains and open many doors of many minds. You have the key to all things in the palm of your hand. With that key you have the power to unlock the doors of doubts and leave open the pathways to the true spirit connections.

To be well read about spirituality does not mean that people have read the right things, and to be learned is only to follow the thoughts and ideas of others. To dissect these and then come to a conclusion, whatever way that leads, is the essence of all things. You must learn many things to see the one true thing. I have said to Aleisha many times that whilst first learning my words you should not read those of others, true or false, who write about spirituality. For if you had done so you would have become confused and would not have been able to use your knowledge to understand that which is right and that which is wrong or false. I now have no doubt that Aleisha can see for herself or use her knowledgeable instincts to do these things. So it is not now wrong for her to read the words of others. However, you must know that many people to whom you may speak are not in the same warm position of enlightenment. They take a word here and a word there, or a philosophy that seems logical, and grasp hold of something else because it has a fancy name, at the same time never learning the truth, only what they think makes sense. Only in questioning their so called beliefs will you get them to do so for themselves and see that if there is no logical and simple answer to their query, then the idea is built on sand and is about to collapse before their eyes. With this in mind, I ask Aleisha to speak to them from the heart with my words, from myself or from her own knowledge. We are together in harmony in spirit.

Chapter One

Spiritual Aspects

"In order to see the truth you must learn all things
to fully expand your concepts."

**Please teach me about spirituality; why I am here and
how I can know in which direction to go in my life when I am
at a cross roads not knowing what decision to take.**

Firstly with the laws of spirituality you must remember one
thing. You are a spirit with a body and not a body with a spirit.
Your spirituality is what makes your body alive. Your mind
is not your spirit. Your mind is part of your brain and is only
motivated by your spirit. Your spirit is you, your personality and
your experience through many lives which has brought you to
the stage of development that you are today. The spirit which
you are has reincarnated through many lives in your world and
in each life it has learnt many lessons. If we take the whole path
of your spirituality you will learn that spirit is an entity only.
The advancement of the spirit to reach the highest of planes
of existence is the ultimate. The home of the spirit entity is a
plane of existence called the next plane of existence from you
in your world. From this plane of existence we keep returning

1

to your world for one purpose only, and that is to learn. Before we return to earth we plan our journey and know what lessons we have chosen to learn and experience. As the advancement of the spirit entity is the ultimate, many spirits, not all, choose to have lots of lessons in one life in order to learn and pass the test so to speak and move on more quickly in their road of progress in the spiritual plane of existence. This is why some people on your earth have many problems and others have peaceful and idyllic lives because they chose not to experience lessons and tests.

When planning your return to earth you do so, let us say, stating certain aspects you want to experience, and these aspects cannot be changed however much you pray to the Holy Spirit to do so. That is why some people on your earth who say have asked to experience humility or pain of dying, when experiencing them will ask for help and then cry because help does not come. All other things in your life can be changed if you ask for help from your guides or the Holy Spirit. But when praying you must believe that help will be given. Help will only be given if it is right for the laws of Karma and asked for the right reason. This does not include wealth, power, self esteem or any aspect of hatred or violence.

Love is the essence of all things and all things can be conquered by love. Love is the whole meaning of life and it is the power of the spirit over all things. Love can conquer all vices and violence. You cannot break the spirit of the love of a person. If you cannot connect with a person through pure love, it is not love. Love has no boundaries and it has no questions or distrust. If you distrust, it is not love. Love is given freely without a price. You cannot abuse someone in any way and say you have love for that person. To try and degrade the soul or spirit of another person is not love. Love can come in many forms that is not between a man and a woman who are in love with each other. Love is the power and love is the essence of all things spiritual, whether on the earth plane or the spiritual plane. If there are questions and doubt then there is not pure love.

Next, you must know about your guides. You have several guides who are with you at any one time of the day or night. Your main guide is always with you; the others come and go as you need them. Your main guide was chosen by you before you came back to earth in the life you are in now. Also your guide chose you to be the person from whom they could learn lessons to help make up their own spiritual advancement. You may have connected with this guide before in another life and had a strong bond. Other guides have different purposes. In your case you have your grandmother as one of your guides who is there only to protect, help and be with you for your prayers and guidance. She has chosen to do this work with you. You did not choose her to do so. She does so in this case with pure love. Her own advancement is stopped temporarily whilst she stays with you. She is more helpful to you from the next plane of existence (where her spirit is now) than she would be in your world where she would not be so wise and supportive to you.

You may ask how your guides give you help and why so many things happen in your lives that are upsetting, frustrating and sometimes cruel or hard. Firstly, although some aspects of your life may have been chosen by you, others have not. But you may find that you have crossed the paths of other people and their lessons are having a knock on effect on you personally. Your guides will help if you talk to them. They will give you warnings and feelings by instinct. Sometimes if you feel instinctively that you do not want to do a thing, then it could be your guide warning you that things will not be good if you take that path. They have no other way of talking to you other than by instinct or through meditation, although you may hear the voice of reason if you ask for help or advice on a certain situation. If you choose not to heed their advice and take the path that instinct is telling you not to take, the road will be blocked and you will not progress in the most satisfactory direction. If you listen to your instinct, which is always and always right, then doors will open for you and you will have the correct direction. Your instinct will tell you that it is the right decision and you will feel good within yourself, even if you think this is merely because you did not do what was feeling wrong. Your instinct is your gift of spirituality.

Lastly, for the purpose of reviewing the basic laws of spirituality you must never look to the future, only today. You must never distrust spirit but must believe that all things will be right. Only in trusting spirit will these things be given. It is a hard lesson when we think we are in control of our own destiny, but this is not the case. We are in control of our own spirituality and the way we choose to use it, but our body and its brain cannot control our correct path in life. Spirit connecting with spirituality can do this with trust and belief that this is happening. Nothing else will work. If say your instinct tells you not to take a path but the alternative is grim, it is not for you to question that the other path is not correct. You do not know what is planned along the alternative path.

So you see that you as a spiritual being are inhabiting a body for one purpose only and that is to learn and experience and be richer to progress in your spiritual advancement only. The lessons are hard and many people in your world appear to have wealthy, idyllic lives which are very enviable. It is spiritual wealth that you should desire, not monetary wealth. Money brings power and power is wrong. Money brings envy and discontent and these are wrong too. You can go back to earth in many lives. In some you may have chosen not to have bad lessons and learn, and in others you may have opted out or not given the right answers in life to the tests. But in either case, when you return to the next plane of existence you will not have accumulated any points towards your advancement, so to speak, so the life is wasted. Somehow you must learn not to crave and desire things, but to trust in your own instincts which are your guidelines, and have a strong belief that there is a mass of spiritual love which will see that you have all that you need. This is not necessarily what you think you need, but then you are looking at it from a human perspective; they are looking at it with pure spiritual love, just for you.

One spiritual teacher says that the world has strings, which connect it to the universe and spirituality itself. I thought that if I opened up then there was a clear tunnel, for want of a better word, from here to you? Which is correct?

You are using a simplistic version of the same thing. He is trying to see a scientific version that is all. With faith you open yourselves to spirit, whether it is by a spring rotation, a straight line or a puff of smoke, it happens all the same. You do not need to know more, for you have only the comprehension to see an open pathway. That is what you believe and that is what happens in your comprehension. As you become more enlightened then you may shift to see it in a slightly different complex, but for all true believers there is a short route to spirit that needs no frills or fancy names. It is there. Tap into it with simplicity and you will have an easy connection. If you want to see more, there will be confusion.

How do I explain it to others, who have no comprehension of spirituality, how to connect?

You explain in a simple way that you talk and speak to spirit as easily as you open your eyes each morning, with the ease that you smile or frown or see through your own imagination that which pleases you. There is no question in your mind as to how you do these things. You say that there should be no question as to how you connect to spirit. You can ask a doctor to explain why you have the spontaneous action to open and close your eyes. He will give you medical jargon as to why this happens. To most of you, it is instinct and that is all you want to know. To the doctor he needs a more technical explanation. If you want this too, then study it, for there is an explanation that is also true of course.

It is daunting to think we are not one, but part of a whole.

You are nothing if you are not part of the whole. For from the whole you have your life force which is your being. Life is not just as life in a body as you are now. It is a force that is life that animates you into any power of being that is chosen. You must see that to be is only saying that you are being and being is becoming part of the other, which is the whole. I would say to you that when you understand that you are part of a whole you will learn and absorb from the whole and not be singular in your outlook to the oneness of yourself. In contradiction to this statement I would say that you are in control in the evolution of your own spirituality and your own destiny. Nothing can detract from this fact. But what I am saying is that being part of the large spiritual body which is the life force and animation of all things, you are inspired and moved by that force and so it therefore gives you the destiny and the inspiration to move forward. If there was no force you would remain still and static because there would be no inspiration in all things. At the head of the force there is a greater force and so on as I have told you many times. You must look into the vastness and you will see the whole more clearly. You look at a star and then at a multitude of stars. One star makes up part of the whole. As the whole you look at the large whole which is the universe and so on. So look at your life and you will see the smallness and at the same time the largeness of it all. I am trying to get you to see the full spectrum that is all.

Are there seven levels of consciousness after we leave our world and reach the level where you are today?

But you see I am not on one level I am on two. How you ask? Well I am a teacher so I had to rise, so to speak, and then come back to a level to be able to communicate with you. I could not do so from where I was. This transition is done easily and I move between the two at times, especially if I need more advice and guidance. Where is the ultimate you ask - is it only seven levels away? The term of seven levels has been passed down in your books and transcriptions, in that the seven levels make up each stage so to speak. There are many levels or planes, not just seven. They go on infinitely. But seven is a significant number so you could say that these are stages, although that is not at all true.

It is difficult to understand and I have difficulty in explaining. I know that you trust my explanation.

Is consciousness simply being aware every minute, of yourself, your actions, and how others may perceive you? Or is there much more to consciousness than this?

Consciousness is the level of spirituality at which you are at any one time. It is the progress of your spirit. It is not where you are in your perception of everything within your lifespan. It is more who you are in spirit. You are looking at it as being conscious in your living state not in your spiritual state. You are conscious and breathing within your living state but your level of consciousness is either on earth or at home on the spiritual plane. I will explain. When you are on the spiritual plane, that is the time between lives, then you are on the spiritual level of consciousness. When you are living in a life on earth you are therefore on the earthly level of consciousness. It is either one or the other. When you are on the earthly plane, then you are deemed to be on that level of consciousness.

Is the mere satisfaction of knowing you are making efforts every moment to be non-violent, honest and wishing everyone well, enlightenment itself?

No not at all. Enlightenment is being aware of the spiritual laws and having perceptions of the whole spiritual sphere. Living within the laws of karma and the spiritual laws is what your life on earth is all about. If you do not understand the laws and you break these laws it is understandable. If you learn the laws and then break them, that is different. You must learn and then you will be richer for the knowledge because your path is clear and your understanding much better for the way that you walk your path on earth. The laws of karma are in fact the rules of spirituality that are explicit to your own spiritual development. Karma is your own spiritual file so to speak. So the laws of karma are the rules of how you must or should live so that your own karma is correct.

Do we have to be free of desires in order to find these high spirits, or be in tune with them?

Desire is a lesson which you must learn in its varying degrees. You must be without desire for some things yet aware of desire of the lessons of the life in which you must learn them. So yes you must desire the aspects of your specific lessons which are the ultimate of understanding. But no you must not have desire for things which are not relevant to these lessons,

Why are you, Ishamcvan, answering my questions?

Because you ask me questions and I must answer all those children who do not know the way to progress. I am a teacher in a classroom of children. Some are eager; some think they know the answers and the rest are eager to learn all that it is given to them. Some ask every question imaginable and this is in itself the best of all because an inquiring mind will get the answers to every question. There is no question beyond my answering. Keep the questions coming from any person at any time and I will answer. Where is my path? Am I to progress in my present location? You must learn and then move. Do not move and then try and progress because it will be hampered by uncertainty. As you learn all will be unfolded. You will gain peace of mind in your present situation if you learn as you go. Spirituality is not frightening, or frustrating, it is a wealth of knowledge that is given through my writings for all of you to understand. I would say that yes you must move to a more peaceful and spiritual environment although I will not say to you where. You must find your own path through life and this is part of your tests. But I will say to you that you must change from the materialistic world with all its stress to the spiritual world of love and understanding. You must think only of your karma and your spiritual development. Nothing else is of importance. You must progress, that is your purpose so that you will not waste your life on earth by being frustrated.

I don't think I have any special gifts from spirituality, am I correct?

I would say to you, you have gifts in abundance. You have those which are important to spirituality and these are many. It is not necessary to see or hear spirit but if you feel spirit with you and learn on a daily basis, then you are more knowledgeable than many of those around you.

Please talk about the various planes or levels of spirituality and where we progress to when we leave the body we have now?

I will say to you that your idea about cause and effect has a great bearing here as does your idea of gaining points on earth to help your evolvement. Your progress as a soul entity is to gain the ultimate. What is the ultimate? It is very far away but it is there. We are all on a journey that is affected greatly by the others that we touch on that journey. I am touched by you. You are touched by you. You are touched by your acquaintances and friends, as you are by your children and all those people in earthly bodies who you harm and give your love. It is all necessary for us to see from our actions and situations the actions of others. Say that you have a lesson to learn, a severe problem for example. Many people react in different ways to your problem. Some gave you love, help and support and by doing so they show that their souls hold compassion and this is good. Others are either not interested in your problems or scoff or laugh at your misfortune. Do you not marvel at those who are helpful and compassionate and sometimes many of those are people you had only briefly touched in your present life on earth? So when you progress back fully into spirit your reaction to your lessons is recorded, although that is a much simplified version of what happens. So do the actions of others, however small. You ask do you have to prove good in your lessons to progress and I say to you to progress, yes. To stay at the level of consciousness that I am in now, no.

Is it not said by many that one must be desireless before he or she can find God and enlightenment? And if that is so, how can one whole-heartedly seek these things without the desire to do so?

There are many aspects to this question, so I will take them one at a time. Firstly you must understand the perception of your word God. God is a consciousness not a person. God is not a man sitting on a cloud to whom you pay homage during life or when you die. The word God is a human word. So look at it this way. On the spiritual plane or planes there are various levels of consciousness. We will look at the spiritual plane to which you return when your body dies and call it the next level of consciousness. When you have learnt all your lessons at the next level of consciousness you graduate so to speak, and move on to a higher level and a higher level and so on. Over each level of consciousness there are higher spirits, in charge if you like. Now the next plane of existence, which you return to when you die, the next level of consciousness, has supreme or high spirits in charge. These are in various degrees and this is what you call God.

Does one have free will, whether that will lies within the soul, the spirit, the mind or any part of the individual? Or is all we do, think and feel preordained?

You have pre-set many things in your life before you return to earth. These things you cannot change. That is your parents, your death and your lessons. With regard to your lessons these are important for they are the reason you have returned to earth. To learn and enrich your spirit so your spirit can move on higher and higher, which is its only purpose and desire. For all other things, and the way that you work through or fail your lessons, you have free will. If you did not, then your lessons would be pre-set and of no importance to you.

Is the human race evolving toward an over-all increasing enlightenment and awareness of God? And if this is so, why does it seem to be that fewer things are held as sacred in today's society?

Mankind is at many different levels of spirituality. You have on earth spirit or souls as you call them, at different levels of advancement or maturity. Many are wise and experienced and living lives as to the rules of karma, others are young and not heeding these rules. For all lessons man has freewill so he can ignore the lesson or act in a way that is against his basic instincts of correctness, or shall we say kindness to mankind in general. The whole purpose of man is to be loving to his fellow man, for love is the key to all things. Without love then horrors such as persecution, power mongering, wars, abuse, murder and everything will take place. So it is obvious that it is essential for man to study the laws of spirituality in order for these not to happen. But with all of your spiritualities at different levels of advancement, it is not possible for this to happen. The awareness of spirituality, or as you call it God, is different for everyone. Some do not want to see, some see and fight against what is asked, and some are walking the path trying very hard to do those things which they know will help their karma. They do not want to have to come back and have to face the situations again and again. They want to move on.

Could you just summarise spiritual understanding again for us please.

Perhaps we can just go over things today to make some of them clear in your mind so that you do not have times of uncertainty and problems in comprehending all the vast amount of knowledge that I am trying to put into your mind. Perhaps from your perspective these things are overwhelming and complicated. From here they are simple and easy to comprehend. I can see and feel what you feel only to a degree and from my perception I do not see that you could possibly have a problem in seeing what I see. But the spiritual consciousness is so very vast that this is the thing that is proving to be difficult for you. I was told that this could be the block, which would determine whether or not you

11

would move quickly and rapidly in your understanding. I will try again to make you see that the vastness of it all must be brought down in your mind into a simple and small sphere. Let us look at the sky and the stars and you will see that if you look at the whole there are many millions of stars that you can see, but none that you can relate to. If you look at the moon, which is bigger, you will be able to imagine the surface of the moon, the highs and lows and the density of light and darkness. But for the stars they are too vast in number to visualize. So you see with everything in the spiritual world or in life you must break it down into little segments in your mind if you want to comprehend the meaning and connection. If you think suddenly of all the starving people in the world you cannot relate. If you think of starving people in your home town that you see on the streets or you know, then you can relate. But you must try and see the whole only after you can relate to the small portion that you understand. So after visualizing the moon, try to visualize a star and another star and another. Once you can relate to a starving man that you see or know, think of another in a similar circumstance and another in another country and so on. So with the spiritual vastness that I try to teach you, take one small portion that you understand and then go to the next and the next and then lump them together under a heading and then go on to the next until you fully understand the whole. The spiritual world is vast but the concept is not. The concept is simple and that is the key that I use to teach you. There is nothing complex about it all. I do not refrain from using long complicated words because I do not feel you can understand them, (as you suspect), but merely because they are not necessary either for yourselves or for any of the people who will hear the words of Ishamcvan through your writings. I do not insult you by saying you would not understand if the meaning was written in a more complex way, only that it is not necessary.

Do you see the sunshine?

Yes we see the sunshine and you see the rain. That is why I say to you that your world is grey and ours is bright and beautiful.

All things bright and beautiful are in the spirit world. All things corrupt and bad and dreary are in your world however bright you see it. There is no comparison. It is as different as is night from day. You cannot see when you are experiencing a beautiful sunny summer's day that your world is pale in comparison to mine. But I say to you that it is. The reason is many things apart from spirit. If I said to you that you are affected by the spirituality of the people around you and the ones who are working and being close to you, you may perhaps see that this has some bearing. You have heard that if all the people in the world were like minded and like spirited to the fullest extent, and they all stood for a moment and contemplated or chanted to spirit, there would be a tremendous surge of power and you may see a small proportion of what I say to you. Your very being of spirituality is your power. Also the lack of spirituality is a doom. So to be near people who are not spiritually minded would be to cast doom and gloom over the world. And that is exactly what has happened.

If we live spiritually, will it affect others around us even if they do not want to embrace the knowledge themselves?

The point that you make upon society by having values sent from spirit will be very small indeed, but this must be done. The millions of people that do not think as you do will have no consequence upon your values, but the statement has been made all the same. If I were to say to you that you must not do something for one reason, I do so from spirit and this is an important point to remember. Spirit has a perception that is correct by the laws of karma. I am not just a person in your world giving you an opinion that you may argue with or criticize; this is a fact not an opinion. If you choose to ignore the advice, then the choice is yours, nothing more. Time is of the essence in your world and you must try and achieve the ultimate. Do not shrug things off and say that, well I can always come back in another life and pay the price for the things I do not choose to do in this life. You do not want to come back, that is not the purpose. You want to go on. You want to learn. When you return, any of you who say these things will be so upset that they did not listen to the wise words of Ishamcvan. There is no other way. You can fool yourselves but you can't fool spirit. Spirit knows when you cheat, or ignore the advice and there is no way that you can escape the gaze of the Holy Spirit every second of your breathing life. I say to you, is it worth the risk of coming back to live again? I do not think you understand the importance. Nothing is worth ignoring, in order to satisfy yourself in this life, to necessitate coming back to experience again in another life.

Do you know everything that is happening in our world?

Yes of course I do, the world of spirit is connected because we are one. We know all of us in spirit what is happening to all other spirit entities. We know exactly. There is no question. The same as we know what is happening to every single spirit entity living on your world at the same time. I can see you in Canada and a child in Africa at the same time. I can see millions of people individually at the same time. I can connect with one spirit or hundreds of millions of spirits at the same time. I know which spirit is working with which person and so on. There is no question.

Will scientists ever be able to see your spiritual world?

No they will not. That is quite definite. There is no proof from your world. Only an awareness of those people who are gifted to know that spirit is there and they are picking up the vibrations because they are allowing their spirituality to do this thing. If you look at any thing from a scientific angle it is explainable. Everything in your world has a scientific explanation. That is as it must be. You are talking about physical things of matter, not of spiritual things, that is the difference. If you talk of spiritual things, you are referring to a universe full of things beyond your explanation. The things that have been taught to you by your teacher are nothing in proportion to the things that are there to learn. So how can a scientific person on your world, dealing only with physical things and their explanations, possibly put a meaning onto spirituality as would fit in with his tests and experiments with a meaning that is explainable? There is no proof. There is only awareness and belief.

Will there ever be a time when everyone in our world will believe in all things spiritual?

This is difficult. No I must say that there will never be a time when everyone will believe that all things are spiritual. For you to journey in your life on earth it is to experience all things as lessons. These lessons also include the fact that you must come to your own understanding of the laws of spirituality from the perspective of the grey unspiritual place of your living. If the people all on your world believed that there was a spiritual place then there would be no lessons. What we want from you all is for you to teach the natural laws of spirituality so that they may be spread amongst the people of your world. But unfortunately there will always be sceptics and disbelievers and this is just a matter of equations. I know that you are keen to teach and there are many, many hundred of thousands of people who are eager to hear. I would say to you that if there is only one person willing to hear then your job will be very well received from both that person and from spirit. You will be a very successful teacher. But not all the people will listen. Some will refuse to listen and that will always be so. You have the freedom of choice, all of you. And it will always be that way.

I have met a very unhappy person who asks for answers but will not accept any spiritual teachings. What should I tell him?

You must tell your inquirer two things that he is failing to observe. One, he is spirit and not a body that is governed by his mind. His spirit has been him for many lives and this spirit is advancing in its development. It is in that body for a purpose to learn lessons which will add to his advancement. He says that many things that have happened to him have been self inflicted. Some have been by error of judgment. Many were chosen by him to be experienced in this life. The way that he dealt with the experience was changeable, but it is not necessarily that he dealt with them in the wrong way. They were powerful tests and he is stronger for their experiences. Secondly he is ignoring his own spirituality and automatically trying to find an argument in all things. I do not say that he should not question, that is good and like yourself he has to have a great deal of convictions passed to him before he will give himself over to believing what is the obvious. But he is nervous to say that what he says he believes he actually accepts as his beliefs. There is a great difference. He must be like a sponge and soak up as much knowledge as possible and then put forward arguments. Not keep to his old ideas and not consider taking any new ones and changing his way of looking at things. You cannot always do that which is right by staying with your old ways. Look, observe and listen and then tell spirit that you reject their laws because you have an argument which is stronger. There is always an argument against any statement and any idea. For the positive there must be a negative. But you don't have to always look for the negative as being correct. Maybe the simpler and non scientific explanation is correct and man over the years has ignored this in the view that this simplicity is too simple to be true. You must keep talking to him and let him make you a sounding board for all his theories and ideas. Do not say to him that his ideas are wrong, only try and show him the way by observation and calmness in all things. Tell him to trust his instinct, which he is not doing. In the past a great many of the bad things which he says have happened to him have indeed been because he has not listened to his own instinct. His guides speaking to him and telling him that he must have doubts because the path he is taking is not going to be good for him. But he ignored this advice being whispered to him or thought he knew best and then when things went wrong he says that they were self inflicted. Perhaps they could be viewed in this way. But still he does this. Still he does not stop and sit and muse and wonder why he is going to do something which is not with passion and belief that a true straight path is being taken leading him to his desired destiny. Look, listen and only when you are sure move forward. If you are not sure or you have any doubts at all, stay until you have another path shown to you.

How do I know if a person has understood the answer to their question?

Spiritually there is a difference between the person who thinks they understand and those who feel or receive the message with its understanding without realizing initially that they have even grasped the answer. That is the difference with a spirit knowing that the answer is true because of their path through lessons of spirituality, and the person who is not advanced and will automatically question and break into pieces what is being said before trying to understand

Are all people blessed with the same amount of spirituality?

There is a story I would like to tell you and it is about the poor man who was rich and the rich man who was poor. You see it is not a question of riches because they are not with spirit. So to be rich of spirit is the essence of all things. You can be poor with no money but in fact richer than the rich man. And the rich man can be poor in spirit and therefore poorer than the poor man. For all things that you desire, ask only to be rich of spirit. Ask to be able to learn wholly and fast. Ask nothing else and your whole world will change. Not necessarily by our doings but by your own perception of things changing your view and making you see things as they really are. I will not say that you will ever lack anything material for your sustenance but you will never have riches of money if you choose to work with spirit. It cannot be. Who would listen to you if you live in a grand mansion and have a fancy plane or car to take you everywhere? People would not relate to you. But to be one of them and having experienced things that they tell you, the work of spirit will come through and they will trust you. It is hard but always we will take care of your needs to survive.

It seems that many people look at spirituality differently? Is this ok?

Every one of you has a different approach to the subject of spirituality and it is because you have the natural acceptance of all things, good or bad, that come at you that your perspective is different from the others who are all different to each other. Some people accept bad things as a normality of living and accept good things with surprise. This is the difference. Other people bemoan and question every bad thing that comes at them and find it strange. You question and get upset but you know from whence they came and you are not surprised, just irritated. Now perhaps you can see how all of your group has a different outlook. Some are set in their ways, some try too hard and some are eager and inquisitive. But all are on the same path and have the same goal so what does it matter? I have told you many times that your spirit is individual; it is like no other. This is because of the path that it has taken. A path is to be walked on its own with the crossing of its path by others, but not the affecting of its journey by others. You are alone. This is a statement you must accept. You are not an appendage of any other person. You do not think or see or feel the same as any other person. So you see the people in your group are all different.

What is pure spirit?

I refer often to pure spirit and often to an advanced or old spirit. You have to be advanced within the realms of karma to become a pure spirit. On each level of consciousness, including the one I am on now and the next level of consciousness where I hope I will go on to next, these levels all have levels of progression, so to speak. The advancement is towards the spirit's maturity and ability to pass over to the next level. In the level you and I are in now, that is being at this level and going backwards and forward to lives to learn, starts with you being a new spirit, (that is one who is not knowledgeable by lessons and passing of tests) to a mature or pure spirit which is by the highest degree ready to pass on to the next level of consciousness or plain of existence. So you ask are all babies pure spirits because they are not yet tainted by the worldly ways of your fellow man. I would say to you that not all babies are pure spirit. They are as they are within their own spiritual advancement. If the spirit of the baby is mature then it is closer to becoming a pure spirit than the spirit of a baby which is a new spirit or not yet educated by your lessons of purification. So the answer to your question is that a pure spirit of any spirit entity is by its advancement only. Pure is the highest on that level of consciousness. But a pure spirit could pass to the next level and become a novice in the learnings of that level. It is like a boy in school who becomes head boy at college and then goes on to University to become a freshman.

Why do some people have such complicated theories about spirituality?

In all things there is simplicity and in the word of spirit there is nothing but simplicity. Do not let people weave a blanket of intrigue that is not there. The world of spirit, as is the world of nature which is fed by water, grows and matures and then dies, seemingly to return its dead body to the earth. Mother nature as you call it, is pure simplicity and so is your life and the world of spirit. Spirit is everlasting. You will never see the beginning or the end. It is a process of evolvement and this journey is of enlightenment to your own individuality and nothing else. There is only one journey of importance to yourself and that is your own. Only you can learn the lessons you wish and you choose and all the decisions and risk taking is from your own decisions. You carve the path through the woods never knowing the end destination. So in reality this journey should be a voyage of wonder at the new sights and experiences you see, not a horror of unpleasantness and upsets when they happen. I will say to you that for all dark things there is light. There is always the light. Do not screw up your eyes so you face and focus away from the light for this is your growth and your energy to strive forward. Never can you advance if you do not face the light. The light is spirit and is positive and good. Your guides will turn you to the light if you ask and many human forms will try and turn you away so that you see a false light or the glitter of things which appear brighter and more appealing than the pure white light of the Holy Ghost, which is the world of spirit and all spiritual beings. If you decide that the world of spirit is anything more than simplicity and love then you do not know spirit. To know spirit is a gradual process of recognition in all respects. You cannot know a person in your world by a few casual words and walking on your way. You know a person by familiarity and loving to understand and fathom out their innermost thoughts; to know their moods, their highs and their lows; to sense their very being if that person is exceptionally close to you in love. So it should be with spirit. You will not know your guides or your teacher if you do not work at learning their ways and their meanings and their implications. When you have this trust and understanding, then you will advance in your learning because the spirits who are with you are wanting to teach you all that there is to know.

What is the proportion of people on earth believing in spirituality against those who do not?

I will say to you that for every man that there is on this planet of yours that is of the merest understanding, there is one thousand that are being the same as him. And for every man that has the fullest of understanding, there are one thousand who understand nothing. That is all.

My life is so bad that I cannot seem able to turn myself around. What should I do?

I will say to you that all is darkness until you choose to focus on that small dot of light that is to become a larger dot and then a flash of light before it is an uncontrollable sphere of illumination. If you did not believe in that true speck of light, the brightness would not develop, nor see the brightness which will ensue. Always look for the beginning and then focus on the end. But the beginning is already there and is growing within your sight. The whole of the end encompasses many people and many things. You cannot see the people who are within this realm or the others who are not included because of their own insecurities, their fears, and their lack of understanding or their pure jealousy. It is not your place to see this thing. Trust in the power, love and understanding of the Holy Spirit and all will be true. You must have this true belief and connection before the forward progress will advance to fruition.

It was said somewhere that there are people in the spirit world who do not believe in life on earth, and vice versa. Does that mean that these spirits have not led lives on earth?

Spirits, not people, you must be corrected. This question is the same as the one before. Spirits who do not recognize life on earth are few and are so because they choose to look elsewhere or to bask in spirituality and not learn their lessons. Yes all have been in your world at some time except the very new spirits, which maybe have not yet returned. Even so they observe the world by concept and understand it before they return. It is the spirits who are returned that do not necessarily want to be connected with earth for some time, so therefore do not wish to observe.

Please explain protection from spirit and from yourself.

I will say to you that you are always protected from spirit; from your guides and from higher spirits when necessary. Your guides may ask for higher protection. That is always the case. Now, you may not accept that this is happening. You may say you do not believe in spirit and you do not see that spirit can protect you. That is as is may be. For you to accept is of the utmost importance. You may say that you believe in the protection of spirit and you think that you have to do something also to add to your protection. To do this you just ask spirit for protection, that is all. Now you ask why do you need to protect yourself? From whom are you asking for protection? I have told you many times that there are vibrations from people and individual persons which could affect your own karma if you are not aware of what is happening. In other words if you let others affect you with their own persona then they will. If you choose to not let this thing happen then it will not. In other words you ask for protection and you will receive it. But in fact what you are doing is saying that you are aware that the other person or persons are giving off this aura that you do not want and you see this thing. That is good that you see this thing. For you are then aware which is the ultimate of all things of perception. You know it is there and you wish not to have it yourself. So you ask for protection for this thing only. You cannot meet a person who you perceive to be evil in your words and say that they can harm you. They cannot in fact harm your spirit unless you choose to let them do so. If you glue yourself to your beliefs and your protection from spirit then it will not happen. You are aware of spirit that is all.

In many things your words are not as we would have expected. I am questioning too about our friend who was upset with your words, which were not as she had foreseen.

Are my words ever such? They are the meaning and the truth. What is the truth is not always as you see the truth. But they may be in fact better than the interpretation that you yourselves have on things. To say that she is not yet at terms with the spirituality which is inside herself ready to burst forth into good and healing and bringing the peace to others, is in itself greater than saying that that which she has now is the thing which is good. She has further to go and more magnificent things to see and do. Is that not better? Is it not? For I say to you that for many of you the things that you have seen and done are nothing in comparison to what can and will be achieved. You are all young and naive in your learning whilst you are all old and wise in your experiences. For to experience is the ultimate of learning. You cannot be a scholar if you have not learnt and you cannot graduate if you have not achieved a level of superiority over those who have not taken the time to learn and progress through the classrooms of life. For the ultimate is to go on. For to progress is not only to myself and to spirit, it is beyond and on and on and on. You are the beam of light that does not change direction but fades beyond the sphere of what the eye can see and on and on. You are my childlings and my charges. You are the infants that I nurture. You are my baby to see grow and become adult in your learning. I will hold your hand and guide you through the maze that is life and onto the confidence that is taught and given to you by a wiser and more knowledgeable father. I am that father. Spirit is the grandfather who is wiser still and the Great White Spirit is the even wise great grandfather. Do you understand?

Are you doing other things with other people while you talk to us?

Yes I can do so. If I choose to, that is. Sometimes we focus on one thing. Sometimes it is many thousands of different things. We can be in many places at the same time. Spirit can fragment or travel from the whole whilst still being part of the whole. Spirit is never totally one. That is not possible. Your spirit is within a body for the time being, it is also part of the mass of spirituality that is on this plane of existence and within your world also. The spirituality of others in your world or their lack of spirituality affects you in a way that you do not fully understand. If the harmony of spirituality around you makes you feel at peace then this is good and you should stay amongst this environment. But if the harmony is bad you will be seriously affected by this and should step back and walk away until you enter a new field of understanding and peace.

Where do humans originate from?

You ask about the body of humans, not the spirituality which is the source and uses the human body for its journey through life on earth. There is a big difference. I will explain both so that you understand. You must think first that you are spirit with a body not body with spirituality. Your spirituality is everlasting. It cannot be destroyed so that it is nothing. That is not possible. The spirit returns to the next plane of existence, where I am now, and from there returns to earth, using many bodies, until it learns all its lessons and is spiritually mature enough to move on to another plane of existence which is its purpose. For each journey to earth it chooses its human body, whether male or female, healthy or deformed. This body you must think of as like a butterfly. Your journey on earth is like being trapped in a chrysalis (your body) from which your spirit leaves and flies like a butterfly home to base to evaluate its existence on earth. While you are a chrysalis you do not see the wonders of the big wide world or spirituality because you are confined to a small vision expanse. It is only when you become a butterfly again that you see the whole spectrum. So your question was where do humans come from. The human body has evolved from animals. Animals grow and change from one species to another, as you know. The world you live on grows from ashes through the sprouting of seeds and becomes a lush green world. Then man destroys it and it returns to ashes again, only to have the whole process happen all over again. The animals change with it. But for your spirituality, your existence, the you inside the body, that is different. You have reached the maturity of your spirituality through a long process of learning. Let me say that you started a known path, say from an amoeba, although there was of course a long path before that. There is no beginning in your understanding in the path of the spirit and there is no end. It is ad infinitum.

Should we give ourselves over to spirit, wholly or partially?

To be is to give. If you give of yourself then you are in fact being unselfish with the essence of all things. I say to you to be and not to try. In all things you all put too much wasted energy in trying too hard. If you just flowed, everything would happen. To exercise any sort of energy is to in fact go in reverse of your own spiritual flow. To send a definite thought is negative against the flowing with the spirituality which lies within you all. Anger is energy and peace is spirituality. So be at peace with yourself and relax into the being that is your own spiritual enlightenment. You will not find the lessons of spirituality in anything but peace. If you think you see them in aggression or in anger then you are deceived.

Do higher spirits ever get angry at the wrong doings of man, say like the horrors done to people by terrorist leaders?

Anger is a word that is only for the likes of man. Spirit has love, not anger. But you ask are we affected by the wrong doings of men? Only in as much as we see that it is futile that man will not listen and will not see what is so bright a light in his eyes. Why when spirituality is being told to you from every angle do you not stop, listen and obey its very small needs? To be with spirit is the answer to your life. There is no other. When many of you come home and say that you were too busy to listen to spirit or too vain to not want to be in control of a situation and too angry to not give in to an argument, then we are sorry that this has happened to you. No we are not angry, just disappointed that you have to go through it all again.

Should we always try and work out the answer to things for ourselves?

Please I say to you at this time, remember and remember and ask yourself the answer not the question. For there is more than can be seen by yourself and for this reason then you must be with me and see as only we can see. I have the answer but not the question. I want the question and you want the answer. For if there is hope in any situation there has first to be redemption, because this is the key. For all people that have done wrong, then they may be as that or reform themselves, and that is all. You are not to know the answer for it is not there for you to see. The mystery of the universe is only what it is. Now ask yourself for your words of wisdom, which come not from yourself, and you will see. The anguish of the worldly beings is many times dependent on their own arrogance and misunderstanding, rather than the true words which are lying deep in their hearts. You play the games of life and for the prize you do not necessarily get to be the winner, is that not true? If only you would pause and look to see deep into your hearts and then perhaps you would attack a so-called problem from a different angle. Admit that you love. Do not compromise and say that one thing is this or that just because you do not want to truly see that which is there. For the truth is the key. Open up your hearts to the truth and all else will fall into place. You all have your lessons, and you are all too part of the lessons of others. You anguish and you cry at your lot, but I say to you rejoice for you are a pawn in the game of life and by being so you are so close to the board that you can see the players as only they themselves know. You must observe and act. Is that not what you think? Be at all times yourself and yet yourself with the power of spirit and you will see that spirit is the guiding force and there is never a situation when this is not important. Take the man that is devoid of spirit, or should I say with spirit depressed, and you have an empty soul, even though they may appear to be a very nice person. There is something missing; a very important missing part. I say to you that it is better to have a person who has wronged and is with spirit than have a perfectionist who has nothing that is spiritual in his beliefs or his actions.

If spirit wants many people to learn, why is your message not being distributed at a far greater rate? Why do you not have more people doing it?

There are many people who tell the message in many different ways. But many of them are not heard or even considered as being wise in the knowledge of the life ever after and spirituality. If you were swamped with prophets, then they would not have the impact because everyone would be used to their message and would dismiss them in fun. With fewer more powerful prophets then the people have to make the effort to learn and that is more rewarding.

There must be many people who will never hear the words of Ishamcvan or any other prophet. Spirit cannot reach them all.

But yes it can because each person has a connection to spirit through their own guide. They already have the link.

Yet most of these do not even know their own guides. Why is it essential to tell people about their guides when they are born with them? Surely they themselves denounced them early on in life.

It is not quite as simple as that, but yes they choose not to see and hear their guides. It is a gift they have which they choose not to acknowledge for various reasons. Yet many people always have the knowledge that there is something there, even though they may not understand spirituality itself. They are curious to learn for they have the feeling.

What aspects of my spirituality are hidden?

It is merely that they are not yet awakened. For you to practice spirituality then you must understand more than you do now. I would say that the hidden aspects are perhaps better described as ones that are not yet within your experiences, only that.

Lots of things seem to be going wrong in my life. I try not to be angry, but what should I do?

I know you are not angry but you must stop and stare for to do so will give you a richness that is beyond your belief. I do not know the words to tell you, I only know that you must do this thing. This is the greatest lesson of all in your life. To take in all that is encompassed in your realm of living. Miss not one thing. Clear your mind of all things material. Ask not for help in giving you anything but your spirituality, for this is the most important aspect of your life. See the spirituality of others and observe. Connect with people through your spirituality. Do not pass by on the other side if you see someone who is not to your liking. They may teach you more than you can ever dream of.

I have just started to sit in a circle and have been told we have a higher self. Could you enlighten me about this? My feelings are that it is our own spirit, which can be both on the earth plane and on your world at the same time.

For every person there is body and spirit. Body is earthly and spirit is higher on the spirit plane from whence it came. Spirit is in a body on earth and therefore in itself it is divided between the two planes. It is the higher self from the body, in the description these people are using. I would prefer to say that spirit is the common denominator and body is the attachment for your life on earth. No more, no less.

Is your plane in a physical direction from our earth? If so which direction is it?

It is all around you. It is neither north or west or anywhere else. It is not matter, or volume or substance. It is air. Spirit is like a cloud made up of tiny molecules that are in themselves spirits, which are parts of other spirits. We are one but nothing more than a puff of the wind.

Why must we just be?

The secret of life is to be and not to think too hard about what happens to you on a daily basis. If you take the basic natural way of life, without all your modern day trimmings, you would know that your predecessors lived simple lives and did not worry too much what was going to happen to them tomorrow. I would say to you that your world is now so evolved in mechanics and materialism that people think in a mechanical and material way all of the time. Their wealth and their status is the most important thing for them. When Jesus said to the people throw away your possessions and follow me, he meant not just that fact but also to build up a trust that they would be cared for from spirit if they did so. I am not saying to you that you should throw away all your possessions, only that they are not necessarily needed for your life on earth. Many people do so and lead fulfilling lives. Many people do so and become drop outs dependent upon society instead of living by rules of virtue and goodness to others. Your attitude whilst you live on earth is a very important factor. Your attitude is of course governed by your own spiritual advancement. I mean your attitude to not only life itself but to all those other people with whom you come into contact on a daily basis. You will say to me I know that the attitude of people and yourself is dependent upon the pressures and problems that you encounter at the time. I will say to you that your attitude at these times is the test. Can you still behave in a good way under duress or do you break down and lose your control by speaking bad words or doing bad deeds? It is easy for people to be good when everything around them is good but to be good natured and pleasant to others when all around you is bad and difficult to handle is another thing. Is it not better to face your enemies or those who are trying to persecute you and be pleasant in the face of adversity? It does not matter what another person does to you, they are in the wrong. It is their problem, not yours. Do not take on the problems of others. You will never be able to solve the problems of others. You can watch but you cannot live the problem for them. If they deal with the problem in an unsatisfactory way in your eyes, you should say to yourself the fact that you have observed that they handled the problem in a bad way is enough and feel sorry that they did this thing. Do not look at them as they hurt you and get aggressive and send anger back. What good would it do? If you react to a situation in this way then you have the problem by association. You have taken on board an aggression or an attitude that you did not want to have. You only have it because you have not advanced enough in your own personal karma to see that it is not your problem how other people react to you. If they have jealousy, envy, or any attitude for unknown reasons, they are the one that is wrong.

It is difficult for us looking at the aspects of people on our earth, their complexities, their different cultures and lifestyles so does everyone come together in the spirit world?

Some of you believe that groups are formed in the spirit world with like attracting like and not mixing with the rest who are different. This is an amusing observation. We are all spirit who are the same because they are spirits. In the spirit world we do not differentiate nation against nation or beggar against rich man. All are the same. The spirit is the same. It is the birth right or the body or the standard of living that is different. When Jesus said you must love one another he was so right and you must learn to do this. If you all only got rid of prejudices against nations and class it would be a start.

What is our inner voice?

Your inner voice is your instinct. They are the same. So what are these things? They are the voice of your own spirituality. They are the voices of your guides and the voices of spirits from higher realms through them telling you the answer to your questions or your problems. They are the truth that you will either accept or refuse to acknowledge. They are the truth if only you will listen.

How can I better listen and understand what my inner voice says to me.

Listen, that is all. Do not try and take over as if you know best. You do not know best. Your inner voice or your spirituality knows best. Remember at all times you are here to learn. The lesson is not always clear to you and you do not know the answers. You have to work through them in the hope that you are on the right track. Your voice or spirituality, which is experienced and knowledgeable in all things, will help by whispering in your ear. If you choose not to acknowledge that you hear the voice or that it is right, then you will not heed them and then take the wrong path if you choose that route. If you presume that your instinct, your inner voice is right and work always in that direction, you will be the richer and life will move onward in the right direction. If you choose not to listen you will remain static, or should I say going round in circles and not progressing. Listen to you heart and not your ear. That is all.

Of what purpose is a person's sense of humour and why do they differ from person to person.

Every person is different. They differ in their outward appearance, by that I mean the body, which they are using to carry their spirituality through this life on earth, but the personality of the person, or should we say the spirituality which is apparent of that person is another matter. That is spirit which is experiencing life on your earth. So if we look at the spirituality of the body as being the importance that is paramount, if we ignore the body then the things like sensitivity, humour, loving nature, hatred are all things which are expressions of the maturity of the spirit. Now I know you will want to ask why it is that a spiritual person who is quiet and inward feeling does not appear to have a sense of humour, whilst a robust person who roars with laughter is said to have a better sense of humour. That is not so. It is just not visible that is all. So I say to you that for every person you meet you must try and see the spirit within the body, not the body and then the spirit. With practice you will see that it is easy to read people and see those who are putting up false fronts so to speak, and who have very little experience in their own karma.

From what you have told us about souls, it would stand to reason that the number of souls in existence remains constant. Is that true?

It is only true if you look at the whole vastness of it all. There is spiritual life ad infinitum. There is no beginning and there is no end. For this reason we cannot count. But I would say to you that there is never a few and never so many that there is no room at the inn. The sphere is vast at this level alone. The

31

other spheres or planes are beyond counting. We do not count anyway. We have no figures, no numbers and no sense of time. We have no need to count. That is an earthly thing.

Would it be possible to know how I am progressing in this life?

No. Life is a lesson. You must never know how you are doing or you would be complacent and stop trying. Read my words and you will see for yourself the answer and the hope.

From your previous lesson to me you said spiritually I am on a journey of my own and with no appendages of other people. Could you explain this?

It is your spirituality that is on the path. You are experiencing the life on your world to learn the lessons. Other people will come into your life but not your spiritual path. You are on your own in that respect. When I said no appendages I meant that the spiritual path of another person is not yours. You are on your own. Yes you have other people that are with you in body and some in spirit too, but your spirituality is individual and therefore only you. Do not let any other person invade that sanctum.

If you gave us an insight into the future it would help us to bear our suffering would it not?

Probably, but you miss the essence of my lesson to you. Your spirit chose to come back to your world to learn certain lessons to enrich it, which in turn would allow it to evolve higher and higher which is its destiny and desire. As with all lessons, if you know the answer in advance then the lesson is lost. Maybe if you know even that the suffering will go soon, which in your case it will, then you may have a better attitude. I do not mind saying that all will be well, but I will not give you details of how or let you know what is going to happen. That is not my purpose. My purpose is to teach the concept of spiritual evolvement and from understanding this you will be better equipped to deal with all that life throws at you.

I do get the feeling that the majority of us living on this planet (for what is a really short time) have to struggle from one problem or bad experience to another, with only the occasional good experience or happening thrown in to keep us going! I know now that these are "our tests", but does that mean that this planet is only inhabited for this purpose, and that as human beings here, ad infinitum, we will never become totally happy?

Yes I will say to you that the earth is a classroom for learning. But in a life you experience many things, depending on your spiritual advancement and your vision and observation. If you are not spiritually advanced, then many, many things may pass you by. For you to say that the lives are to experience only the bad and intolerable things is to say that you are seeing only one aspect of your life. Many people have many lessons. The extent of those lessons and their perspectives is dependant only on the choice of the experiences that their spirit felt it needed to experience in order to be wise in that experience for having taken it, and then to move on. Let us say that all wise spirits choose many experiences and some of them will be bad. If you look at life from the eyes of a spiritually aware person you will see many more things than if you are not enlightened in your own karma. So to say that life is full of woe is not true. Life is as you want to perceive it and how you want the problems in life to influence you. If you do not want the experiences to damage your shell of spirituality, then it will not. You will be the richer for the experience. If you say that practically all people are having hardships, yes this may be true. But you forget the people who are richer for them and smile and are happy with themselves and their loved ones, even so. There is not all doom and gloom. In countries where people are starving, there is still infinite love for families and they are aware of each other and their feelings to a much deeper degree than in a city where people live rich and meaningless existences without probably loving at all. Love is the key. To give undivided love, to always feel the other person's pain, not just imagine it, is what is perhaps the ultimate of all lessons. For love is the key.

Does there ever become a time when spirits have learned everything that is possible? And what then? All this learning, to what purpose, what end, what good does it do and to whom?

Have I not told you all the purpose many times? It is to progress. I know that you cannot perceive why you should want to progress, but I say to you why would you want to live and die and not have a life everlasting? So let us look at the scenario again. You are a spirit not a body. Your spirit is infinite in its wisdom. It is as expressed in your body today only a mere proportion of its capabilities. You are nothing. Spirit is everything. Your spirit is a seed that is growing into a plant and then a vine and then a huge plant that goes on and on till you cannot see the end of the tentacle. From the beginning of the seed, you cannot see for it was too far ago and too small to perceive. The end of where you are going is also out of sight. I will give you a parable. Look to the caterpillar on the ground, which is eating the leaves of a plant. It is happy eating the plant. It is without purpose other than to learn how to become a butterfly. When it is a caterpillar it does not see the sky or the field the other side of the hedge. It is content. Many people in your world live their lives not seeing further than your world. It is not possible to do so, neither is it possible for the caterpillar to see over the hedge. But one day the caterpillar becomes a butterfly, which is beauty beyond all understanding of the caterpillar and the butterfly goes from plant to plant drinking the sweet honey. Even then it only sees a small proportion of the sky and does not see a country the other side of the ocean. It is all another world. But you will ask me why does the butterfly not have lessons? Of course it does, it is a spirit developing all the same. But much further down the line, so the lessons are not of the same intensity.

When we come back in another life on earth, is it all in future time, or do we go back and forth.

We have no time from this level and can view everything, anywhere at any timeframe all at one time. It is difficult for you to understand, but think it through. Yes you move on in progression but not in time. In your world you move forward in time, but in other worlds it may be back and forth.

If Aleisha or I spoke another language and not English, would you still be able to communicate with us. Could you speak any language if it were necessary?

I do not speak any language. I am spirit. She is spirit and body. My spirituality speaks to her spirituality with no words. I am inside her, telling her, but not speaking. I am saying into her mind. She is a tool for me to communicate. I do say, but I do not speak. You must understand if she hears, she does not. For we do not need words. We need to communicate and that is the difference. It would not matter if she was deaf and dumb she would hear and speak all the same. Me to her and her to me. For to speak is not necessarily to understand. To communicate with spirit is to give oneself up to understand,

I understand about coming home, but what I find very difficult is about the levels. You say there is no beginning and no end. The purpose is learning, learning what? Do souls who have progressed higher ever come back to this or other planets? If they don't, what is the purpose of all this learning?

The learning is nothing more than to make you spiritual in all respects to a higher and higher degree. The lessons on earth or anywhere else are not about learning, shall we say, of how to be tolerant of others. The lesson for your spiritual development is how you deal with the problem of tolerance from a spiritual perspective, nothing more. If you do not deal with tolerance in the correct way of using a spiritual approach, then you will not be in possession of overcoming the lessons of tolerance. You ask if high souls come back to earth or other planets. It would depend on how high they become. From your world, you pass to the plain of spirituality and back. When your soul has matured through learning, then you move to the next level and so on. Worlds, which are used as classrooms, are only on the present level of learning, not on the next 7 stages. For them there is another concept. The whole purpose of your spirituality is to become higher and higher in your consciousness until you are the white light that attracts the moth. The moth does not question the light; it just knows it must be there. But the difference is that the light destroys the moth, whereas the light of spirituality purifies the soul. The soul has a purpose to want to be purified, that is all. If only you could remember the purpose you have from this plane of understanding, none of you would ever, ever do anything that is not without spiritual intension.

What possesses a Spirit to want to inhabit the body of anyone who is evil and wicked? Do they get to choose?
It is not the body that is evil and wicked; it is the way that the soul chooses to be whilst inhabiting the body. So the soul which wants to go back to earth to learn again may choose to be born of parents and inhabit a body in the scenario of this situation, which will give it obstacles or lessons so it will have to face and act accordingly. But, if the spirit has tried the lesson many times and failed to respond the spiritual way, it may have the lesson given again and again in one life, which is frustrating. The person, or should we say the spirit or soul in the body, may react with evilness and wickedness and make the whole situation much worse. Yet if it could remember back to the time when it chose that body and that situation of birth and what it wanted to achieve, it would in fact act quite the reverse. Hence the entity must not remember the spirituality of the lesson. If it did, then there would be an instant answer and not the soul/spirit making up its own decisions to the spiritual situation.

Is human spirituality changing and if so by what measure e.g. time, vibration?
Spirit within a body is as it ever was. There is no change. Spirit is on a path and uses a body solely for that purpose to learn as it goes through a life cycle. If you ask is spirit being abused by man in today's world, I would agree, that yes it is more difficult because of your lifestyles. But the power you have to set your

own path, against all the distractions and ridicule that you may experience, is only defining that your spirit, which is you, is rich and cannot be swayed from that which you know to be the true way to achieve your answers as is correct from the power of spirits higher than yourselves.

What is your source of energy?

We have no energy. That is a word from man to explain the spiritual progression. If you ask how are we powered to progression, I would say that we flow with our own experiences and desires to evolve higher and higher. We are not fired from another source. We are as one with ourselves. We are in no way connected to another source. We are as one with all other spirits, yet alone as one spirit. As is a molecule of a cloud. We need the mass, but each molecule is singular in its own right. Not dependant on the other molecules, unless it wishes to be one large mass. But spirit is powerful as a mass or singularly. The more mature the spirit the stronger it is in all respects.

What are the things about your realm of consciousness which you find most difficult?

With all things, it is the lessons which have to be learnt and overcome. However, from this plane of existence we know that to learn is a pleasure and essential at the same time. It is not that it is a tiresome thing to be overcome before repeating the exercise over and over again and becoming more and more boring. For myself and my current lesson of frustration, I am having to overcome many aspects which were not apparent to my spirit, although of course known to my teachers. All teachers set their pupils lessons for which they themselves know the answers. But I learn and I observe and I am richer for the experience.

What is the importance of our sun to us spiritually?

It is a symbol of hope and light, that is all. It does nothing more than symbolize. However it has been a great symbol to your forefathers who held it in high regards.

What is blocking my spiritual growth most of the time?

Nothing is blocking your growth except your own willingness to do all those things, which are set out as not being accepted. There are no grey areas. If it is said that a thing is not permissible, then you cannot change this to suit yourself. That is all.

Is a creative outlet such as painting or growing things a way to improve ones spiritual awareness?

I would agree that it is good to take time and go within yourself in activities such as painting. You are expressing yourself with no interference from fellow men. You are taking time to contemplate, are you not? With plants and any living things, if you are in tune with them, you are becoming more aware and astute in your feelings and observations

I want to enjoy life and so I have set myself up in a very happy life, will this slow my learning?

Yes. The lessons of life are not necessarily to have a good time, although it is good if you can radiate happiness and warmth to all you come into contact with.

Do we ever achieve all that is to be learned for one lifetime or do we just run out of physical time?

You are given enough time to complete the lesson. You do not always want to complete the lesson when you look at it from the earthly perspective. You sometimes ignore what is staring you in the face. You don't want to address it.

I have a favourite saying, which is "perspective is everything" do you agree?

No I do not agree that perspective is everything. I agree it is extremely important. If you mean from perspective all other things derive, I would be more inclined to say yes. From your perspective observation of others, there then becomes compassion and tolerance and love. Then yes it is important.

But I would say to you that to learn observation is probably one of the most important lessons to overcome, for by doing so you then automatically make yourself open to learn many other aspects relating from this action

Is there something that we can do for you, Ishamcvan?
Learn the truth. For you all to learn through my link is to benefit spirituality as a whole because it is our purpose to give you all the tools to learn. For those of you who understand, our task and frustration is worthy, for those of you who do not, then at least we have tried. But remember you are given the rules of Karma (the rules of life) and it is your choice whether or not you want to agree with them and apply them to your own situation. If you observe people who question or disagree, you must understand that they have the freedom of choice. It is not your place to make them alter their choice. You must not judge them to be right or wrong. They have the same knowledge, if they seek it, as you yourself. They must interpret it in their own way. This is not easy to bear from this perspective. For all of us who have knowledge in whatever aspect or profession, when we pass on that information, it is frustrating to not have it accepted with open arms. We all know our individual subject matter, the pupil does not. Why does the pupil not learn? Why does he turn his head and say that he is not sure if that is right? One thing in your world, which is the biggest problem, is that there are many prophets who are false. But they wear shiny cloaks of errors which man, if he is not spiritually evolved enough to see through to the charlatan underneath, will claim to be the authority which they must follow.

You have said before that some music is full of anger and bad for our spirituality, but if a person enjoys this music and it makes them feel good, is that a bad thing?
It would be hard for any of you not to understand that a person enjoying music with a violent theme or that is full of anger, is someone who is at the same time enjoying a spiritual experience as could be the case with other music. Anger is bad

as is any demonstration of anger. You would not hesitate to understand that a person beating another person is not spiritual even though it is done in the form of sport or jest. It is a deprivation of one person of another, therefore in itself non-spiritual. Music is spiritual in most cases because it raises the vibrations around the listener and becomes part of the zoning in, for a better explanation, of the person to a more spiritual environment. On the other hand, extreme, loud, angry music is the reverse of this situation and will if allowed, incite anger and aggression. More like a brainwashing and incitement to do something harmful whilst in a semi-trance that this music has created. I question that any such music would make a person feel spiritual. To say it makes them feel good makes me suspect that they enjoy being hyped into anger. Many people like to have anger.

I am aware of the benefits of taking time to stop and see nature, but is it bad to spend too much time alone, even amongst nature?

Quite definitely it is. In life you must enjoy as well as experience the moods and actions of other people in order to learn. If you are devoid of giving to other people you are low in spirituality. I am not saying that you should not enjoy solitude because at these times you can reflect with yourself and meditate and absorb nature to enrich you. I merely say that to be too long in solitude is not good for your lessons. You must find the equilibrium.

I find that when I encounter certain situations that I have come across before, I handle them differently and hope that this is an indication of spiritual growth. But if those situations are hurtful, the pain is still the same. Surely if one were growing spiritually, one's feelings would alter accordingly?

You are very much growing with your spirituality, there is no question of that. But you are still too emotional about being hurt and this is a lesson you have in life and you must continue

40

to learn. No one likes to be hurt but I say to you personally that you must always take two steps back from the situation and ask yourself why the other person is behaving the way they are. What is their reason? Are you feeling persecuted when there is really no cause? There is no question that you are dealing with these problems in a much more sensitive way, but unfortunately you have to rid yourself of the problem of feeling hurt. If you can project yourself to stand behind the other person as they face you with the hurtful problem, then perhaps you will begin to understand. You have paraded before you a series of people who will try and hurt you. That is your lesson on earth. You must learn from my words to address this lesson and turn it around to your advantage. For example, if you give out love to the person who is hurtful to you, at the same time turning your back and moving on, then not only will the person be confused, but you yourself will walk with your head tall and perhaps this time your lesson will be over. One day, when you position yourself correctly, you will find peace and contentment and love in abundance. Your lesson of hurt will be no more.

Some modern day prophets tell us that we come from the source. Please explain the source?

You all come from a whole which you may call many things, including of course the obvious which is the source. You came from a source. The evolution of spirit is the source of all things. So yes it is true, you all come from the source.

Chapter Two

Spirit Entities

"I am the air that you breathe, the wind on your back
and the essence of all your understandings."

How would you define spirit?

It is nothing. There is no substance. Spirit is not there, yet
it is. It is without volume yet it is the largest and strongest force
around you. How do you see me, like nothing is there? How do
I feel you, with the touch of a feather on your face. Is it there? Is
it not? Spirit is elusive. It is the master of deception. Just when
you think you know it, there is another surprise in store. Just
like a lover. You unfold with love, layer upon layer of mystique
and intrigue, always showing wonder and yet another surprise
in store. That is spirit. That is the ultimate of essences, greater
than man and less than the higher spirit above it. A nothing that
is in a series of encounters that makes it wiser and stronger. An
evolution that will never be studied because the progress of this
essence is beyond science and understanding. You think you
know spirit. You wait till you see spirit again face to face, or should
I say, breeze to breeze. I say again. I am the air that you breathe,
the wind on your back and the essence of all your understandings.

In me you are yourself, nothing more. I am the spirit of you and you are the spirit in me. We are one, with each other and with all other spirits. There are no more singular beings, for we are one with ourselves. Not beings; not things; not even a grain of sand in a mountain of sand. Nothing more than nothing.

Where do new spirits come from?

Infinity. There is no beginning and no end in the progression of a spirit entity that is within your powers of understanding. But let me say to you that the highest of our high spirits which you may call your God, made all the little specks of dust which are baby spirits and set them on their journey. They came from nothing and go to nothing because to explain further you would just not perceive. This explanation is perhaps the most simple I can say to you.

Where about in our bodies is our spirit located?

Your spirituality is a presence, not a part of your body. It is separate from your body. I know you will find this difficult to understand but it is correct. I will say therefore that your spirituality is an essence that surrounds you and is part of everything you do. It encompasses you and is you.

Are some spirits/souls on earth actually part of other souls? For example one soul divided into several souls all living on the earth plane at the same time, not necessarily in contact with each other but able to tap in and drain the energy of one or the other. Is this so?

Firstly you must remember that spirit whilst it is at this plane of existence is one with itself but at the same time is one with all other spirits also. This is difficult for you to imagine. Also there are no elements of time, only from your perspective on earth. Now, if you can imagine that spirit is one but is on your earth and here at the same time then this will be a start. But having perceived this concept you must also think that whilst on earth it does not remember the spirit world. This is purposely and obviously for the whole aspect of it learning its lessons. If it remembered the spirit world then it would know its tests and there would be no purpose. But, the spirit is connected from the spirit world to your world by a thread of connection, so to speak, that is there all the time it is living in a body on your world. It is said, mythically, that when death occurs the thread is broken. There is not an actual thread, but this is a description only. Also, as I have told you the spirit will return to my world when you sleep - for some of the sleep time. Now let us look at the aspect of the spirit being fragmented into various bodies when it is living its life on earth. It could be said that if spirit is one on this plane that for any progression to your world it would have to become fragmented. But to do so it returns to its individuality and it is more that spirit is individual but also part of others when it is here, rather than it returns to a larger lump. For this reason a single spirit such as yourself is only as one when on your world. There is certainly no other spirit, which is a fragmented part of its oneness that can drain its energy or be living in a body in another place with or without any connection. However what can happen is that spirits around you can drain your energy if that is an explanation. But as I have said before many times, you must position your life away from persons and places and vibrations of those which drain your energy and your spirituality. So in short the answer to the question is No.

What is the difference between spirit and soul?

Nothing, they are the same. A soul is an earthly description of the spirit in a body. It is describing that the soul of a person is it's being which is what fires the body into life. Like an electrical appliance (the body) which will not work unless it is connected to an electrical outlet (the spiritual plane).

Can a human experience the entering (via the solar plexus), of a soul from the world of spirit who was known to them whilst on the earth plane?

You can experience the spirit or soul of a person who has passed over to our side. They can be with you as much as they choose. You cannot summon them. They do not travel through space. They are with you with a blink of an eye. But they do not enter your body. They stay outside your body. They do not control you or take over you in any way. I do not take over Aleisha; it is her choice to let me into her sphere. People you knew in your world are no more. Their spirituality passed over, not the person. You are spirit in a body and that body makes somewhat your personality for your life, although that is not really the case. So the personality is the person. In this life you may be angry and violent, but your spirituality when you reach home is peaceful and reticent. No spirit will harm you unless you want it to.

Please explain what is possession of a body?

A spirit from this plain of existence will plan a journey back to earth and choose its parents. From these parents a body is born and the spirit will inhabit this body for its life on earth. When the body dies the spirit returns home. During its lifetime no other spirit will enter that body. But I will say to you that as you observe some people you may think to yourselves that they appear to be lots of different types of people yet all in the same body. The reason for this is usually some malfunction of the brain of the body which sends different messages to the body on how it should behave. If the brain is not clear then the body will act in many different personalities. Such as if your arm hurts you will not be able to raise it above your head because your brain tells you that the pain will be worse if you do so. Just so the brain of the body will say that the person should be very weird in their behaviour and the body will believe that is the correct thing to do. Illness of the brain is the same in its manifestation as that of the illness of the body.

Can a body be possessed by one or more spirits?
The body can have only one spirit during its lifetime.

Could a spirit who has passed over and wishes to progress within your level of consciousness be held back from their

45

progression by the power of prayer (asking for help) from many, many people collectively, on the earth plane? I ask for this has been said of a princess who recently died.

No, that is not possible. You only progress because of your own spiritual experience and level of understanding. If you do not pass the tests you will not move on. People in your world are not on the same level as here. They are inhibited in their level of helping. People who idolize a person on your world do so for many reasons, personal and being in awe of someone they admire. I am not saying that the person you mention was not spiritually advanced, more that she was on her own path and will learn by her own lessons. You must remember too that her life on your world was short and her lessons few in order to advance. When the lessons were experienced she moved on and came home. There was no reason for her to stay and live longer in your world. I died in my middle years too. I had to move back home.

Is spirit visible in the spirit world?

There are waves. That is how I can describe to you parts of the spirit world. Can you imagine waves of incense as it drifts around the room? It has many areas, which it covers. There is no beginning other than the flame and there is no end as such either, it just burns out slowly. We spirits are like that incense. We were created initially but we grew from nothing, it is so hard to explain. I have dwelt long and hard on how to explain to you about the start of the spirit from nothing. It is never from nothing. There was never a beginning. You will not accept I know that there was never a beginning, and if I tell you that there is not an end you will be equally perturbed. We are infinite in the spirit world. We never really knew when we started and we certainly will never know when we reach an end. Did not your parents say to you when you were small that you were never satisfied? As soon as you achieved something you had to strive for more. It is the same with spirit. We strive for perfection so that we may evolve higher in our spiritual understanding, but when we do that after much hardship and pain in our lives, we strive for higher again and it never ends. But here to achieve spirituality at its various stages is not a struggle as it is on earth. It is spiritual learning which is achieved but by much different means. It will take me long and hard lessons to teach you the full spectrum. But some of your group asks how long I have been aware of my evolvement as a spirit and I will say to you always. I never remember anything before my spirit being there. I do not remember being an unwise spirit but of course I was at some stage. This is because we have no time to measure it by. And how much longer will it be before I reach three planes from my earthly existence? I do not know, it is as simple as that. If I knew would tell you. None of us knows. We are all students in the hands of our teachers.

I would like to ask a question about earth bound spirits and how some of them prefer to not leave the earth when their body dies.

They are very few and it is not usual for this to happen. It is usually because they suffer a sudden or horrific death or both at the same time. I have told you how spirit must leave their body in their own time. Do you remember I said this with respect to transplants where the body is killed early to take the organ needed and then spirit was in shock because it did not leave the body as it had planned, in a quiet or slow way, or whatever it had chosen? The decision was taken away and another being or beings took control of the spirit returning home in its own time. The same is with earth bound spirits as you call them. For some reason the spirit entity has the same problem. It is not able to return home as it had planned or still believes that it is in a body when in fact the body has died. The spirit does not believe the body is dead. This is strange to believe but it is true. Do you remember we talked about near death experiences? I told you that the spirit leaves the body temporarily and it is preparing to return home when for some reason the time is not right, or it changes its mind for want of another phrase, and knows that all its lessons on earth have not yet been completed. So it returns into the body. The spirit has control in this case, but even so it glimpses our world so it remembers when it returns to the body. With violent death the spirit is not prepared to leave. It does not have any clues that the body is going to die. With illness, however trivial, the spirit is somewhat prepared. The same with accidents, although not always. The spirit sees that death will occur even for what seems to you to be a fraction of a moment. Spirit is ready. Not always, but usually. But with some rare cases the spirit does not know or does not accept that the body is dead. This is the only case where spirits are earth bound. Usually this is very temporary but sometimes it is for a little while in our terms that the spirit remains, but to your terms it may be many years. This is what is described in your world as a ghost when spirit appears and is not sure whether it is spirit with or without a body. This is also very rare. What happens then you ask? Well in most cases spirit will be guided by ourselves or by its guides to return. Very rarely this does not happen because the spirit is governed by the things which happened to it during the death of its body. It is in shock so to speak and cannot be reached by another spirit. Always it returns eventually. Sometimes it is quicker than others.

Are all murders changing the pre-set date of death?
Yes. The pre-set date is dying of natural causes.

If a person is murdered before their pre-set date of death, would the spirit, when returning to the spirit world, need to complete any unfinished lessons. Do they come back to earth or do they learn them from the spiritual plane?
The first thing that happens is that the murdered spirit will have to observe many things on your world which are related to the murder or death. You could say that the lessons they were learning on earth were cut short but a whole new set of observations and learning lessons will happen without them going back to earth. You could say that the lessons are then re-shuffled and next time they go back to earth they may not have to do the lessons that they learnt when they were observing the murderer and subsequent events.

You say that some ghosts are souls who have not come to terms with dying, why is this so if every person chooses when they die?

A ghost is your earthly term, not ours. I will try and explain by saying that a ghost is an appearance of spirit in its last life. To say to you that a ghost is a figuration of the body before it reaches this plane of existence is not perhaps quite true. So we will start with the death of the body of a person when death is not expected. The spirit always knows at the point of death when it is to die. But if, say, the act of death is so fast that the body was not expecting it, then there is a problem. Most people dying know and prepare for the passing of the soul or spirit back home to this level of existence. But in some cases of death this awareness is not necessarily apparent. So the spirit you could say is not ready. In another scenario perhaps the spirit does not want to leave the body because it has great loves on your earth or concerns for people it leaves behind and this creates a problem with its journey home. In both cases and several others, the spirit is fighting death and it tries to cling to earth when it should have a straight passage back home. In these cases then the apparition of the spirit trying to cling to its dead body will occur. In time the spirit will be helped back whether with words from your world or whether from its own guide or spiritual leaders from here.

If there were less population in the world in say 1900 and many times more today, where did all the spirits come from? Did you make new spirits to fit the bodies?

I would say to you that the spirit world is endless and the planes of existence are ad-infinitum so that the people on your world are a drop in the ocean compared with spirituality. So you have increased the population of the earth. You can never have even a small proportion of the people needing spirits to even make it noticeable from this perspective. Spirits evolve not only into people on your earth but into bodies of people on other planets and other worlds. There are millions of other worlds. Millions of planets. Some are inhabited now; some were, some will never be; so that shows you that the fact that your world has increased its population is nothing of importance. It is two grains of rice in a bowl of rice instead of one grain of rice. The souls or spirits available are several sacks of rice.

How do we recognize the levels of souls and their stages of advancement when in a body in our world?

You know by instinct those souls which are new or novice and those souls which are old or mature do you not? You are probably doing this by observing the way that that person is behaving. You see that people who behave in irrational manners or without care and consideration are new souls and those that behave calmly and with caring are old souls. That is true and the two extremes are easy to recognize although you will see that there are a far greater proportion of new souls than there are those who are mature. The significations of their characteristics are not always that simple so you will never know for certain. Some souls or spirit entities within bodies mature during the course of their lives on earth, and this is of course the purpose of a life. They may start out on their paths of lessons very ignorant of what to do and which way to behave, but they learn as they go along and some of these become progressively more mature very quickly. I know you will ask how we know those spirit entities which are at the intermediate stage between the two. Those souls who are beyond the novice and still not yet mature. These are the greater majority and you cannot classify them all into the same category because they are not. Each spirit is at a different stage of its development to its neighbour wherever they are on the ladder of progression. No two are the same. You will observe that there are sensitive people doing humane acts of kindness and compassion in your world, who do these from instinct to the situation they see or by voice from spirit which they recognize and act upon. These are your true mature spirit entities. At the other end of the spectrum there are those people who abuse others, belittle them in speech or violence, and desire money, power and fame. These are your uneducated or novice souls.

Somewhere in the middle are others who are working through their lessons. Some act in the acceptable and good way and advance accordingly, others make the wrong decisions or choose not to act in the correct way to the laws of karma and they do not progress. They have to face the lesson again in another life in another time. The whole essence of reincarnation is to be faced with lessons, to act in the correct way as laid down by the Holy Spirit and the laws of karma, and then to progress. All spirits or souls on this plane want to progress. It is only when they get back to your world with its greed, temptations and power that they get swayed and forget their purpose. These novice souls or those who are not progressing are not aware of the voice of their guides or their spirit helpers guiding them into the right ways. They are blind and they do not choose to see, they are deaf and they choose not to hear. They are having a great time in their lives on earth and whilst there nothing else is of importance. Why should they listen to spirit they think, when life is wonderful, plentiful and full of self gratification and wealth? It is only at death and their return home that they see the error of a wasted life and no progression. As I have said before their actions are not wrong, they can do just as they please, but if it does not fit with the laws of karma they will not progress.

Please give us your definition of a new or old spirit? Is it how long they have been in existence?

All spirits start out as novices. As they learn lessons and the essence of spirituality then they are enriched and considered more mature. If they choose to ignore the tests then they will not progress however long they have been in existence.

What do you spirit entities do all day on your plane of existence?

You cannot compare life in a body to that of a spirit entity in this existence. There is nothing in similarity at all. We do not do or be anything. We have no need to measure time or occupations. Time does not exist. If time does not exist then no actions are of importance. Actions do not happen. Thoughts happen. Observations happen. Observations of your world and other worlds and the learning of lives everywhere. It is difficult to explain and is one of the most complex aspects that I have to teach you. When you return home as I have told you, you become one with spirit. As one you do not act or do things, I cannot explain more elaborately. You are with the Holy Spirit and you learn from the Holy Spirit as you are given guidance and help, but you are not an entity that can do as it pleases as respect to advancement. You must work with other spirits in finding out your level of consciousness and where your spirit, or rather you as a spirit entity, is progressing along the pathway to evolvement and achievement of the ultimate goals of progressing forward. You as a spirit entity are able to see anything you please and you can visit your loved ones on earth or purely observe life on earth if this is your wish, but you are not a free entity as such, you are part of the mass of one and therefore need to be released with permission, so to speak, although this is rather a severe way of putting things. Also some of you ask about like attracting like in the company that the spirit keeps while existing as a spirit entity. This is confusing to know how to be specific about this point. The only way that this could apply is for me to say to you that there are various stages within the next plane of existence that could be somehow put in this terminology. In this level of consciousness there are advanced or mature spirit entities who usually work in some capacity such as learning to teach people in your world such as yourself, or learning to become guides or channels etc., and these souls or spirits will be at a level where they have more direct contact with the Holy Spirit or the higher spirit levels within this plane. But the lower or novice spirit entities are also being assisted, although this is not the correct word, by higher spirits within the realm of consciousness as are those in the middle. So although all spirit entities are labelled so to speak for their advancement they still mix with all spirits in order to learn and be one. So you see all spirits mingle. They are conscious of their levels within the level of consciousness and are knowledgeable of other spirits being more advanced or less advanced, but they still are all one as spirit. There is no sectioning off at all and certainly no discrimination of groupings or types of spirits. So I must say to you that you cannot say that like attracts like. It is just not true. Spirit is one. One cannot be split. If it split it would become two or three or more and I say to you that spirit is one and only one.

Do not try to make the whole vision of our plane of existence or the teachings of the Holy Spirit more complex than my teachings. I have told you that everything is very simple and that is how it must be. Your world has become great analyzers and you read too much into everything that you see and hear. Be grateful that simplicity is best and there is no need whatsoever for anything complex to be written or read about this existence. If you read such then question the wisdom of the words and ask yourself for what purpose has the author made the whole scene difficult to understand? Be at peace with yourself at all times and by putting yourself into this mood of tranquillity you will experience much more pleasures than you ever imagined possible. You are too complex in your every day life and you are missing the beauty of the day. Stop and smell the flowers. They are always there whatever the season and the weather.

I have heard that lost souls are attracted to go towards the light. Will you explain please?

Lost souls are lost spirits which are not ready to go back to the next plane of existence. I have told you that these are not in great numbers but they are there all the same. A spirit entity, as I have told you, is usually prepared to leave the body it has been occupying but in some rare cases this is not happening. It may be that the spirit knows that it does not want to return to our plane because it was having such a good time in your world, maybe with its riches, or power or hatred. Or maybe it is just suspended in a limbo state. There are many reasons but whatever the case these spirits must return at some stage and it is better sooner rather than later. If you sit in a spirit circle or rather a circle trying to contact spirit or with spirit trying to contact you, then this is seen clearly from our world like the rays from a beacon in the dark. Because you in your group have great power and this is seen by spirit as a great white light around you all. The Holy Spirit has helped by putting this light around you because you are trying to contact and get close to spirit. It is this light that attracts spirits to you all when you are together. So when you meditate or pray and have strong vibrations together this light rises and is not only seen from our level but also by those lost souls as well. Sometimes, but not always, the lost souls will recognize the light as being a beacon from your world to our world. They will see the connection and follow it home.

Could spirit in your spiritual plane of existence influence those of us who are still in the earthly plane of life?

I will say to you that yes they can if they so choose. But those spirits which choose are only those who are not so experienced in doing that which is right. Spirit is always with you, but in the most they know that they are there to help with answers by instance to those things you wish to have advice on and those aspects which you find a problem. Most spirits will assist you within the laws of karma. There are of course those spirits which are young spirits or are not good spirits which will try and influence you by means of jest or wrong doings and these are not good. I will say to you that this is very rare, but it does happen. Mostly the person on your earth will pick this up, as perhaps evil doings and will protect themselves in some way so that this does not happen. The spirit will act playfully as perhaps a ghost or a phenomenon which your world finds frightening, but this is rare. So I will say to you that yes a spirit could influence a person in your world who is open to being used and that is all. Normal spiritual people will not be influenced and neither will they be approached in the first place. And these spirits are rare anyway who do these things. But perhaps you ask whether spirits can influence you to do good things? I will say that to ask if spirit can influence you is different from asking if they can affect you by attracting your attention. It is rare that spirit can influence a person. A person can use their instinct to pick up a warning or a strong message from spirit, but I would not put that in the category of influence.

Do you in the spirit world know what other spirit entities are doing?

We know all of us in spirit what is happening to all other spirit entities. We know exactly. There is no question. The same as we know what is happening to every single soul on your world at the same time. I can see you in Canada and a child in Africa at the same time. I can see millions of people individually at the same time. I can connect with one spirit or hundreds of millions of spirits at the same time. I know which spirit is working with which person and so on. There is no question.

What are soul groups?

I will explain about the spirit of you being part of a whole group of spirits which are part of another group of spirits and so on. I would say that the group of spirits which you go to when you return to this plain of existence are divided in the following manner only. Each spiritual group on this level is at various other levels according to the advancement of the spirit entity itself. So if you yourself are an advanced spirit you will go to one group and another person who is a new or beginner spirit will go to another. Therefore all spirits of the same advancement level are in one group, so to speak. So you cannot say that a family will all be in one group. That is not so because all members of a family are not necessarily of the same spiritual level. However, you as a spirit are connected with all other groups at your level and below your level and can visit them, if this is the right word. You cannot visit levels above you and that is why you strive to gain admission by evolving higher in your own spirituality. I would say that as love is the essence of all things that is all that is important in this world of spirit. You are not concerned with your earthly ties and you will not crave necessarily to be only part of those you loved on earth. That is not important and you must begin to understand that your ties on earth are nothing more than your parts of lessons. There are the exceptions. These are the strong spiritual ties that you have had over many lives and those which are exceptionally spiritual which you have met firstly in the life that you are in now. That is all.

If you are part of spirit here and part of spirit there are you segregated as your life on earth or are you at the same time one.

You are part of spirit which is a whole and whilst on earth you are so as well, although you live your life as one and are independent whilst on your world. Never within the realms of your own spirituality are you alone in your spirituality. You are part of the whole. So if this is the case then whilst you are on earth you are doing so as a part of your life here. You travel in your sleep back to here just the same as when you are back on this plane of existence permanently again you can visit your world to observe and be a part of touching people through a medium or direct contact with those you love. Say for example, from the spiritual plane you could be with a love one who is dying. You visit their bedside to give them love and spirituality. You are still living here but you visit. Living in your world you visit the spiritual world whilst you sleep. It is the same. You are in both worlds at the same time. You are spirit not human. That is the difference. Spirit is one with spirit. Human form is alone.

Someone I know wonders if there is a connection with the visions she sees and the closeness she feels with some spirits who were with her as humans in her life on earth. She wonders if they are one or are different.

I will answer that which is in her mind. I would say to you as we mentioned before that spirit is one not segments. To see spirit as one guide or one vision is not a separate part as a human being living on your earth is as separate parts. Spirit is one in its fragmentations; a vision of her father or her grandmother or her guides. Not as different people in human form. So to say to her that she is with spirit is enough to understand. Then to say that spirit is as different forms of identification only, is another vision to understand. Spirit surrounds and protects you all. Spirit is one with you. Spirit is connecting to your spirit. Spirit is one.

Do people such as the seventh son of a seventh son actually inherit spirituality?

It is nothing more in fact than the advanced spirit choosing an advanced spirit to be born through, that is all. All spirits on the more advanced level of their existence on this plane will be very choosy who they are born through. They have a very short and meaningful life to have to learn the final lessons so it must be chosen with more care than if they are new or novice spirits.

Does spirit only talk to us to help us with our lessons?

From the aspect of spirituality, all spirits wish to make known the laws of spirituality to you all there, except the new spirits who are not yet in a position to be educated enough to succeed. So the spirit world does not send the love to the bodies on your earth, they connect with the spirits inhabiting the bodies of people on your earth. Spirit is eager for spirits in your world to learn their lessons. But few spirits are good teachers because this is not an easy thing. Many try to attract the attention by speaking through the minds of mediums and this in itself does attract the attention of many people. But the message is thin and of no consequence. These spirits are trying to talk to ones they loved on earth - spirits they loved. So the answer to the question, all spirit is concerned with is that spirits in your world learn these lessons and evolve higher.

Where do new souls come from and can they die out?

They do not come for there is no beginning. They do not die for there is no end. The existence of your soul or your spirituality, which is the same, is perpetual. You start to learn and you continue to learn and there is no other way. If you fail to learn you remain static. If you learn you advance. In your advancement there is no end. For always there is more and more learning. So the spirit cannot die. The spirit can become weak within a lifetime. Or it can become strong which is the effect of learning. But it cannot fade away and die. That does not happen.

Is it possible for a spirit to be on this earth in two separate bodies at the same time?

No

How do you communicate and interact with other spirits on your plane of existence? Do you use language?

No we do not. We know all things. Spirit is one. Spirit is not segregated. Spirit communicates by thought. Not actually, but this is the nearest you will understand. If you in your world could read the minds of your fellow man you would not need to communicate with words. You would know. We know all things, in this world and in yours all at the same time. We would not stop to communicate with another spirit and then go on a talk to another. That involves time. We have no time. Everything is done simultaneously. It is hard for you to understand.

Is there any classical music that is bad for your spirit because of its anger?

Not for spirit; for your mind and body yes. But your spirituality is above reproach in that way. It may make you feel angry, upset or depressed, but your spirit should rise above it and still be at peace. On the other hand, soft music will lull the spirit into feeling safe and thus raise the spiritual vibrations. Why does it not work in reverse? Because for the angry music it is a test of tolerance, for the soothing music it is like coming home to spirit.

You have mentioned that I am an 'advanced' spirit. I am having some trouble accepting this idea. I do not feel very advanced at all. In fact I feel quite strongly that I'm flailing around in the mud much of the time. I've made some really

poor choices and am quite judgmental and critical. I thought that people who were advanced were generally calm and giving. Can you clear up my confusion?

You are an advanced spirit, not a high spirit. There is a huge difference. To be advanced on the ladder of spiritual understanding you can be half way up and therefore more advanced than those people below you, but not as advanced as those above you. It is not required that you know, whilst in your life on earth, where exactly you are in your progression. All I say to you is that you are not a new spirit, for you are advanced and wise in many things. But, you also have much to learn, so you have been positioned, as have all of you, for these lessons to be shown to you. Not in one way, but in many ways. When you then come home, you will see how you have advanced further and you will see the complete purpose of all your experiences on earth. For these are all there in a contrived pattern. They are not random acts or experiences that just happen to you and have no consequence in the whole scheme of things. However, although you have your path set and your experiences in place, you have free choice, so you may yourselves choose to not go beyond experience #1 or you may race through them with an exhilarating passion right through to the finishing line of that particular life. It is all a matter of your choice. So you see that is why you think you are flaying around in the dark. Not because you are not as advanced as you would like to be, but the reason being that you are advanced enough to understand that you have to face everything head on and take whatever is thrown at you. Your frustration is not in the lesson but in how to climb over it and get to the next. That in itself shows your advancement. Another person may ask me if they are advanced and I may say also that they are. Do you see that this is an extremely open question and you will only be told that which is right for you to know? However, I did not say that you were a new spirit, did I?

Are people who have the ability to 'see' or otherwise sense energy or who get visual or other non-physical impressions

(like medical intuitivism) more spiritually advanced than those who cannot? Or is this merely another kind of skill like having a natural athletic talent?

Not all people who say they can see or feel do in fact do this. They believe they do, but that is very far from the truth in a large proportion of them. This is the fashionable thing to do so many people imagine that they have this gift. For a true person who works with a spiritual connection, yes they are certainly more advanced than most people on your earth. But this person is single minded in their belief with their connection and never ever varies from that. That is the difference. If you see a person who has a "so called gift of vision or intuition" then test them by asking them about various theories you have heard about other types of spiritual connections or ways, and see what they reply. It is pretty easy for you to work out one from the other. Also we have your intuition to use, as well, and yours being good should in fact give you a quick answer.

We would like you to explain the theory of a person we know, who says a time of enlightenment is coming, and a queue of spirits are waiting to get into bodies.

Your spirit enters your body at the time of birth and it leaves your body when your body dies and it returns home. When a spirit wishes to return to your world, it looks for its parents and then a body is made for it. You cannot say that for people to be enlightened half way through their lives a new spirit will enter, neither can it be said that a great deal of spirits are waiting to come back into bodies in your earth. There are always spirits waiting to return. But what would be the purpose, as it is said, of coming to your earth in order to be enlightened? The spiritual plane is the plane of enlightenment, not your world. Spirits do not wish to re-enter your world for any other purpose than for it to be beneficial in their own path of learning and evolving. You learn during a life from others and your predestined lessons. I cannot say to you that this could possibly be achieved in any other way.

Outside this physical realm, is there a structure and form which does not change?

Outside your physical realm is spirituality and other physical realms as well. From the spiritual realm, as you call it, there is no structure and form. For the others there is at the time that entities are in those realms to learn, experience and advance. Their structure and form varies as do the experiences. It is difficult to define in one short question.

Is it possible for our spirit to leave us whilst we are on earth? I have read this in a book.

Souls or spirit entities even on earth are in this plane of existence as well at the same time when viewed from here and not earth. From earth you appear to leave your bodies during meditation or sleep. In that case you are in both places at the same time. But when a spirit entity returns home after death of the body, it is not greeted by all other souls that it chooses, it is greeted by all other souls within its group as knowledge and a feeling of being there only. The returning spirit will visualize particular spirits and greet them if you want to use this terminology, although I do think that it would confuse you to look at it in this way. The description in the book is too earthly to be true.

According to one author, associated souls identify themselves by assuming earthly features by way of recognition. Why would they want to do this? Similarly he also says that the schools of learning are associated with recognizable buildings familiar from earth?

Spirit in the spirit world is nothing more than nothing in appearance. Spirit recognizes spirit without features, without anything in fact. It knows. That is all. There is no need to see because there are no eyes. If spirit wants to see a spirit, which was in a body, it does not need a picture of that body to know which spirit was in that body. For you see we connect spirit to spirit and not spirit to body. In no case do we do this. As for the temples of learning, it is the same. However there are times when spirit is shown a place on earth and a situation where a particular lesson is being shown. Then spirit will see earth. Or spirit can visualize earth and a building if it wants to at any time. During lessons or teaching it may choose to do this. That is all.

This author has also given two possible interpretations about displaced souls. Will you please tell us your version?
I will say nothing more than that souls go to earth and return, that is all. Souls/spirit entities which are displaced come back just the same. They hover a bit longer on the journey back, that is all. But when spirit arrives back it goes through the same process of observation as any other returning spirit.

Are souls who have harmed others during the life cycle put into seclusion upon entering the spirit world before being placed within their own group? If so, what remedial action takes place?
They go through the same process as the others, but their counseling is more intense. They are still within their cluster when this happens, because all spirits return to their own clusters. If they have been really innocent, then they are shown the error of their ways. If really bad then they must return more or less immediately to learn again. So isolation they do not have because all other spirits within that cluster are on that level, as I prefer to describe it, and they learn from each other too. If the spirit was isolated then the others do not have the close vicinity to observe. Remedial action is by making the spirit see for itself the things which are against the laws of karma.

Our guides touch us with spirit, do they not?
Yes, but your guides are with you all the time and teach you and help you on a daily basis. When things get really bad, then you may be sent an angel to clarify a point or touch you with spirit when you are in a time of suffering. They touch too your guide. He takes strength too from angels. I am taught by angels. Angels are my guides, if you understand.

Could you please describe the shades of light/brightness associated with the speed of travel as an entity?

When the soul leaves the body, there is no light. As souls travel home, there is no light. As souls enter the cluster there is light around them depending on how they fared in their life on earth. Bright lights are the pure souls, and dim lights are around those who need lots of help and guidance. To see a spirit in my world, or as an aura, or as a bright light is nothing more than a pure soul.

Why do we suddenly feel emotional and tearful for no reason? I entered a cathedral once and had this overwhelming emotional surge although I do not follow a religion of any sort. Was it a spirit entity?

Spirit is with you and that in itself makes you have a surge of feeling, usually bringing on tears or joy. In that place emotional vibrations were high. Not religious vibrations but those of people who went there to connect to their God.

Why do I cry every time I have a session with Aleisha and yourself? Is there a connection between relatives I had who have passed over and Aleisha?

Crying sometimes can be due to the energy and vibrations, I think you will understand. When you connect with this environment, whether consciously or not, you will be overpowered by it and your emotions will be softened and you will feel you want to cry. That is all. There is no connection with your family and Aleisha

Can I ask you please, Ishamcvan, if a place or a house has vibrations of other people, which we can feel and may make us upset or uneasy? Does the same thing happen with objects such as jewellery or stones? Can they give us bad vibrations too? It is said that a ring keeps the aura of the person who first wore it. Is that true?

In theory yes, because in all things around you there is a part of your aura which stays. The more spiritually advanced you are then the more peaceful the aura. The younger the spirit entity, then the more aggression or disharmony will remain. With regard to possessions of that person, then yes they do have this aura, but in a much lesser degree. It is because they do not wear the article all the time, they take it on and off and break the pattern. The aura of the person in a place is consistent; it is not fragmented and thus has more effect. You ask about a ring. My answer is yes and no, it all depends on the owner, even though it is possible to have strong vibrations in extremely bad cases.

What about stones such as crystals? Do they have good spiritual vibrations? Does it matter who has touched them? Could, say, the person who pick-axed them out of the rock put a bad vibration on them if they happened to be that sort of person.? Is that why we have to cleanse it in the sea and dry it in the sun? Could I do the same thing with a doomed ring?

Some stones have more feelings than others. You may be in tune with crystals but those alone. You may be one of those people who can get various things from different stones. But yes they have to be cleansed of their former handlers first. Can you do this with a doomed ring? Not so easily because you have the substance which is manufactured and not natural. The process in making the ring is complex in the way that various metals and stones are brought together, which sometimes means that these components are not necessarily in harmony with each other.

Throughout my adult life I have had many people approach me thinking I am someone else. This happens a lot! Are they recognizing something in my non-physical aura that makes them think they know me? Is this possible?

Some spirit entities will recognise others as being on the same level of progress as themselves or having been connected before in previous lives. You must remember that before you return to earth you choose some guides or spirits to be part of your life, say your brother or your husband. They, in the next life, may be connected to you also, but in a different way. An entity may have been with you several lives ago but in this life merely passed by you in a small role or not in any active part. So you see that it is possible to recognise a spirit in a body yet not know why.

Could you describe the individuality of a spirit entity that has left an earthly body?

We are not individual spirits of people who have passed over; we are one spirit that is broken down into lots of spirit particles. I describe this for your comprehension and understanding only. All spirits are part of a one spirit. The one spirit has a higher spirit and that higher spirit is then encompassed with the lower spirits and that becomes a larger group of spirits controlled (for your understanding) by a yet higher spirit and ad infinitum. So you see the spirit of people who have passed over is then part of a whole. When someone from your world passes over to this side their spirit, because that is all there is, is encompassed by the group of spirits, so to speak. That spirit just passed over from earth is then part of the spirit group. It is difficult to help you understand and I am trying many different ways to make you aware of the situation. All spirits on this level of consciousness could be aware of anything that is happening on earth. The spirit entity has to have the will to say, want to connect with the spirit of a person they loved on earth to reach them through a medium. They must know where the person is going to be so that they can communicate through a medium to speak to them. This is not a long complicated process for the spirit to find the person and so on. It is an instantaneous thing. So you see that if a spirit entity here had strong ties still with an earthly entity inside a body still, it could watch or contact that spirit. Always remember that it is spirit contacting spirit. It is not spirit contacting body. The instincts of the body, if fully or greatly developed, will pick up the spirit entity trying to contact them.

If a person is to pass over with a sudden death does the spirit know beforehand? It doesn't seem the same as a person dying from a long illness.

Listen to my previous lessons. Read what I have said. I have already told you that everything we do from spirit to your world is with the blink of an eye. It makes no difference if a person is dying over a period of, say, several of your years and the death is expected, or whether the death is instant with no prior expectation, the death is a death as it is planned. We know when it will happen. Everything is destined to happen. It is not some error on your earth or someone's fault that this happens. It is meant to be. So you see because it is destined spirit knows that it will happen. As all spirits that have passed over previously are one and not individual, all will know that this will happen. To ask whether loved ones will try and reach the person about to die or their close loved ones on earth prior to the death, my answer is sometimes yes. Not always. But sometimes yes. Spirit or spirits may surround the person destined to die or the loved ones in the hope of soothing them. Sometimes people in your world say that they had a premonition that something was going to happen. It is spirit with you. It may not necessarily be spirit from people they knew who had previously passed over, it may be guides or spirits of entities that they do not recognize. Spirit can always be in a position to give help in a way by just being there.

When a spirit entity passes over are they met by spirits in the guise of people they can recognize, and will they stay with the newly arrived spirit to help them settle into the spirit world?

I say to you that this is not exactly the case. Spirit has no body and a body of your last existence can only be seen if an entity chooses to do this. Loved ones may initially momentarily put on a guise so that they can be recognized but a spirit will recognize spirits anyway by instinct, so to speak. It is not necessary to do anything else.

If more than one guide is assisting a person in our world with a particular problem or experience, is it ever the case that those guides will disagree with what is best. If so, what would happen then?

Never would that be the case. From the world of spirit, the answers are always the same. The allocation of guides to a spirit in a body is for the purpose of assisting them through the troubles of living in a world of matter. Each guide is the same in spirit; none are right or wrong. They work only within the laws of spirituality and these are the same. Spirit has no opinion, only love and understanding. All spirits who act as guides are on the same level.

Will all spirit guides on your level teach the same or are there some with other experiences who will teach differently?

It all depends on where they are in their own level of spiritual evolvement. The more they evolve, the more they are wise. If they are wise then they teach with more purity of learning. If they are new spirits and are not experienced then they will maybe give a more muddled or non-clear view. But I speak of spirits, you speak of guides. To be a guide, that is a spirit that is with you throughout your life, then that spirit has to be more spiritually evolved. But not all are at the same level. Some may be there to learn also. The spirit guide learns from the person on earth, as I do with Aleisha. If this spirit is at a lower level, then that guide may not be as wise as another who is that much higher up the scale of spirits in their classrooms.

Is there such a thing as a male or female gender for spirit?

Spirit does not have a gender. However spirit will refer to itself with the gender appertaining to that of what it lived in its last life on earth. For example if I was a hill farmer in Greece or Turkey and was married with children and a wife I therefore would be classed as a male. So I refer myself to you as being a male. I do not say to you I am a male but I infer that I am of the male gender so that you, with your limited understanding can relate to me as a male rather than a nothing thing.

So, if you connect with other spirits, say two, who were females in their last lives, would you say you were a male or female entity?

I would refer to us as a group spirit entity as female. That is because two are greater than one and so we come as female. It is not necessary to come as anything except for you to feel a connection.

Is it possible for a soul/spirit entity to enter a wrong body?

No, because the circumstances of the birth into which your spirit will live is chosen a long time before the birth. The parents are chosen, the lessons are chosen and the life is planned. For that reason the spirit cannot go into the wrong body. However you may think that maybe your choice was odd and you think it is the wrong body, but I say to you that this is chosen for a reason of your lessons and is not false.

Do we and our parents choose before birth to come down into the same family?

Not exactly. The parents choose their parents and their lessons and they are born to a life. The baby, let's call it, chooses the same and is then attached to the parents to teach them lessons, good or bad, or should I say hard. The parents have no choice in the spirit coming as their child. It is the child who decides that one.

Do we continue to connect with the same family over and over again?

Sometimes, but usually only a couple of times, not continuously over several lives. If I said to you for example that your parents chose their parents and then you come along as their child. Perhaps you die young and they had a very hard time with that. Perhaps when you are ready to be born again many years later you may choose them as an aunt and uncle or a sister and so on.

Could you explain the evolution of the spirit entity of a pet? Is it a lower level than ours before they evolve to human form or how do they mature spiritually?

Theirs is not part of your evolution. There is a parallel existence of spirit. In fact they are chosen to take this branch in the road. If you can imagine that they are a sect that is helping you all in your journey you may then try to understand. If I said to you that these animals are in a one-off existence of spirit in order to be with various people in a chosen form, usually one pet will be attached only to one person. There is a strong connection. If you went to a dog pound and found a dog that had already been with another owner, it does not mean that the former owner is the chosen connection of that dog. This is because the connection had not yet happened and you may be the person that is part of that connection. However if a pet has a strong connection to its owner and the owner dies, then the pet is in limbo until that itself dies. The new owner will not be a substitute in any form. Also you have to know that often a pet that has that close connection to you will allow its body to be taken over by a spirit that is in your dimension of transgression in human form. You will look at the pet and see the spirit and perhaps the likeness in spiritual connection of someone who was close to you and had passed over. You will not see in an animal the spirit of someone passed with whom you did not have love or any connection.

Please explain how a spirit as a pet comes to live with a human. Are they finished with their spiritual journey on this level or are they just beginning? Or do they come back for this life. How many times can they come back?

Spirit, wherever it is in its own journey, can take time out to come back as a pet. This existence as a pet is not actually part of their lessons, but it is helping people in your world by being with them. The spirit will agree to come back as a pet. It is a one off time out for the spirit. Can they come back at various times, usually not but it is possible to do so twice. I cannot say to you that it is preferable to come back twice but I do say that it is usually to the same person. If it is necessary they the spirit will be allowed to come again to that person if that person is in dire need of help and the animal can provide this. However this is generally not the case and the side journey is one time only.

Is it true that one spirit can have a contract with another?
Let us say that two spirits in the spirit world would have an agreement to help each other through a life or be at a certain place at a certain time in the other person's life to be support or help. But you all have freewill so that once you are living a life back on your world then this can be broken, sometimes merely because you do not remember the contract or do not want to engage with that person. It could be that one person appears in your life yet you do not want them to be close to you or part of your existence when in fact that is what you have arranged with that spirit to do. Then two people part and the contract is broken.

Can you have a life on earth without a contract with another spirit?
Yes it is not necessary for your life.

About how many contracts can a person arrange for one life?
One only.

How difficult is it to shed the concept of the body and be fully in spirit?
Very easy.

Is there a way to help the spirit of a dying person to pass over to the spirit world?
Yes. You must talk to the mind of the person. Not the body or the brain, but the mind which is the vessel of the spirit in the

body. You talk with no words. You say to the spirit with your mind that it is time to leave the body and return to its home. The time has come to leave and it is just ok for that to happen. If they are worried about leaving loved ones on earth, you must tell them that they can observe all of their loved ones from the world of spirit. They will be able to not only see the people but they can be with the people daily, hourly or all the time. That may seem strange for me to say and you will ask how you can be with them say with their loved husband on earth and in the spirit world at the same time. Once the dying person can grasp that concept then they will be better equipped to flow with the dying process.

What is the difference in moving between earth and the spirit world and being in both simultaneously?

They are in fact always simultaneous. If I said to you that the spirit would move back and forward between earth and the spirit world, I am saying that it is all happening at the same time. From the spirit world all actions have no time. A spirit can be here all the time or on earth all the time, but every action on the earth plane is leaving the spirit on the spirit plane at the same time.

Could spirit on your plane of existence be with more than one earthly person at the same time if these people are in different places?

Yes because it is all simultaneous.

If we had no thoughts or memories could we live just in the now with no time?

Precisely. But earth has to have time. Lessons in your classroom have to have structure and these have to have time. It has to have a past and a future and it has to have memories and thoughts because that is how the body is designed. If you had no body yet were living an existence in a smoke say, not a body, then you would not need time. This will happen in other concepts

71

in other worlds. But the lessons are different because they are much, much more advanced. As you are in your progression you need to have bodies and you need to therefore have time. As you progress to things you need to learn that are more complex than living you will see that thoughts, actions and deeds will be without time. But love will be paramount in these lessons, more so than you see it today. Does love not need time? Yes it always does. From the world of spirit love is always present and if a spirit visits your world because it is simultaneous then the love in the spirit world will be the same strength of love in the spirit visiting a loved one on earth. It is not possible for a spirit to return with hatred or anger, it only has love.

When does the spirit enter the body or egg of a baby?

I will generalize because it varies with different times. Sometimes it is soon after conception, sometimes in the early months, but sometimes it comes and goes and comes back at the birthing. A spirit in an egg or a small baby needs not be there all the time. I have told you that your own spirits return home during sleep, or can do, so it is the same thing. You call it astral travel, not a name I like.

Can you tell us more about the transition of spirit in his return home?

When the spirit is ready to leave the body it does know so, of course. Many times it will leave the body for a moment and then return. It will do this several times. It is more like a pulse rate. You can count the minutes and see the regularity of the movement backwards and forwards. When it decides to go and not quickly return back it is guided by the person's main guide. The body is discarded like a chrysalis. The butterfly flies home with the guide at its side. When it reaches the mass which is spirit on this level of spirituality it enters the mass and is home. Once there it is surrounded by spirits. Some of these it can feel it knows, some not. In either case the spirit is relieved to be again surrounded in the eternal love which is spirit.

How long does it take for a spirit to recognise that they are no longer in a body?

Instantly.

Is there an acclimatization period once you are in the mass of spirit?

I cannot say to you that this is a good description. What happens is that you are in the process of looking over your life for a while, although we have no time of course. You analyze that which has gone before. As doing such you are maybe not as another spirit who is past that stage. But this is an extreme description because it is not that simple. It is a gradual progression of movement or swirl of the cloud, the mass, the smoke. A movement from A to B which is not a movement. Very difficult to describe.

Is the time of our death pre-set and are there exceptions?

The time of death is always pre-set. That is the actual time that you are supposed to die. You cannot take your life before that pre-set time. However with murder another person can take your life before the pre-set time. That will cut off your life on earth too early when perhaps you have not learnt all your lessons. I said to you that your time of death is preset and cannot be changed. But another person does have the option to change that if they choose by free will to do so. You can commit suicide if you use your free will. But it is not allowed. No death is allowed by the higher spirit other than the one pre-set.

If someone murders another and cuts that person's set life time short, does the murdered person have to return again quickly to earth to finish the lessons as does a person who committed suicide?

The action of one person killing another is never allowed. You cannot take a life, whether a fellow human or an animal. For the person doing those things they have stopped the chosen lifespan of the spirit in that body. It is important to remember that aspect more than the fact that the body itself was brutalized. So the spiritual advancement of the murderer of animal or man is curtailed or damaged as a consequence. That spirit of the murderer will have to return many times to your world with relevant lessons resulting from not learning about murder before its advancement will re-commence. For the victim then there is no affect to the spirit. However the lessons the spirit was working through in a life on earth have to be completed at some stage, on earth or by observations from the spirit world. If you look at the fact that say, a man was murdered at age 20 when his lifespan was to the age of 45 and only minimum lessons were learnt, then in the next life it will be allowed to maybe only have to return for another 25 years, so in consequence it is a shorter life next time. But this is too precise an example and is only for you to see my point. In addition, this murdered body spirit will have learnt lessons from the murder of the body so he may have gained some points from the experience which could or could not be offset in his whole spiritual assessment.

Do we need to send help to someone who has died from this world? Is there a value to our prayers?

Once the spirit returns to this plane of existence then there is no need for your help. They are surrounded by love and the elders or the higher spirits are there with an abundance of love and understanding. Whatever has happened is not so severe once these spirits take charge, so to speak.

Would you agree that a soul progresses by trying to overcome all negative emotions, specifically connected to fear, through many lifetimes? Can a soul return home bruised and hurt because of this and how is the damage repaid.

Negative emotions are lessons. The spirit, dependent on their advancement, has the power to play out the lesson and overcome the emotion whilst on earth. I have told you many times that greed, frustration, anger, love and tolerance of others are all amongst the long list of lessons. If one of these is given for your life on earth you will have lots of things set in your path for us to make sure that you have overcome this aspect whichever way it comes at you. If you do not overcome it and you return home, none the wiser, then you will feel bruised. Higher guides then set you right in observing where you went wrong and send you straight back to do it all again.

Chapter Three

Mind, Body & Spirit

"Your mind is a processing centre; your body a vessel;
your spirit the ultimate you"

**Is it true that children who are born severely disabled
are the most pure of all souls? Are all of us born as such at
some stage?**

To be born of a body with a disability is the supreme test
of understanding and it could be said that to do so the spirit has
to have reached a certain level of progression to be allowed this
privilege. The spirit must be advanced. The spirit is nearly pure
in its realm of progression within this level of consciousness. So
it could be called a pure soul or to be exact a nearly pure soul or
spirit. It still has to live that life with all its hardships to progress
to the pure stage. But all these children are very spiritual and it is
obvious in their appearance to all that see them. They are wise in
spirit and lame in body. You ask if all spirits have to come to earth
in such a body. I will say to you that this is not the case. There are
many ways of learning your lessons and these are different for
each spirit. Some may choose to come back that way, others may
choose a different path that gives the same results and tests.

If someone received a transplant of say a kidney or heart, could the donated organ affect the characteristics or personality of the recipient?

You must remember that there is spirituality first and body second. The body is only the vessel to carry the spirit on its journey of lessons through life. When the spirit returns home then the body dies and becomes again dust. So the body, although it is energized by spirit, is nothing when spirit leaves it. The organs and the body itself do not keep the spirituality, for the spirit leaves and goes home. So for an organ to be taken from the dead body, and I repeat the dead body, and given to another body, it is of no consequence. For it is like saying that you took a wheel off an old car and put it on your new car. You are not affected by the owners of the old car, for they did not affect the wheel. The person with the new body part makes it their own.

From where do humans originate?

You ask about the body of humans not the spirituality, which is the source. The spirit uses the human body for its journey through life on earth. There is a big difference. I will explain both so that you understand. You must think first that you are spirit with a body, not body with spirituality. Your spirituality is everlasting. It cannot be destroyed so that it is nothing. That is not possible. The spirit returns to the next plane of existence, where I am now, and from there returns to earth, using many bodies, until it learns all its lessons and is spiritually mature enough to move on to another plane of existence, which is its purpose. For each journey to earth it chooses its human body, whether male or female, healthy or deformed. This body you must think of as like a butterfly. Your journey on earth is like being trapped in a chrysalis (your body) from which your spirit leaves and flies like a butterfly home to base to evaluate its existence on earth. While you are a chrysalis you do not see the wonders of the big wide world of spirituality because you are confined to a small vision expanse. It is only when you become a butterfly again that you see the whole spectrum.

So your question was where do humans come from. The human body has evolved from animals. Animals grow and change from one species to another, as you know. The world you live on grows from ashes through the sprouting of seeds and becomes a lush green world. Then man destroys it and it returns to ashes again, only to have the whole process happen all over again. The animals change with it. But for your spirituality, your existence, the you inside the body, that is different. You have reached the maturity of your spirituality through a long process of learning. Let me say that you started a known path, say from an amoeba, although there was of course a long path before that. There is no beginning in your understanding in the path of the spirit and there is no end. It is ad infinitum.

Could you talk about abortion?

The reason I did not discuss this before was because it may cause some distress to certain members of your group and I wanted them to think calmly and carefully to my answers and not be too emotional and irrational, if that is the word, with themselves and their involvement. So here is the word of Ishamcvan and the advice from higher spirit as to the interpretation that must be given to you all. Abortion is sometimes right, but is usually wrong. When it is right is when it is thought that the child may have inherited certain bad characteristics from its father or mother such as insanity from rape or abuse or similar. Where the growth of the fetus is in the wrong position and causes severe complications for the mother and will never grow in that position anyway. Where abortion is wrong is where it is used as a means of having sex and then discarding the fetus because it is not wanted. This is not an act of love, it is an act of sex. I have told you before in great detail the difference between love and sexual lust. If in a relationship love has gone then so should sex. If sex continues when love has gone then it is the same as sexual lust only. To conceive a child with sexual lust and not use a form of birth control other than that of abortion is irresponsible in the first place and not allowed. If a child is conceived from love then usually, although not always, the parents try every way to keep the child whatever the circumstances because it is the natural thing to do. Abortion is not the easiest option in such circumstances and causes more problems, probably, than keeping the child. You will see from all this that it is a very complex issue and I hope I am putting this over to you with the right message. Let us take the hundreds of thousands of abortions that are taking place purely because a child has been started in error and this is the easiest and quickest thing to do. There are very few of these cases that are justified. Probably none at all unless they fit in the spectrum I have mentioned before. Many of those mothers could have the child and then give it to another person who cannot have a child of their own. This is good. It will be done with love for the child and love to the person who is receiving the child. Many of those mothers were put in that position from spirit to see their reactions and the way that they took to overcome their dilemma could change their personality and the path of their lives whichever decision they took. Of course now with technology and science doctors can tell when a fetus is growing that it is damaged with defects or disease, and then they decide to abort the child. In most cases this is acceptable to spirit and in a great number of these circumstances the baby would die before birth anyway. So you see that when these deformed children enter the world they then set up another area for discussion and variations of lessons to their parents and those people directly connected to the child. I hope you have understood the teachings of Ishamcvan on this subject. I do have to say to you that on the spiritual plane abortion is definite to these rules, although as with everything else there are circumstances to be taken into account and allowances made to the spirit and his karma. But the biggest thing to avoid is trying to make excuses for an act to fit into the category of allowances. This aspect applies to all things I have taught you that are not going to necessarily advance you in your next return to our world. For an abortion to happen in exceptional circumstances as I have mentioned, it is not a problem. For an abortion to happen for convenience only to the mother and no other circumstances, it is a problem. In the middle there are lots of other cases for consideration by spirit.

What about birth control? Is that allowed?

You still seem to be uncertain as to the definite opinions of Ishamcvan and the laws of spirit in this respect. I have told you many times, as today, about the difference of love between two people and a loving sexual act which will eventually result in children, and a lustful sexual act which is not intended as an act of love or for children. For a loving couple to control the size of their family and the timing of their children, this is acceptable especially when the family is poor and feeding the children is a great problem when there are too many. To use birth control methods only to perform acts of lust it is not permitted, neither is abortion as a birth control method in this case. The law on this issue is simple and easy to understand. A loving couple does not have to be married necessarily; it is just that they are in love with each other when the act is done as an extension of this.

Our question is about defects of the body or mind, which make a person do peculiar or abusive things. Is it merely that they have inherited the wrong genes which makes them behave in this way?

If the person is of sound mind and not mentally retarded, then I say to you that the peculiarity that they feel they have to participate in is only a test. I have told you about homosexuals and these other people are the same. A situation is put to them in their lives and they have the choice to do one thing or another. They chose the test from the spiritual plane. They asked for it to be hard; particularly hard in some cases. If, say, a person is faced with a barrier between being female or male as is rarely the case, then this person has the choice to act in the sex of the person it chooses or to have treatment to keep it to the sex which it was born with, which is correct by the law of karma. The same thing would happen to a pervert who abuses children. It could be that there is a peculiarity that needs treatment, but the person themselves will know that the thing that they urge to do is not acceptable. They either give into this thing by making excuses such as a defect of the cells, hormones or the brain and carry on doing the thing, or they fight it and ask for help and treatment. These things all have an answer and treatment is there if they chose to take that route. The choice is theirs. The lesson is theirs. Always there is a choice. Even, as I have said before, a homosexual has a choice to get help. Many though love to be that way so they choose to have a good time and not ask for help. The choice is theirs.

If we think something, is it as bad as actually doing it?

Well it is strange to see the coming and goings of all of you and from this perspective the views of your silent thoughts, which are only available for scrutiny from the world of spirit. You must never forget that your thoughts are your deeds of the mind and it is the mind that is tempted to do and think things which are not necessarily the needs or desires of spirit. But the flesh is weak and the spiritual advancement is curtailed or restricted by these actions. So if you can control your mind by your spirit then you have won the game so to speak. It is your mind that is in control of your body, not in the spiritual sense but on a day to day basis when you are not being aware of your spirituality and its laws above all other things.

Is it our minds and our intelligence which governs our thoughts of what might happen?

It is one of the most wonderful of all things to be certain of a thing and be proved that this was in fact as certain as you had known it would be. So if you follow this thought pattern and nothing else you will soon see that things change for the better. If you think negative you get negative. If you hope and believe, then it will happen. There is no other way. You cannot ask spirit for help if you do not believe that help will be given. It may not be given in the way you expect but it will always be given if you ask. So I will say to you once more that you must trust in spirit.

You do not know or wish to know why you are moved in certain directions. It may be for the benefit and learning of others that you are manoeuvred in a position to help and assist them. You will never know because it is not relevant to you. The only thing that you must do is drift with the tide, knowing that your journey is planned and will take the correct path if you do not paddle against the tide with your own variations of what you think is correct and the way to go. The way is not always clear to you, but it is to me and I say to you that you must trust. We are trying to get you to learn to trust. I would say that this is the most important aspect at this time.

Will there ever be a cure for cancer?

For all illnesses man will find a cure and then new ones will emerge. But if you take the fact that all persons on your earth choose the way that they die then you may find that this adds confusion. I did not say to you that a person will choose to die of cancer. I said to you that a person may choose to suffer a great deal of pain and humiliation before they die. It is the suffering that is the key, not the disease. The spirit does not choose to die of cancer. The person chooses to die in that way. A person may choose to die in a train crash, but not in itself more than it chooses to die in those circumstances at a particular time not on a particular train, do you understand? If the train that was due to run at that time was in for repair another train of another colour and style would be put on to run in its place. It is the same with a fatal disease, if doctors in their evolvement of learning find a cure, then new diseases will be put in their place such as aids. There must always be a means of death and suffering, otherwise how would spirit learn its lessons.

By giving up those things which are abusing our bodies, do we in fact become more spiritual? Is the difference that easy?

I have told you all many times in my lessons that to abuse your body with any substance is not acceptable. Whilst I tell you

82

that the spirit is more important than the body which you are using for your path through this life, it is also essential that you have the spirituality which is advanced enough not to succumb to any temptation which is harmful. For you to go against the laws of spirituality, with the knowledge that this thing is wrong, is in itself curbing your advancement. So if you look at these points, then by making yourself more clean, so to speak, you are more spiritual. It proves that the karma needs this thing to happen. By being more spiritual you are better. You cannot make this thing happen by wishing it to happen. But you have achieved this by listening to the words of Ishamcvan and proving that by doing as is requested then you will be richer in body and spirit. So look for more, and try to overcome all that you know is required. I am not being strict or hard, I am saying these things for your own advancement that is all.

What are your views on masturbation?

This is a complex question for there is no definite answer. I would say that for many people it is wrong. This is because it leads to other things such as abuse and crime such as rape. One thing leads to another if it is done in excess. Man loses control. It becomes a disease that grows and grows and man has justification to himself to permit him to do this thing in excess. I have told you all many times that you must not abuse your spirituality or your body by any substance or act, and masturbation would fall into this realm if done in excess. But also we must look on it as being permitted also. For it is. There is nothing wrong if it is done in the right circumstances. If it is not an obsession. Every time is different. Every decision by man is for him to decide with clarity if it is right or wrong. I say to you again there is no right or wrong. If man decides to do a thing whether it is masturbate or kill somebody, it is his decision, that is all.

From where did AIDS originate?

From spirit. As did all illnesses and diseases. Without illness there would be no suffering. Without suffering there would be no lessons.

With regards to procreation and over population, because women are fertile every 4 weeks, wouldn't population control be easier if, like some animals, we become fertile just once a year?

Probably, but that is not how it was chosen to be. We are back to cause and effect. If your women only had the feeling to mate once a year, the whole rules and temptations of mankind would have to be rewritten and the tests would be less in accordance. The effect would be less in the population and more in the problems of behavior. One problem goes and another arises. So never do you have an ideal situation. You must look at your experience of life in a body as being a lesson, not an easy ride. You should want lots of problems for this is what makes you richer in spirit.

With regard to a baby with a dreadful illness or disability, a baby is not aware of life, God, meanings etc. A baby can't be suffering the uncertainty of spirituality in its first year – it doesn't have the brain or knowledge. What is the point of the handicap?

A brain is part of your body. It is physical, so is the body. Your spirit and its path are both physical when you are in a body for a life on your world. What the brain thinks or the intelligence tells you is not what makes your spirituality more mature. Understanding the concept by using your brain does. But a baby may have a spirituality that is old yet a body that is young. That spirit may have chosen a concentrated lesson on your world for a short space of time. The body and the brain of the baby are not the ones that are learning the lesson. It is the spirit of that body that is having to endure the frustration and the spiritual pain, not the physical pain. The baby will feel the physical pain and be distressed and the spirit will understand and learn. That is all.

Why does the human body have to be so complicated?

It is not. It is merely like any engine. One part leads to the progress of the other. If one part is faulty then the machine breaks down. It is not complicated at all. It is simple. The going wrong of various parts may be construed as being complicated but the machinery itself and how it works is not complex at all.

It is said that a healthy body creates a healthy mind, would a person's spirituality be boosted by this comment too?

Not at all. The spirit of a person in a body that is riddled with disease or deformity would probably be better than that of the spirit in a body that is perfect. It doesn't matter ever if the body is not good, to the spirituality that is. They are two completely different things.

Could you explain whether it is possible for a person to connect spiritually to a spirit trapped within a deformed body with no power of speech?

I rebuke that the spirit is trapped within the body. It is there freely and joyfully, as you of course know. Spirit in a deformed body is learning much faster than you. Now I will say to you that you feel and sense people, their moods, motives, reasons for actions etc. This is something you have developed because of your spirituality. Now, let us take a spirit as you have described and I will say to you that this spirit is so much more advanced that it is sensing and seeing far more than you can comprehend. So to say to me also, what is that spirit learning whilst entrapped in such a body, I will say to you that it is learning a hundred fold more than a spirit in a normal body. But the question was can you connect spirit to spirit. Yes of course, and learn from them too.

I would like to know that, if someone's heart fails, but before a transplant heart is available they are put on an artificial heart while waiting, what does this person's spirit feel?

Well, spirit does not feel, it experiences. In the case you describe it works like this. The body which the spirit is inhabiting is being repaired. The spirit is in the body, but it can leave the body and go back which is what happens sometimes when you sleep. But it still has the cord link to the body. It will not let loose that cord link until the body dies and it comes home. So the body is being repaired, but for intense purposes it is not dead. It is being kept alive by machines, and then it works on its own again. The spirit of the person will hover and still be connected. Or it may stay inside the body and experience the machine working. It all depends. If it is time for the spirit to come home, then it will leave, the machine will keep the body only alive and when connected again with another heart, the body will die.

Occasionally I hear a sensation in an ear, more a noise similar to radio frequency. Is this spirit trying to speak to me?

It is a way of attracting attention, if you like. Shall we say that your attention is needed? More so that you should sit down and try and connect through meditation or quiet thoughts. Then you may learn or connect. When Aleisha has this she will go and connect to me. If you are saying or thinking something to which we give verification that you are on the right spiritual track, you will have more of a bodily sensation like tingling or something touching you - a feather - a hand not quite on your shoulder - a presence.

Are you saying that when I get this feeling, that my thoughts or speech is more right than wrong?

No, that particular sensation is nothing to do with what you are doing or thinking. It is just a rap of attention. Like saying stop what you are doing and connect with us. If you get tingling or what I have described, that is relevant to what you were saying. It doesn't work on what you are thinking. That is how a good healer will get a sensation when he is healing. A different but same thing as the tingling. He is doing it right and he gets approval.

Are we born into a particular star sign, in order to best serve our chosen lessons on earth?

Let me say that before you return to your world you decide your path. This includes your parents, the time you are born and some other aspects. The astrological aspects will come into the heading of other aspects. If you are born under one sign your personality will perhaps be different than under another. That is a personality, not a spirituality, which is different. Let us say that a personality is also a test. All this mentioning of tests! So if you want to say that it is serving your lessons on earth to be under one sign or another, I suppose this is correct.

Please be explicit in explaining to me how we function with thought, emotion, and inspiration. My understanding of it so far is that the brain and the rest of the body are basically vehicles. These are solid bodies that we can measure, test, touch and see. But then there are things that we have no way of looking at under a microscope like the mind, our own spirit, guiding spirits; people talk of a soul, chakras and life energy they call prana or chi. How many of these ideas are correct? When an idea comes into a person's head from what seems to be out-of-thin-air, where does it come from? Is it the mind? And what is the mind if it is not the brain? Is the mind somehow connected to one's spirit guide?

There are a lot of questions here so I will break them down into sections so that you understand. Firstly there are two distinct differences between the body - a solid matter - and the spirit, which is without form, although, does have substance as such, even though you cannot see this. The body has many facets such as living parts of the body which function to keep it alive and so on. And then there is the brain, the vessel, which carries the messages to make the other parts of the body actually function. But, you ask me, what makes the brain stimulate the mind into having its thoughts? Well, all I can say to you is that spirit sends messages to the mind which you call instinct or reasoning. From those messages you get maybe your inspirations and your knowing by instinct what is right or wrong for the world of spirit or your own karma. As you progress in your learning these words from spirit become more and more noticeable to you in your body and you then have sixth sense, medium-ship and so on; you are aware easily as to where the messages are coming from and how to interpret them. Even so

I say this, you will be confused. Let me say then this scenario. Say there was no spiritual connection. The mind is there and how will it function? It will still be a part of the brain and the brain will make the mind think and work things out for you, but as for inspiration there will be none. As for instinct there will be none. As for working out mathematical problems and dealing with scientific experiments, yes you will understand for they are parts of the brain's functions and not at all from spirit. Now let us look at the spirit itself. What is it? Is it up there or over there or hiding for you to find it? Not at all. It is you. The same you as you were in the last life and the next and the next. You are your spirit, not your body. You borrow your body for your journey through life, that is all. When you have finished your lessons and you return home to the spiritual plane of existence, then your body dies and returns to the earth. Now we have the scenario of when does the spirit enter the body form and when does it leave? The embryo can be living and the spirit not yet inside it. The body cannot have taken its last breath, but the spirit has left. A body being kept alive by a machine may not have the spirit in it. There is a way the doctors can keep the body alive, but it is not animated by spirit for it is not there. You may sit with a dying person and know when the spirit leaves the body. You can feel it go. So from this let us look at the other questions about charkas and the like. Are they correct? I say to a point, for this is defining the simplicity which is there. They are merely saying the same things in a complex way. Yes you have these centres, but no you do not necessarily have to look at them in this way. Just understand the difference between your body and your spirit and keep them separate. If you can meditate and leave your body and look from your spirit self at your body self from above or from one side, then you will understand there is a big difference between the two.

Given that many diseases are sent from spirit, is it wrong to donate money to their research?

No, for many reasons. You must always try and help your fellow man. There are a great many people who have contracted the disease from circumstances and not being sent from spirit as a direct lesson for their wrong doings. They may have chosen the lesson, but as a secondary effect not a direct effect. Medicine must progress too, it is part of life. Man will try and conquer disease, that will not stop. Suffering will not be ruled out I'm afraid. Everyone has to die, so the choice is theirs. But whether you sit by a dying person and hold their hand or mop their brow to ease their pain, or you donate money to help research help their pain, there is no difference.

What about giving money to beggars on the street if they are going to spend it on drugs that damage their bodies?

You may give money for it is not for you to judge whether they need it or not. If they ask and you have it to give, then do so. If you do not feel it is right, then do not. You must use your powers of observation to decide if you feel it is justified. But as I have said you must not judge. To decide if you want to give or not is not being judgemental.

What do you have to say about incest?

The act of sexual pleasure is primarily for the production of children. It is done in a relationship that is full of love and with this in mind. For this reason incest cannot be allowed under any circumstances.

You say that abortion is ok in cases of insanity caused by rape. How can rape cause insanity?

Where the rapist has mental insanity and then passes that evilness, if you like to call it, onto the child of its victim, then there is an exception to the abortion rule.

We know of a teenage girl in a foster home who has been badly abused by her real family. She will not admit to what has happened and will not see a councilor. She is withdrawn and never goes out or has friends. How can we help her?

Firstly you must break the situation down into many parts. Firstly she was abused and used by people and this had a devastating effect on her. She has partially, and wants totally, to block this out. She thinks that this is the way to act. She does not understand that it was not totally her fault and she feels that the punishment of her parents is not justified. What must be done is for someone to befriend her, but it must be someone whom she will totally trust. I do not think there is yet someone around her who will be right for this part. I wish we could talk to her for that would be a key to open up the dungeon of demons which lurk within her. It is not necessary for her to see a trained councilor; a spiritual person will do, if and only if she will relate to them. So we have a situation where she is withdrawn, because she has so much inside her, which she does not feel she wants to share. She will not go out and mix with people, because how can she trust them? She is afraid and hurt and upset and these things make her unhappy. Ask her if she can get on the internet and talk to Aleisha and then myself. We will succeed where others have failed.

I have been told that as a result of my spiritual progression my physical body is changing. Is there any substance to this?

You can change things in your body by purely wishing them to happen, or not to happen as I have told you many times with regard to illness. Or you body can change because you chose it to do so before you came to your life on earth. By this I mean for tumors to go and diseases to diminish. But for your body to change through a spiritual understanding and progression of your path, I will ask you, my pupils; do you think this could happen? I will test you to see how much you have learnt.

Could you please explain the microcosmic orbit known as "the great heavenly cycle? It is said that as babies in the womb we enjoyed this circular flow of energy naturally and that healing follows this flow?

All things travel in circles. Life, death, rebirth, death and so on. The universe has a circular movement in that all things begin and end and then begin again. Some of your people also say that spirituality is itself a circular movement, but of course it is not. For spirituality is a progression. But progression is a cycle and therefore the movement of spirituality is a cycle in itself. For a baby in the womb there is a time within a cycle and this is an extremely important time that is before birth. So the segments of that circle, or shall we say cycle, is very relevant to a new beginning. For healing you are tapping into the cycle of spirituality. You are opening a hole in which spirit can descend through the healer to make the healing take place. It is all energy and healing itself is tapping into this energy. But the name energy in your world is confusing for it is not energy, as you know it. It is merely a flowing of spirituality and has no power of movement or artificial appendage to the actual flow of things.

I have heard mention of a person having a third eye, but don't understand how this can be.

Your third eye, as you say, should not be taken too literally. It is just a way of saying that you are becoming aware of your spirituality and how to connect with your inner self and the world of higher spirits, our teachers, and their higher spirits, which make up the world of spirituality. You are as a molecule of a cloud. One in yourself but always part of a large whole, yet nothing of substance for your spirituality is you and you are not your body.

Knowing that our bodies are merely vessels for our spirits, is it wrong to refer to ourselves as 'people'? Is there a better, more accurate term?

People or a person in your language refers to a body. As you are a spirit within a body, this can be classed as being correct in your eyes. From our perspective here we would say you are a spirit on your journey on earth for which you borrow a body. You are always a spirit entity whether here or earth bound for the time being.

Chapter Four

Everyday Lives

"Each day is the test of faith of your
own decisions and observations"

How can I avoid being affected spiritually by the problems of others?

There is some confusion generally on this subject which is causing many problems that hamper your progressions. I would like you to be reassured that these things are all noted and are not from spirit directly to upset you to disbelieving. They are the effect of a cause and I have told you many times that the people that you meet on your path may not necessarily give you the strength and good experiences. They may have many problems themselves from which you have an effect. I will try to guide you through the boulders and rocks which they cast in your path. Your guide sees them and you do not. Let me lift your feet into the air so that you float above them and do not feel their harshness and jagged points, which hurt you. I am your eyes and your feelings too. I am your guide. I am your awareness if you let me show you the way. I am not only your love and your friend I am your guardian also. Please think as we two, not as you as a one, to deal with everything on your own. I am the spirit and you are the body. We are one. You are the child and I am the father. I know what is right and wrong, not in a definite sense but in that only of a guardian. You take the steps that I see are safe. You are not to run when I tell you to walk for if you do so you will fall. I will not let you fall. But you still have free will. If you decide to go along without me then so be it. I have no choice but to let you run. I cannot stop you. But we must have the love that is inseparable. We must walk together arm in arm. You must trust me through love, not through reason or because your brain says it is the easy way. I am not the easy way. I am pure love and that I will pass to you for no other reason than because that is as it must be. You are you but I am both of us. You will reunite with me later here on this plain and now if you choose to do so. There is no other way. I will not go away. I will be here whatever you feel, either now or in the future. If you ignore me and then later change and welcome me with open arms, I will be the same. There is nothing that can kill my love. I will wait, that is all.

How can I rise above people who try to put me down?

I would say that you must be independent of any person who is taking from you. You must give only love. Nothing else is important. If other people look for wanting more than love, or do not accept that love is enough, then you must realize that you are the richer and they are the poorer in spirit. Walk tall in the realms of your own spirituality, for that is your protection and your radiance. You need nothing more

How can I make people see they are not acting in their own spiritual interests?

Every person must be in control of their own karma. Every person is alone in this respect. You can help other people to understand, but you cannot make them change their own perspective of spirituality unless they feel it is right for them to do so.

If a person doesn't know why they are going through a situation, how can they react honestly and appropriately?

You are all in control of your own lives, but there will be times when the circumstances of your environment and encounters with other people leave you weak in your own inner strength and this is what often happens. If the person is in this state, then they will not act clearly. It is no ones place to lecture them and the worst thing will be to tell them how wrong they are. With love, care and understanding, and saying sometimes nothing at all, they will gradually come to understand themselves their hurt, and that is all it is. With spiritual strength beside them it will guide their path through the jungle of inner despair.

Am I influenced spiritually by the words of actions of others?

You know the answers to all things from words from spirit. Ask and you will be told. If you choose to go against the words which are being spoken by finding explanations by which you can justify your actions, there is no one who can answer for this except for your self in your own spiritual advancement. Cannot you see that your advancement is in your control only? No one else's. You cannot be affected by the actions or words of others unless you choose to listen. Always you have the control. Always you have the answers because they are being told to you. Listen. You have the key.

There are many people in our world who try to wrong us. What is your perspective on this?

So let us also look at the persecutors of your world. I have told you often that persecutors are power mongers, but they are also murderers and thieves and all other manner of things. They like to control other people for their own ends to give themselves power. You see it all around you in varying degrees. It is a sad and hurting thing to endure but the persecutors seem to always have a reason to themselves for what they do. Sometimes they begin as persecutors but see the error of their ways and repent. Maybe the Holy Spirit will speak to them through their guides and they suddenly stop and look at what they are doing and stop being that way. Sometimes they do not listen and always have a good reason to act that way. The laws of karma do not accept that any man be persecuted by another in whatever way whether it is by mental cruelty or by abuse of the body. Both are wrong and both are not accepted.

What do you think of the crime and violence in many of our big cities?

There are thousands and millions of cities all the same. There are billions of people who are wrong and doing wrong things. They have no imagination of spirituality and the greater part of them does not want to know. It is their choice. Someone from your group asked how you can teach to the people who are surrounded with violence. I will say to you that you can speak and if people choose not to listen then it does not matter. If one person hears your words and listens and is healed spiritually, then the lesson has been good.

What should I do if a person abuses my trust?

If people abuse your trust then you will see them for what they are and then you have the observation and your test of skills to see why and for what reason they did this thing to you. Please observe still, for it is your finest lesson. You may sit beside a road and watch the travelers as they go by and each one will be different. It will not be boring for you to watch all day if necessary for the endless progression of people before you will inspire you with interest not imaginable. So never think that people are what they seem, for this is not true. Neither it is with animals. They may be dumb to your world but they are not. Their spirit speaks to you whatever they are. Spirit has no boundaries and therefore is transmittable through all other beings that have spirit within them. You like to admire and connect with a baby human, why would you not want to connect with a baby spirit - that is I mean a spirit which is a novice or undeveloped. You like to teach a baby human;

you should try and teach a babe spirit too. By teaching you learn to evaluate your own talents and powers. The more you teach the more you learn and the greater in spirituality you will become. To humble yourself to others is the finest of tests to overcome. To humble yourself because you want to do so means that you understand the lesson and act with spirituality and thought and mind which is considerably different. I have told you many times that mind is not spirit. Mind does not control spirit. But spirit controls all things in yourself if you allow it to do so

Please give us some advice about the problem with the actions of others? We find some surprising in their goodness and understanding, and others peculiar in their lack of spirituality.

Forget their wrong and hurtful doings, for you have no control over their path. If the light is there and they close their eyes to it, so be it. If they try and manoeuvre themselves into a position of authority and want power over you, so be it. For it is their path and their understanding which is lacking in its sincerity and goodness. For the man who is surprisingly spiritual when you did not think that he was so far advanced in his journey and lessons of life, I would say to you praise him for his faith and understanding.

How can I look at bad things in a positive way?

I will ask you to look and observe in all that in all there is good and be positive, for that is the answer to all things. For each positive thing that is given you at the moment there are many that are frustrating and peculiar to your mind. But look at the positive and see what beauty and glory there is in these and how they are superior in themselves, way over and above any other things that annoy you for your having to deal with them. The positive things, the gifts have come easily and without pain. Look into the eyes of the baby and see the wonder that is there. Deal with the daily problems and see the input of others which makes them the problem that they are. Ask what cause and effects have made these things yours to deal with. How can they be yours when you are not the cause? But the cause of others in all things will always be yours, for you have been positioned to deal with all effects with the word of spirit to make people understand the reason. There will always be effects and there will always be causes that are not only futile but unnecessary to the happiness and well being of fellow men. When a person takes the time to consider the well being of others, then the cause will diminish and the effects will be no more in the proportion that they are today. Man is no longer in control of his own destiny if he ignores his own spirituality. There are few people in proportion to the population of the world that are aware of the things and beliefs that you take for granted as being the normal. You are in a very minute minority in your understanding. If you were to say to your wise teacher Ishamcvan, tell me what I must do to make these people understand, I will tell you to teach by example. Many of these people are not happy in their lives. But then neither are you, you say. But you are far the more content and at peace than a mere proportion of the happiness that many men believe they must feel. For their outward appearance and façade and the true dismay that they feel inside are two different perspectives. They are not true to themselves. Hopefully you will touch the interest of many people in your simple language. This may be many years before you succeed, but you must work hard at the cause and see for yourself when you look back in retrospect the ripple of the effect on so many which will change their thinking and their reasoning. Many will not dig so deeply in their minds and their background experiences to see that there is room for new thoughts, but then I did not say that you will conquer all forms of argument, that is not true for one person. But you will sow the seed will you not?

I have seen an advertisement from a company who are marketing the concept that the wealth that a person on earth has accumulated during his lifetime should be held in trust until he is reborn. What is the opinion of Ishamcvan on this matter?

Wealth is not important. No person who returned to the world of spirit could wish to acknowledge going back to earth and retrieving wealth. To do so would be against the laws of Karma. You have no memory of definite things when you return to earth in the next life so how could you remember? You have perhaps only brief memories which come and go so spasmodically that they are nothing more than fleeting glimpses. You would not know where to go to retrieve it anyway. You are funny. You world is so naive.

Please explain persecution and abuse of one person to another

I know that you are curious about people that take pleasure in belittling others or finding glory in hurting someone with harsh words or deeds. If a person does something wrong, whatever it is, then it is the sole problem of himself. However, if there are other people directly, and I say directly, connected with this act even if they are not the instigator of the act, then their action as a participant or observer is wrong to their own personal spiritual karma. Any person observing an act and not helping the persecuted person is in fact a participant of the whole. I have told you to observe. If you do so you learn lots about other people. If several people gather together to persecute another then all of them have the same problem to themselves. Why not observe those who are throwing the stones at the persecuted person and see whether they should not have the stones turned around and thrown back at themselves, for they are in fact worse offenders than the instigator of the act because they fuel the fire and make it roar from one solitary flame which could have easily been extinguished before it grew. No person should criticize others of something that they could easily fail in themselves. To fail in a lesson is not wrong. To take a lesson and not learn by it is wrong but to fail in understanding the entire lesson is not. To make a wrong decision or be tempted is to lose the lessons, but it is also good that the lessons were taken. For to take the lessons is to make a step towards progression rather than a step backwards. I am not saying that offenders are right because they offend, only that it is their personal problem to rectify. It should not be the case that the onlookers glory in their downfall and gloat in their unhappiness because they have failed. Spirit will be encouraging them to take the lesson again and if they fail again the whole process is done again and again until it is got right. Is that not the whole essence of returning and returning to your lives on earth if not to take lessons over and over again?

Do bad things come indirectly from spirit through a person on earth acting them out?

There is some confusion at this time which is causing many problems which hamper your progression. I would like you to be reassured that these things are all noted and are not from spirit directly to upset you to disbelieving. They are the effect of a cause and I have told you many times that the people that you meet on your path may not necessarily give you the strength and good experiences. They may have many problems themselves from which you have an effect. I will try to guide you through the boulders and rocks which they cast in your path. I see them and you do not. Let me lift your feet into the air so that you float above them and do not feel their harshness and jagged points which hurt you.

What are your views on war and the people who allow atrocities to happen? There are many modern day terrorists who are causing suffering to lots of people.

The power-mongers of your world are there for a purpose to themselves only. They have no comprehension of the fact that what they are doing to others is wrong. They have a reason to themselves for this act. But of course they are wrong in your eyes and they are wrong with their own spiritual progression. They will one day see that this is not right.

But what about the people who are suffering unnecessarily?

It is all a process of cause and effect. The power-mongers are the cause and the people have the effect. Fairly simple I know, but that is the basis of it.

Did they then ask to suffer this way?

Not all of them. But many did. They are in a situation where the rewards for the suffering from the world of spirit are many. They are teaching others a lesson also. I know that this is difficult to understand from your perspective, because you see the suffering, but it is the case all the same.

But there are so many of them?

And the perpetrators are many too. Not so many, but more than would first appear. Many people see the glory in the fame of the persecutors and they want to bathe in this as well. So they assist in the horrors also. They are vain to themselves and they are weak, which is a test also. For the innocent, they are not to be pitied from a spiritual angle.

What should other countries do to stop the violence? You have always told us that it is wrong to kill. Should man stand by and let the horrors continue or should they risk more lives in order to stop the perpetrators.

This is a difficult question. I would say merely to you that man should stop man from hurting another man. If you look at the situation on a one to one basis, not as a whole, then you will see the answer. If one man was beating a child then it is correct for another man to come in and stop the abductor even if it meant him hurting the other or being hurt himself. It is allowed to kill if you are saving a life. Where it is wrong to kill is if innocent people are killed because of the whole being stopped. In other words dropping bombs on lots of people in the hope that the bad people are killed is putting it very simply. Now you will ask how do you look at an army who is killing thousands of people and adopt the same theory? I will say to you that you must do this thing. Do not allow for it to be done any other way. It is a slower process, but more effective.

Should all countries get involved in trying to help?

Not really. It must be a structured form of attack to stop the violence. Not every country charging in without tactics and logic.

I understand, but where does the persecutor learn that they have not acted in the correct way or shown the necessary feelings of compassion?

When they return home here and look at their life and what they have achieved towards their spiritual advancement ,or rather what has caused them not to advance. Always the spirit is distressed that they have wasted their life. But in most cases the spirit wishes to return to take the tests again. That is why so many choose lives that have encumbrances such as disabilities or hardships, to try and make up points for what they lost by being a persecutor, say, for example, in their last life on earth. But always when the spirit returns to your earth, all plans and reasons must be forgotten, otherwise the lesson would not be such; it would be acting out of an answer.

But you said that everyone has free will. How can you know?

I know because we have no time and the future is simultaneous with the present. So I know what will happen to a certain degree. It is complex. I cannot move people against their will. They have to have the idea of moving. I see that they are moving. I see that they have the inclination not to move. That is all.

What about good actions?

I find it strange that you have to so continually find explanations for your good actions or shrug them off as being of no consequence. Do you not realize that the small things in life are those that count? All those things that are so small you do them without thinking but they are those things which your neighbour will not necessarily react to in the same way. The bad actions you make you know instinctively that you should not have made them, do you not? It is the same.

How should we live and act?

Please continue to live by virtues and beliefs and do not be swayed in any respect by people who do not have these values. Distance yourself from these people in that you do not have infections from their principals or beliefs, such as they may be. Stand alone and firm with the teachings of Ishamcvan and remember that I have taught you well. Never will it be said that you did not have the source to ask any question you chose and have the full knowledge that that question would be answered to the fullest extent.

Is it possible to be talented, famous, rich and loved yet still be highly spiritual? I am thinking of one particular multi millionaire who appears to have it all and yet still acts spiritually towards other people.

Yes any person can be spiritual. You do not have to be insignificant and poor. But, and there is a big but, people are not what they seem. They are what they radiate in the terms of spirituality. For you to be able to see this gift, this personal advancement, is to say that you have advanced enough to tap into this strength.

Could you talk about the persecutors of our world?

Persecutors are power mongers but they are also murderers and thieves and all other manner of other things too. They like to control other people for their own ends, to give themselves power. You see it all around you in varying degrees. It is a sad and hurting thing to endure but the persecutors seem to always have a reason to themselves. Sometimes they begin as persecutors but see the error of their ways and repent. Maybe the Holy Spirit will speak to them through their guides and they suddenly stop and look at what they are doing and stop being that way. Sometimes they do not listen and always have a good reason to act that way. The laws of karma do not accept that any man be persecuted by another in whatever way. Whether it is by mental cruelty or by abuse of the body. Both are wrong and both are not accepted.

What about going back to people I have wronged in the past, to apologise?

Firstly you must understand in yourself how you have wronged people. You must come to terms with it within yourself.

You cannot apologize just for the sake of what you think it will do for you in terms of credits for the mere fact you have apologized. You can't go back and search people out just for the purpose of apologizing. Learn from your mistakes and if you see that person again, and the opportunity arises, then tell them you now see the error of your ways. If you do not see them, then send them kind thoughts anyway. You must never hate however bad a person has been to you, or whatever circumstances have arisen. You must send back love and understanding that is all. For to face the enemy with love and not hate is to disarm them totally.

You have told us that to "people watch" will make us more aware of many things? Why is this an important lesson?

That which appears to be bad is not necessarily bad. And that which appears to be good often is in fact the worst thing possible. People are not what they seem. The wonderful people are with bad motives and the poor quiet people are the rich in spirit and knowledge of wisdom. So you see you must analyze people to a much better degree than any of your group has been doing in the past. You must hold your tongue and not speak when it would appear that speech is important and you must speak out when others fear the reproach of any words uttered.

Can calm people also be strong?

To be a person who is passive can mean that you are in fact the stronger of the two. Do not seem to be angry or agitated for this is not what you are. You have learnt from your teacher that to be calm and observe is to see things as they really are and from this you will perceive the right answer or question as it happens. If not it will pass you by. I will not say that the outcome will be to your liking, but it will be good all the same. For you will be strong and the richer for the experience. You are not to be reckoned with in all things. For you are the answer before the question.

Am I influenced spiritually by the words of actions of others?

You know the answers to all things from word from spirit. Ask and you will be told. If you choose to go against the words which are being spoken by finding explanations by which you can justify your actions, there is no one who can answer for this except for your self in your own spiritual advancement. Cannot you see that your advancement is in your control only? No one else's. You cannot be affected by the actions or words of others unless you choose to be. Always you have the control. Always you have the answers because they are being told to you. Listen. You have the key.

You always say we have freedom of choice, yet you say that we chose our path, lessons and death before we returned. Surely that rules out the choice? It must be such a fine line to walk the path if we have choice to do otherwise.

Yes you do have choice and it is the choices sometimes that you make that also enrich your spiritual karma. Let us say that you have chosen some lessons of behaviour like tolerance. When you reach the lesson in extreme testing, then you have the choice to learn or the choice to walk away. Just because the lesson is chosen does not mean that you will necessarily choose to take it when the time comes. If you understand spirit, you will, purely because you know the lesson for what it is. If you fight, get angry, be abusive to others who are around at the time without really being in the way, you are definitely not listening or learning. So you still have a choice, but not points for the lesson. It must be taken again and again and again if necessary until your free will is using its spiritual learning to say that the lesson is important to learn. That is all.

Surely it is not still necessary for you to have me experience things over and over again? Have I not learnt well?

Actually you are not repeating the lessons. They are all new with a different twist. You are progressing forward, but you are always impatient and cannot see that the rate is faster than you feel.

Do you think that if I have a focus on anything in my life, that with determination I can achieve that goal? Or is it to be determined by outside factors such as having pre-arranged my life?

No, I have told you the things that you choose before your return to your world. You did not choose your path, only your lessons. The rest is up to you. For all your lessons you can take the result of these one way or another and these will in fact put you on another path. Your future tests may then hit you from another direction, but the lessons will be the same in their intensity or their inner meaning. So I will say to you yes, you can focus on something you want and with will and determination you can in fact make it happen.

Is it right then, that positive thinking brings about great energy, which will actually make things happen?

In theory yes, but of course it is not quite as simple as that. But I will say to you that if you are singularly focused on what you want then it will certainly happen against all odds. If you doubt yourself it will be more difficult.

So what about the theory of putting all my thoughts and wishes into a pink bubble whilst in meditation, letting it drift into the universe and in fact knowing that these things will actually happen? Can this effect be the positive thinking to which you refer?

Yes. By doing this you are bringing it out into the open and making a statement of what you want to achieve. By being precise about each element you are in fact telling yourself what blocks you need to put into place to make this thing happen. You are in meditation making your plan. Yes this is good.

But what about asking or setting our monetary gains in order to be a component of the overall plan? You have told me that I must never ask for money or make it of any importance.

But in my case now, if I do not ask for money I cannot see that the end result will happen. Then is it all right to ask for money?

I will not say to you that it is wrong to ask or tell yourself that you need money in order to fulfil something that you want to happen, but I will say to you if you ask for money and you do in fact receive it then you must not keep it for any means other than the purpose of the question. You cannot ask for wealth to use as you will, you can ask for money in order to say build a sanctuary in order to help others who are less fortunate than yourself. You cannot ask for money to buy a new car or a new hat or an expensive meal. That would be wrong. But if you ask for money for a purpose, and that purpose has say a spiritual background, then that is a different matter. So although I tell you all you must not have materialistic ambitions, there are exceptions and there are the obvious ones to be excluded.

What lessons am I suppose to be learning from my recent relationship breakup?

I am not sure you really want to know the answer, but since you have asked I will tell you. You must overcome first the problem of being singular minded and selfish. You do not think that you are these things, but I must say to you that they are there. You must learn to put one other person, whoever that may be, before yourself. Think of another person and how they feel and act and respond. Wonder why they are, or they do, or they think, the way that they do. Learn by observation. When you have learnt this thing, you will be so much richer in spirit. To be rich in spirit is the essence of all things. You cannot evolve in the world of spirit if you are not in control of your own destiny. To do this thing you have to be in tune with not only nature, the universe and the environment, but with all other persons as well. By the time you are evolved in this level of consciousness, and ready to proceed to the next level, you will have mastered all things. There are many aspects such as humility, patience, understanding, tolerance and so on. You must learn to be less selfish and know that you are not the most important person in every situation. It is just as important to stand back, observe and learn. You are much more beneficial to the other person if you understand. The wisest people in your world are those that understand and are tolerant to the needs of others. That is all.

But if I do all those things and am in a relationship that doesn't seem right for me, is it better that I leave and end it?

At no time should you be anywhere where you are not comfortable with the vibrations or actions of a partner. If you are being verbally, mentally or physically abused, then you must distance yourself from the situation. It is neither right to abuse or mistreat another person and it is not right to stay and suffer when it is not necessary to do so. The other person will continue as long as you allow this to happen. If they continue after you have distanced yourself from them, however trivial their actions appeared then this is still a situation where they are totally wrong. This does not give you comfort at the time because you already realised they are wrong, but what I am saying to you is that you are right for ending the relationship and would have been wrong to continue and suffer just because you thought it was wrong to hurt the feelings of the other person. Of course all situations are different and I only generalise.

I do not fully understand why there have to be so many components to make up this lesson. Surely as one or two are worked through then we must have learnt and do not need more?

But the lesson is not learnt and that is the key. For a test will be given, maybe with much anguish in its learning. When that test is done the reaction of the person in how he or she plays out the experience is essential to their persona. So if that person lives through the test and learns from it then that is acceptable. But, if that person breathes a sign of relief that the lesson is passed and then wants to do things that show that the lesson is not learnt, then more tests have to be given to show the lesson from a different angle in the hope that the meaning of the test is absorbed. It does not mean that if you take a test and get through it that you have really deep down learnt the lesson. Unfortunately it will come in many guises until eventually the lesson is learnt.

I have been reading your words and have some questions in regard to them. You have said that homosexuality is a test or lesson chosen by the spirit and imply that it is something to be overcome. You say that sex between people who are not in love is wrong in the eyes of spirit. I don't have a problem with that. You also said that in the eyes of spirit, sex should be reserved as an expression of love. Again, I don't have a problem with that. What I cannot believe is that spirit would put more importance on the gender of people in love than the fact that they are in love. I thought that love was the most important thing. If this is the case, how can the mere detail of the gender of the people negate that love? Are you saying that people of the same gender cannot be in love in the same way that people of opposite genders can? I do not believe that either.

You are quite correct in saying that love is the most important aspect of all things. There are many different types of love though. There is the love of a mother for her child, which is not the same in its description as, say, the love for a woman and her friends. Exactly in its description, but different shall we say in its intensity of its direction. It is love all the same and equally as important, but love distributed in a different way. The love for a man to a man and a woman to a woman should be categorized as being different than that of a man and a woman, which in many cases results in the proclamation of the birth of a child as a result of this type of union and love. To have the act of sex as a result of a love of a man and a woman, as I have described before in great detail, is a sacred act and should only be performed as such and as a result of an intense love. All other acts of sexual union is for the act of sex and not as the act of immense love for the purpose of sanctioning that love from which children may or may not occur. So bearing this in mind, the act of a man with a man then becomes a sexual act only even though these men may say they are in love. The love they feel for each other is a different type of love than that which is between the unions of a couple of different sexes. There is nothing wrong with a man and a man having immense love for each other, but the sexual act is not therefore permitted. A man may love his brother or his friend with immense passion, but that love must not be sexual passion, no matter how much they think that is what they are feeling. They must see the difference for it is there to see, not for them to ignore and give in to the apparent passion which is manifesting itself. The human body has been designed for the sexual act only between different genders. Any other sexual acts therefore are not sanctioned the same from a spiritual perspective.

Chapter Five

Dreams

"The power of the mind is especially vulnerable
at the times when you sleep"

**What are dreams and how much attention should we
pay to them?**

Dreams are varied and mean very many things. I will try
and list them for you. Firstly they may be things being acted out
which are in your mind or your brain. They may be problems
you are experiencing or similar and it is your brain which plays
tricks and enacts them out in many strange ways. They may be
premonitions that your spirituality is saying you should observe
and in these there may be a hidden meaning, which you will learn
to interpret. Or they may be your guides telling you something
that you have not heard them say to you in your waking day.

**Why do some people seem to remember their dreams
more than others?**

To remember a dream you have to have a certain set of
meanings. You have to tune into the dream as it is happening. For
you to remember is not necessary. Some people may imagine

what is happening in their dreams and they make the dreams more vivid and wonderful or horrific. It is they themselves that embroider this dream. They will remember. Others may not if the dream is for a different meaning, such as advice from spirit. It is remembered by your spirituality and maybe what you call an instinctive way to deal with a situation whilst not remembering the dream or from whence the advice came to you. It depends on the circumstances of the dream.

Do we dream of things we would like to happen?

When I say to you that you must act on your dreams of what you would like to achieve, I do not mean that you have to dream this thing whilst you sleep. Firstly to fantasize is to dream. To dream is to want something that is sometimes unobtainable. It is not silly to want something that is at present unobtainable if you have the will to strive towards obtaining this thing.

Could you please teach me a meaning to my dream which I cannot find in books about dreams?

Dreams are a complex subject. We will have to break them down into several sections because that is the way that they happen. Firstly dreams can be a revelation of your traveling whilst you sleep; your astral traveling or your spirit traveling. I have told you before that spirit will leave your body when you sleep. Not all the time, but most of the time. When it does so, you can return to this plane with astral travel, not dreams. From this plane, so to speak, you can observe many things and these can appear as fragments in dreams occasionally. Next you can relive things in your life or your past life during sleeping, which you found distressing, worrying or caused you anxiety. This too you will remember when you awake. This is happening because of an anxious state of your mind. This is not spirit connecting. But the third thing is that spirit speaks to you when you sleep. When spirit is trying to tell you something, or give you reassurance, then spirit will spirit speak to you when you sleep in the hope that you will remember the message and interpret it when you awake. Sometimes it is difficult

111

to interpret the message, or the wrong interpretation is given by yourselves. So you see this third dream experience which should be the easiest way to receive messages from spirit, is often the most wrongly received message interpretation.

I am experiencing recurrent episodes of what science calls "Sleep Paralysis". It seems I am awake but my body is asleep. These are extremely frightening and often I find myself fallen on the floor, unable to move, screaming for help but no one comes for me. During the most recent episode, I was screaming for my mother over and over again, which I found particularly disturbing.

These are in fact dreams. They do not appear to be but they are. You are asleep but your mind appears to be awake. You may move around, walk, fall out of bed or anything else but you are not awake, you are asleep. The dreams have a meaning and they are drastic in their appearance, because you need to take heed of what is the underlying message. You have to admit that your life at this time is frightening in many ways. You feel you are not in control of things and this is upsetting you. But you must detach yourself from things in order to be of help. This may be very difficult for you to understand. You cannot be of help in putting these things in order if you are in a distressed or panic mode. I am not saying to you that you should detach your emotions entirely for that is not possible, but you must look at the situations, all of them, like an observer, and from that you will see that you are powerless to control the destiny, only being able to control the effect of the cause on yourself. For many times the destiny of other people and the way they are dealing with this destiny, or shall be say pre-set tests, is difficult to live with. You cannot understand how they are behaving; whether it is another person who is using you for his own ends or a spiteful word here or a person in anguish there, it is their problem and you can only help as best you can. You cannot change the root cause any more than you can take control of the situation, however frustrating it appears. That is the dream. That is for you to see. You don't want to be in charge, you want to crawl up in a ball and go back to being a child with your mother telling you soothing words of comfort. It is a bad time, but with all bad things, they pass. For a roaring waterfall eventually lies in a tranquil pool does it not?

My dreams do appear to be significant; are they messages and warnings of events to come, or are they due to my fears and insecurities only? Many I find distressing, involving former and current partners. Others show me specific dates which correspond exactly to previous events that hurt me.

Dreams, many times, do give you an insight to many things. But as you observe your mental state of worry or anxiety, whether conscious or not, these can bring about fantasies as well. I would say to you that most of your dreams are the latter and you are going through an extremely emotional time at the moment. I would also say that with regard to love, you must not hurry. There is a person in your future, who will far surpass all the others who have gone before. Do not accept second best for the ultimate will come to you. Forget the past and its people for they are behind you. Live for today for it is precious. Look to tomorrow as a mystery which will be a wonderful surprise. Be only what your spirit tells you is best. Live within yourself for you are a temple that no man must destroy. Make your decisions by what your spirit tells you instinctively is right. Do not argue with yourself and try and make things fit.

One of my most common dreams is a sensation of falling? What does it mean?

It is a shift. Something new. A sensation not experienced before. A feeling of inadequacy sometimes. A loss of power. It can mean many things to many situations. These are just some of them.

Do babies dream?

Spirit still talks to babies and they respond because it is the natural thing to do. To adults the same thing happens but the grown person has put up barriers which put the dreams into a fictitious category. Babies dream of their past lives, their loves, their people experiences. They also dream of feeding and being held and of animals around them to whom they connect spirit to spirit too.

Is there any significance if one dreams in colour rather than black and white?

None whatsoever. Some need one and some need the other.

What causes nightmares?

Suppressed anxiety. Trying to find a solution to a problem. Something you have read or seen and in many cases a fantasy that you have which only expresses itself at night. Many times, though, spirit will shock you into seeing what you don't want to see, but spirit will not frighten you, so if this is happening it is your inner thoughts and not spirit.

It is said that we all dream several dreams each night. You have spoken about dreams before, but why is it that some people remember many more dreams than others?

Some people actually like dreaming and living in a fantasy world. They have pleasure in enacting out that which deludes them in their ordinary lives. It is an adventure. As such they take the memory of the dream with them as precious baggage when they awake and have to face the hum drum reality of life.

I only remember about one dream every few months usually; is there any significance to the ones that I remember over all the others that I don't?

Maybe you do remember the messages which spirit sends to you and you discard the dream fantasies which you live in your sleep. If this is the case then you will be richer for the fact that you are listening to spirit even though it is perhaps conceived by you as doing so unconsciously.

Can we ask for help in our dreams?

The power of the mind is especially vulnerable at the time when you sleep. All actions of the dream are done unconsciously. But always remember that you are an observer of dreams even though it may appear that you are a participant. Your mind is making you one, that is all. So for this reason you cannot ask for help whilst in the dream state. During meditation you can ask for help and this would be the best way to contact spirit, although it can be done anytime during waking hours by just asking help from your guide. The power of the mind is almighty in its excellence. You can perform the most wonderful of miracles if you believe that you can do that thing. I say to you that if you believe then so it shall be. For you to ask for help and believe that you will get help is in itself making the thing happen. Do you understand? So if you manifest a dream to be a reality you are nearly there in achieving it. If you ask in a weak way instead of one that is all powerful, then it will not happen. So I say to you that for the believers there is always the salvation and satisfaction of achievement. For with achievement they will have the cleansing of their very souls. The spirit will understand the miracle and will be at peace with itself. For the time being, that is. You will be aware of your development - not in many things that are large but in things that are small and insignificant. Believe that if you have confidence in yourself in that this is happening to you, then you will grow and grow so that you have belief in yourself in larger things. For your compassion grows too as does your spirituality. If you stop and take time in all things without panic or power or contempt of others, then you will be rich in spirit.

Can you please explain why some people recall their dreams and others do not?

There are many types of dreams and the interpretation and memory of each of them is by the owner of the dream. I could say to you that many times a brain will make more beautiful something which is not necessarily shown. For example a dream can be your mind causing you to be anxious about something and then the dream is an acting out of this thing. Or it could be a message from your guide to your subconscious. Or it can be nothing more than a fantasy, however logical that may appear. So as vivid the dream or as meaningful, then in the same proportion will it be remembered. If it is a message from your guide you would think that would be remembered, but not at all. Such a message is played directly to your subconscious that is all.

How can I improve how I remember my dreams?

Dreams come to you via your subconscious and that is something over which you have little control. If you dream then it could be a message from spirit or something that concerns you or gives you joy. There is nothing that you can do to make this happen. How do you remember dreams? That is something you cannot plan.

Why do I sometimes have the same dream over and over again?

If spirit is trying to tell you something in a dream it could mean that you have not yet addressed this issue. If it is a dream manifested by yourself through pictures from your mind, then you are worrying about something that is not yet resolved.

Is it normal for people to have nightmares?

Normal? Nightmares happen always from your mind giving you thoughts and actions which you may have seen and are enacted, or which you have created in your imagination. Nightmares never come as a message from spirit.

Can dreams predict the future?

Usually not but they can give you warning signs to heed. Not a prediction exactly but more of a sense of something.

Can I control my dreams? Is this possible?

Not at all other than being less anxious and more calm about your daily life. You have your dreams as an observer, not a participant, even though this may appear not to be the case. You are not in control at any time but you may wake up if you find it distressing.

On an average, how many dreams does a person usually have in one night?

There is no average. Many people do not dream at all on a regular basis and other have lots of dreams.

Does a person dream on and off all night?

People dream for a very short time. The dream is very fast indeed whatever the duration but you remember it as being of normal speed. Think of fast forwarding a film. You do not think in the waking state that you could see everything, but in a dream state you do.

Would you please tell me why some people say they do not dream?

Everyone dreams. They just don't remember.

Do children's dreams mean the same as adults? If not what is the difference?

Children are contacted by spirit in their dreams more so than adults. This is because they are not long removed from the spirit world. As they get older then the dreams fit into another pattern, dependant on the adult of course, and what anxieties and imaginations they have.

Is it possible for our daily activities to affect the content of our dreams?

They give you scenarios which your mind fantasies with or makes you concerned enough for you to re-enact them in your dreams. It is rare that pleasant things from daily activities formulate themselves in your minds to become dreams. It is more the troubling things which do so.

What should we pay attention to when analyzing our dreams?

I would prefer you to just try and find the meaning of the dream and know whether it is from your mind, your anxiety or in fact a message from spirit. Once you have categorized the dream then try and see what is said.

What does it mean when you dream about the same person over and over again?

Either that this person has been sent to help you with something and it is a message from your guides, or that your mind has made that person important to you and for this reason you do not clear your mind of it when you sleep. It is always one thing or the other,

Are there any differences in male and female dream patterns?

None whatsoever. It depends on the person themselves.

Why is it that our dreams rarely follow a logical pattern?

But they do. It is you remembering the dreams that put them into a different pattern because you do not remember ever all that you dream, you only remember a part or parts of the dream sequences.

The other night I went through a rough night of sleep. What are these dream states that I am experiencing? Is there anything I can do to prevent them?

The dreams are a manifestation of your own anxieties. These are from the past as well as the new life you are making for yourself, of which you are nervous. Because of your anxieties in your sleeping time your mind will still be thinking of them and shall we say does not switch off into sleep mode. What can you do? Many things. Firstly you must meditate on a regular basis. During meditation sometimes ask for help in clearing your anxieties. Ask for help to show you the way forward and ask for help generally to know the right decisions when a situation arises. You can learn to talk to spirit as a friend. You do not need to say words, you must merely say them with your mind in your awake state before you go to sleep and in a meditation devoted to asking spirit to assist you. These techniques will help you to relax more and induce a peaceful sleep. Do not dwell too much on whether you will or will not dream that night, just presume that you will not rather than the reverse. This is in fact an act of positive thinking. If you can see that you become more relaxed with your anxieties and then they will in fact dissipate.

I am feeling energy and vibrations during some dream states. Is this spiritual energy, a build up in me trying to release?

This has nothing to do with spiritual energy, which is a peaceful energy which will ebb and flow and will not be strong in any way. Sometimes it is more like the spray from a waterfall in your face or a breeze on a hot summer day. That is spiritual energy, not a force that comes and goes like a thunder storm. What you feel is strong anxiety, nothing more.

Why do I feel a lot of fear whilst in some dreams? Is it other spirits that I am feeling?

Your guide, main guide, will continually be whispering to you and trying to guide you in your life. He will try and get you to calm your anxieties. You yourself are not seeing the dreams as anxieties yet and so you associate them with fear. There is no such thing as evil, and spirit would only appear to you as gentle and loving, so as you will see we have a contradiction in this statement. Other spirits will only come to you with the permission of your main guide. So even if other spirits were sent to you for a specific purpose, and that may be for you to view an example, you will not feel fear from any of them. Spirits, true spirits, are loving and only want to guide you for the better. Fictitious spirits made up in your mind may be anything you believe they can be. You must learn to notice the difference.

When we dream of people who have passed on, do those spirits know that they are in our dream?

Dreams vary in their content and meaning. Sometimes a person may be on your mind and in your dream you act out a scenario with them which comes from memories or is make believe because you want to be with them in any given scenario. Other times they may be wanting to connect to you so they will whisper to you when you are sleeping and send you visions which you call a dream. It is one or the other, that is if you see or dream with someone you know. There are other cases that are shown to you but do not relate to past loved ones. But the more you love someone the more frequent the dreams or contact with them. Is that not true? All loved ones who have passed over to our world become pure spirit and as such they can ask to contact you in your dreams depending on their spiritual advancement and the permission of your main guide.

Why do we dream about many things and not about anyone specifically and several dreams in one night?

Some are messages from your guides about situations that you have had or will have, and these should be heeded because they are words of wisdom. Some are purely your imagination and others are people in the spirit world who are trying to get your attention. Not by just contacting you by showing you a play in which you will be a player, but more that they play mind games with you in a playful way. What you should do if you get lots of dreams is tell spirit generally that you don't like them and to take them away because you need to sleep. If you do not do so they will come more frequently and you will be attracting them for their own sake alone. If they appear to be messages then heed them. The best way is to write down everything you can remember about each and every dream. Then when you look at your notes you will see a pattern of those with a meaning and those that don't. Those people who say they don't dream actually do. The message is given and absorbed by your own spirituality

120

so that you can say to any given situation that you suddenly know the answer.

Do animals dream too?

Yes they do. All living creatures of a certain evolvement do dream.

Do people who are blind from birth ever dream? If so what are their dreams like?

Yes they do but usually colours and shapes which also contain the messages from spirit. The dreams of the mind will come to them in the same way that they see people through their senses when awake. The way they live when awake will be transformed in the same way into their dreams. They see with their senses and this is the same in their dream state too. But colours and shapes they definitely see, and many blind people will tell you that during meditation or dreaming they very much enjoy this seeing of things.

How long do dreams last?

They are reasonably quick by your time standards but they may appear to you to last much longer. That is because the spirit world has no time and all things happen simultaneously. But whereas dreams are different from astral travel they do sometimes have messages from your guides, so involve usually a spiritual element. Hence the no time zone does apply. To you a dream can seem to last for some considerable time, especially if in a nightmare, but I can assure you this is not the case. Most of the night you sleep without dreams except when you are off astral travelling. For these reasons you will see that your sleep time is broken up into sleeping, dreaming and astral travel. Dreaming you do not necessarily do every night though. However, dreaming and astral travel can occur simultaneously.

Is it a good idea to record my dreams?

Yes if you are interested in finding any hidden meanings of advice it is best to write down everything you remember.

What does just seeing colors mean in dreams?

Colours only with no other interaction usually are associated with a spiritual connection. Your guides can send you messages with colours. Sometimes you will hear a whisper from them whilst the colours are showing. Also you can refer to the meaning of colours to associate the content of a possible message.

Is it normal to always remember nightmares but only occasionally remember dreams?

Nightmares are from your overactive mind and because they are not only frightening as well as being a product of your mind, you will be able to remember them more easily. So you see your mind makes it and therefore the memory of it is already in your mind to recall.

What does it mean when people say they had a dream within a dream?

This is a strange question. In a dream they see themselves as dreaming. How can that be possible? During Astral travel they may recall they saw themselves asleep and dreaming but that is all. Any other concept is their own imagination playing tricks on them.

Do all dreams contain a hidden meaning?

Not all of them. I have explained the different types of dreams, the ones from spirit with a hidden message and the ones created by your own mind which do not. Messages from spirit acted out in a dream or showing you a colour with a message do have meanings but ones created out of your own pleasures, anxieties and other bodily and mind functions only have the meanings which are deep set in your mind already, or those which you yearn to happen.

Are dreams influenced by fears or stress or any other factors?

The types of dreams which are manifested from your own mind and incorporate your fears, stress or anxieties are real and are in fact an acting out of these factors. Dreams from spirit guides with messages are not influenced by your mind so are independent.

Do drugs influence dreaming?

Definitely. I would say they turn dreams into hallucinations however minor they may appear. Hallucinations are not dreams.

Why don't children seem to recall their dreams? Are they not having as many as adults?

Yes they do but because children are closer to the spirit world having just left it, they will absorb messages from spirit and not feel it necessary to recall their dreams to other people. However, many remember them just for themselves the same way as they often see spirit and do not tell people of that either. A child will also act out scenarios from what they have been doing the day before, or stories they have been read or in fact problems with siblings or adults which may not appear as problems to those around them. To tell of such fantasies, good or bad, about people usually means that they prefer to say little in case it is misconstrued. So in short, children either do not feel it necessary to recall dreams or in fact forget them when they wake up. As the child becomes an adult then the mind of the adult wants to remember whereas the child does not want to remember.

What is lucid dreaming?

Lucid dreaming is one of your modern day interpretations by someone who was trying to analyse dreams and had no knowledge of what dreaming was about. It is said that a lucid dream is a man made dream by the person in order to act out something or see in a clear manner what they want to see. Nothing more.

During lucid dreaming can a person have control over their dream?

Because this type of dream is manufactured by their mind and nothing else, they do fantasise that they can be part of the dream and control the way the dream goes. But I say to you that this is a fantasy and not a dream from spirit guides. Let us say it is a dream made by the mind on a more elaborate scale.

Is sleepwalking a dream state?

No. This is caused by anxiety of some sort and should be treated as such by your doctors. The person may think that they are dreaming something but this is not the case. The mind has taken over the subconscious and is telling the body to get up and walk. A dream alone will not do this to a person. It is not good, especially in children and when that is the case the child is usually suffering from anxiety which must be investigated and dealt with as soon as possible. It is also manifested as bedwetting and crying unnecessarily. Attention to the child must never be ignored. You may learn something you don't want to hear, but all abuse of a child however trivial, mental or physical must be stopped. Even harsh words between parents to each other may cause the child to have stress.

If a person talks in their sleep are they speaking as part of a dream or observation of a dream?

Usually as part of a dream observation not participation.

Chapter Six

Astral Travel

"Your spirit can travel to many places"

What is the difference between astral projection and astral travel?

They are the same thing with different names, and it is the ability for your spirit entity to leave your physical body. Everyone unconsciously leaves their body whilst asleep at night, but before they do leave, they have to put the physical mind to sleep. Most people don't remember this, but when the physical mind is asleep, the subconscious spiritual you takes over, and this is usually when you do your astral projection. In other words, everybody does it, but they just don't remember doing it. When your physical body sleeps and the astral body leaves, the physical body just rests. No harm can come to you through this.

Could you fully explain further travelling in our sleep, which I think you call astral travel?

So let us see if we can perhaps put into perspective your thoughts and misunderstandings about this concept. So you go to bed and you sleep. You rest your body and your mind because this is essential not only for the life of your body which could not go on without rest, but for your spirit to rest from being in your body also. Now this is something that you fail to fully understand because you cannot understand what would happen if you wake suddenly, perhaps from a fright or a noise, and the spirit is off travelling somewhere. I will say to you as before that in the spirit world there is no time. It is not just that time is slower, there is no time. There is a view point from the spirit world of your lives on earth, your incarnations and the fact that from this perspective they are all happening at the same time. I will say to you that whether your spirit is in your body or whether it is temporarily back on this plane of existence, there is no time frame so it all happens simultaneously. Your spirit leaves your body when you sleep, some of the time, not all of the time. It is still connected to your body and this is an important factor to remember. It is not severed from your body so it is not free. It only goes off visiting. What does it do when it visits? It purely observes and learns and takes advice, so to speak, to your understanding. But the important thing to remember is that it is the spirit which is doing these things, not the mind and not part of the body. When it returns to your world and leaves its body it does not remember its experiences in travelling. Never. But I have not answered the question of what happens if the spirit has left your body, you are asleep and then you are suddenly woken for whatever reason. How can you wake without spirit within you? You can't do this thing. It doesn't matter how quickly you awake, spirit will beat you to it. Spirit will return quicker. Will you feel suddenly bad if this happens? Will you get a start as spirit rushes back? No you will not. You will not feel anything. If your spirit has not left the body when you are suddenly woken and you are dreaming then you will feel fright. But you see you do not dream when your spirit leaves your body. You dream whilst you spirit is in your body. That is the difference.

How would you define the difference between experiencing a dream and experiencing astral travel?

Sometimes it is difficult to know without asking spirit. But I would say the obvious signs are that spirit floats and observes and in no way gets emotional about what it experiences or sees. There is no passion or anger or anything else. It is almost as if these things are happening or you are seeing things which do not move you in any way. Dreams are a concept, not an experience. In a dream you can conceive an idea or you can be told from spirit of advice or a parable of meaning. Spirit can advise you in this capacity. This is spirit talking to your spirit within your body. It is different for spirit to speak to your spirit when it is travelling when you sleep. This is different. So just take a very simple aspect and think only of that until you all understand what Ishamcvan is trying to teach you. Dreaming can be an assortment of different things. You are actually walking or talking or crying or whatever else. You are part of the experience as a person with a body. The dream may be a message to you from spirit about a problem you have or a decision you have to make. But mostly dreams are fantasies of the mind that you watch while your mind alone plays the scenario. They could be because your mind is worried, anxious, frightened or many other things.

Do people remember their astral travel?

Only when done in a meditative state. Not in a sleeping state. In meditation you are not completely unconscious as you are in sleeping, or would appear so. In meditation you are aware somewhat of what is going on around you. You can come out of meditation at any time when you hear a car or a telephone. In sleep you are not conscious of other things going on in the room. So that is why you would not remember an astral travel experience.

How often do we go back to the spirit world when we sleep?

Some of the times when you are in a deep sleep but sometimes not at all.

Why is it that sleep does not refresh me? Is it that I spend too much time travelling that I do not rest my mind and body so that I feel tired when I wake up?

If you are in the world of spiritual travel then you are relaxing and refreshing you mind, your spiritual mind, your inner being. It is worries and stress that make you tired of your physical mind nothing more.

Would it be helpful to me to try to soul travel more?

Astral travel must not be confused with soul travel. By soul travel, you mean connecting to spirit. Yes you should meditate and flow with spirit. Soul travel is man's word. You as a spirit can travel within meditation or sleep. Again it cannot be contrived.

I had what appeared to be astral travel when I was asleep at night and I believed that I was on a spaceship with other beings having a party. Was I dreaming or was I travelling?

If you look at the fact that during astral travel it is unlikely that you would be experiencing being on a space ship, then you will see that this has to be a dream. During astral travel you might go to another country or another planet and observe but you would not participate in anything, especially a party. To be in any sort of vehicle is probably not true. To travel in your sleep happens to you all the time. You may observe other people, you may travel to other places and see what is happening there, you may connect spirit to spirit to someone or some place, but spirit as you know has no body so therefore the participation of any spirit entity's experience is not such as you would recognise as a body experience. That is why it was a dream. However, you will now know that it was a suppression of yourself and how you were feeling at the time and you hoped that you could fly away and party.

What does your soul do while you sleep?

While you are asleep your soul or spirit is travelling astrally some of the time, but not always to this next level. It may go back and forth in your lifetimes to the past as well as the present, or sometimes it may not go anywhere. It can travel and pick up messages from people that it needs to for your own spiritual understanding such as your guides, or guides who are helping you at a particular time. Sometimes it will stay with you if there is no need for any learning or recharging of your spiritual batteries, but this is not particularly common.

How do we know for sure what we see or hear through spiritual travelling and viewing is true?

At the beginning a lot of what you see and hear is not accurate. It is more that you travel and expect to see some things so you do. If you do not have expectations of anything happening then you will progress. I cannot say to you that some things are correct and some things are not, because it would be no use to generalise but you will definitely find that the more proficient you get to do these things then the better you will become. Practice makes perfection does it not? And trust. You must have trust because that is the essence of learning and experiencing all things spiritual.

Can spiritual travelling happen without consciously calming and doing it?

The more you do it during meditation the more you will slip into this without planning. If you flow with the thoughts then this is the way to learn. As you get more proficient then you will do this without thinking.

What is the difference between astral travelling and an out of body experience?

Astral travel is when your spirit leaves your body and either floats around in your vicinity or beyond or back to this spiritual plane. It is usually involuntary but can be done through a meditative state. An out of body experience takes you from your body to look at your body primarily, or where your body is at that time. It can also happen when a person sees themselves and their past and future to the spirit world whilst in a holding position for death of the body. Then the spirit is viewing all that is necessary as a pre-empt to it returning home. Many times this is reversed and the spirit then goes back and is longer in time inhabiting the body.

Could you clarify again please how we determine whether we are dreaming, having an out of body experience, or astral travelling.

Dreams have many sources. Sometimes it is your mind playing tricks and stories or it could be your guides letting you see a scenario and what may happen. This is then given as a warning or advice on what to do. Or dreams can be because you have shut off your mind and you drift into fantasy. Dreams can be viewed and astral travel can be viewed. In an out of body experience your spirit is participating in the experience whether it is moving to stand behind someone and observe them or walking from here to the other side of the country, it is the same. There is a fine line between them all. Dreams you participate in fantasies only and listen to your guides in others. Out of body you observe your body and sometimes your past, and with astral travelling you only observe the spirit world and beyond.

Do I need to meditate to experience astral travel?

You can do astral travelling whilst in meditation or guided meditation. In those cases you are voluntarily trying to do this and are anxious to see what happens. The astral travelling you do when you are asleep is involuntary.

If I leave my physical body isn't there a risk of not being able to return, and could another being take over my body whilst my spirit is away?

This is difficult to explain for you to understand. Let us say as an example that there is a gossamer thread that still attaches you to the body. That thread never breaks until you die of the body, discard the body and return home to the spiritual plane. If you are merely travelling with your spirit then we could say that your spirit is still attached to your body because it is at one with the body all the time the body is living. So in fact you do not leave the body, although of course you do. That is the difficult part for you to understand. Likewise another spirit cannot take over a body that already has a spirit attached to it. All bodies, unless they are dead have a spirit attached to them, so it is not possible that another spirit which you call a being, could take over whilst your spirit is away travelling

What does it feel like to separate your spirit from your physical body?

Feel is a bodily sensation and when you leave your physical body you are spirit as an entity. So there is no feeling. The spirit is used to being a wisp in the breeze so it is no new sensation.

How long does it take to have an astral travelling experience?

Seconds, minutes, hours. It all depends on the circumstances.

What reason can you give me to want to do astral travelling?

Because you want to experience more in the world of spirituality from another perspective, other than firmly implanted on your world.

Will I be able to see, hear, and feel as I do in life?

You will not hear, you will sense sounds. You will sense sights too but feelings are a bodily sensation so you will be at peace and calm and relaxed but not actually feeling what is going on around you because you are an observer, not a participant.

What would you say to a person who is afraid of trying astral projection? Do they have to believe in order for it to happen?

No, I would not recommend that anyone try to do this unless they are at peace with their own understanding of spirituality. There would be no point because they won't be able to do this thing anyway.

Have you Ishamcvan astrally projected to other planets or places where aliens and other beings live? If so, please describe your experiences.

As a spirit entity I have seen many other places apart from your earth. It is endless and from the spirit plane at my level I can see a vast amount. The higher I progress to other levels then the more I can see and understand. Aliens? What is an alien? Something different from you people on earth? Of course. Humans are for your earth. You are a type of body, that is all. There are many types of bodies in many places other than on your world. They do different things from yourselves. But it is not my place to give you those details. The more you advance the more you will be shown different cultures, if you want to call them that. How did I experience the other places? I didn't because I have not lived amongst them all. I viewed them. Was that an experience? No, it was an observation.

Some people have the experience of the body jerking whilst asleep which in fact wakes them up. Is this the astral body returning back to the physical body?

There is no bodily feeling when the spirit leaves the body or returns. The timing is such a split second of a split second that it is nothing in your time scale. The body jerk you mention is a bodily function not a spiritual one.

Does the astral plane feel the same as our world?

It bears no resemblance to your world, which is unique. The astral plane is not a place of substance, it is a vastness of nothing which is everything with no form. It is a spiritual plane. It can be whatever you perceive it to be at any time. It is the spiritual sensations that are important, not the sights you see and feel with what you know as bodily feelings. From the spiritual plane you can see all things and people on your world, but fleetingly and as observation only. You do not stay with them or interact in any way. They will not sense you either.

Are you walking or hovering when you astral project?

You are floating and observing. You project from one area to another, although the area is not form of course. You are not taking part in things but merely sensing what you see as you drift around.

Is it possible to actually see other astral projectors and be able to interact and talk to them?

No, your journey is a singular one. Your spirit is singular to you and everything that you do as a spirit is as a one. You are in this level of consciousness as a one and you are born and die also as a singular spirit entity. When you are living your life on your earth then you are still a spiritual one. When you astral travel you do this with your spirit, not your body. Spirit can sense other spirits with immense perception and visions may be materialised from memories of these other spirits as you knew them on your world, but when you astral project then you travel as one spirit as an observer. You can sense other entities sometimes but not always. It depends on your level of spiritual advancement.

Are there evil entities in the astral world and if so are there any good entities around too when you meet the bad ones?

There are inexperienced and undeveloped spirit entities who are not learning and progressing, but these are not evil. They may be acting as naughty children sometimes but they are not frightening or scary. Only good entities are in the spirit world, even though in varying degrees of sereneness.

When is the best time to go astral travelling?

Of course the best time is when you are relaxed and truly in a meditative state. Not something that you think is a meditative state when your mind is still active and giving you impressions or visions that you believe could be from spirit, but more so when your mind is still and completely blank before you start. You may hear outside noises with your ears but these do not penetrate into your meditative state. If you are not completely in this meditation as I have just described then you will not astral travel or as you call it, astral project. Two of the best times to go into a meditative state more easily are either just before you drop off to sleep or just after you wake in the morning. Both of these times will be when you are neither in nor out of the full sleep cycle. But beware when falling asleep that you do not just do that and then have a dream which you tell yourself is an astral travel experience.

Is it possible to fall in love with another person on the astral plane?

No because spirit is all love and because you travel as a spirit entity only, not an extension of your body and mind, then you cannot fall in love as you know it on your world. You do not actually meet visions of people from other planets or worlds, you view the spirit entities which live within any bodies but see their bodies too of course. You are already loving the entity if you are astral travelling as a spirit so this statement would not apply. Also remember that other worlds may not have a one to one relationship to reproduce and falling in love is an old fashioned statement when looking at the universe as a whole.

Is astral travelling dangerous?

No it is a completely natural thing. The only circumstances where it could be is if your mind imagines things and then you see them as threatening or frightening. But it will be your mind that is making up these things, not the spirit entity that is participating in the travelling.

Could I die whilst on the astral plane?

I presume you mean can your body die. No. Your body is back on earth where you left it. It is only your spirit which leaves your body and goes off. Your spirit must return to your body and will not return permanently to the spiritual plane until your body dies and your guide brings it home here. Your spirit never dies, it is everlasting.

What is there to do on the astral plane?

I think you have a delusion of this travelling so I will explain again. Your spirit which is attached to your body whilst you are in a life will return to the spiritual plane or go to other planes whilst you sleep. This is a regular occurrence. It is nothing to do with your mind or your body. Apart from this thing happening you can also induce the travelling state whilst in a meditative state. So let us say that you try and bring on this thing, then you go through a series of relaxation exercises, like floating above your body and then when you are proficient with that technique then you can venture further. But I must emphasis that this very often is misconstrued as something where your mind has imaginations and bears no reality to astral travelling at all. There could be images, sights and sounds which are nothing more that a self induced dream. It is hard to differentiate between that which is imagined and that which is a spiritual vision, for the participant that is. So it is essential that you listen to my words and not all run away with this new phenomenon and make it what it is not. When you become efficient at the technique then you will see the difference.

Can everyone do astral travelling?

Yes everyone does it involuntary anyway. Not everyone will be able to do this through trance or meditation because it will take an advanced spirit to understand and bring out the initiation of this.

In order to do astral travelling what projects our spirit out of our body?

Spirit will propel spirit. So you could say it is a technique done by your higher spirits. Although if you try to do this yourselves through meditation it could be said that your mind wills your spirit to do this thing by calming itself.

Could you please describe our physical, etheric and astral bodies?

Your physical body is that form which is you when on your earth during a life. It has substance and a mind. The etheric body you could say is your spirit which is continually going to a body in a world and then back to the spiritual plane. The etheric body is your spirit. The astral body is also a spirit but is those other spirits which you see when travelling or is sometimes referred to as your spirit whilst it is travelling because it is as other spirits see you.

Do any herbs such as Salvia help you to relax into a state where astral travelling is easier?

Various substances will relax you and many like this herb when used in excess will bring about visions and hallucinations. This is not what you want if you are trying to relax and let your spirit drift away from the body.

What is the real trigger to leave the body? Where is it located?

There is no location because the spirit, although attached to your body all the time your body has life, is not actually located within the body. It surrounds the body and embraces the body with every fibre of its being. Where is the trigger? If you want to try to do it yourself then I would say it is your will which comes from your mind. But if it happens involuntary it is a natural process which I suppose you could say is divined by spirit and our elders as a process of returning to your world and back to here whilst you sleep.

When astral travelling are we able to use our senses to hear, smell and feel.

You do not use your bodily senses, you use your spiritual senses. You sense everything. You do not see or hear or feel because that is not necessary. Everything in the spiritual world is by sense. So let us say that if you do travel and view other worlds you do just that with your senses. You do not land on a planet and join in the daily tasks of those beings. You view by senses only from afar.

Which position should I take when trying to do astral projection during meditation – lying, sitting or on the floor crossed legged?

The position is not important. Whatever you feel comfortable doing. Look at it as meditation initially and then you will see it has to be a relaxation pose.

Whilst meditating how can I learn to detach my body from my spirit so I can travel?

Practice is my only advice. But you have to learn to shift your mind to another level in order to do this although that is something you learn with meditation too.

Someone told me that I should visualize myself floating out of my body, rising above it and then moving on. Is this correct?

This would be a good exercise for you to try. If you can frequently try to leave your body during meditation and rise above and look at yourself, then you are progressing well and will certainly be able to travel further in the future.

Is astral travelling something everyone can do or is it only for a few spiritually advanced people?

Everyone does involuntary astral travel when they sleep but to induce this state you will need to be proficient at doing meditation. This also means that the more advanced spiritually you are then the further and more intense the true travel experience.

I have tried imagining a spaceship taking me away to start the travelling but it doesn't work.

No it will not. A spaceship is a material thing and bears no relevance to your astral travelling. It is your spirit that is travelling not your body or your mind.

Whilst my spirit is travelling is it possible to move backwards and forwards in time?

Quite definitely. Observing this is something your spirit will be encouraged to do.

Is remote viewing the same as astral travelling?

Viewing is something that you do when you do astral travelling. Remote viewing is something you do during meditation.

You view a place or a person. You do not return to the spiritual plane or other worlds to do this.

Is it possible to go wherever I want when I travel and if so how do I make that happen?

You have the choice to drift where spirit wants to take you but that is all. If you do not give your spirit over to higher spirits to direct you it will not happen.

Can I totally control my travelling or will I be taken to unknown places independent of my wishes?

You will have no wishes because you have no mind. You are spirit and only spirit. As such you are guided by higher spirits and higher spirits who are pure love and will not upset you as an entity in any way. So it would be your mind which would want to do or not do a thing, not your spirit. Once you leave your body you are in the world of spirit and your earthy feelings and rules no longer apply.

Could astral travelling help me to become more spiritually advanced?

Yes all travel to the world of spirit will enrich your own spiritual understanding. Not other worlds and what they are, but by observing spiritual aspects of all that they encompass.

Am I allowed to go into outer space when I astral travel?

You can be directed to other worlds to view them but I would not call that outer space as you know it.

When meditating through my third eye I often see a tunnel with a light at the end. Is it easier if I exit through this tunnel?

Yes if you find it easier. But I would say that the easiest is to see your body and then see your spirit leave that body.

Can I bring back objects from astral travel?

No because you travel as spirit only so there is no substance. Neither is there in anything you sense or see.

Could we gather energy from higher astral planes?

You will not travel to higher astral planes because the only way to do that is to mature with your own spiritual karma. Karma is your record of spiritual progress. If you are rich in karma that means that you have learnt lots and are progressing well. When you return to this plane of existence then you are assessed and will eventually move on to higher planes. I think what you are referring to is more other worlds and this plane of existence which you return to all the time when you sleep. Can you gather energy or spiritual knowledge, yes but it is your life on earth for which you will be judged by the results of your lessons. You will not get points for visiting and observing other worlds.

Is it possible to view people on this earth from the astral plane and see what they are doing?

Yes you can but you observe only as if from afar.

I am trying to do astral travelling but why can't I move enough away from my body to travel? Sometimes I only go a little way away but that is all.

You always go anyway when you sleep. There is no question about that. It just happens. When you try to do it yourself I would say that you have not yet learnt the technique which lets you relax and shift your spirit from your body. Once you have acquired that technique, which will be by your own spiritual understanding and advancement, then and only then will you progress further away from your body.

How do I move around on the astral plane?

It is something that your spirit has the will to do. Nothing is planned. It just happens. Spirit will guide you.

Are there places where we can astral travel which are a copy of our world?

Never. Your world is unique. There are similarities in other worlds but not identical copies.

What is the silver cord and does it ever break?

When you are born to your world into a body and your spirit enters that body there is a symbolic cord which is a description of the fact that the spirit is still connected to the spirit world at any time during your lifetime. When your body dies and your spirit returns to the spiritual plane then the symbolic cord is no longer there. When the spirit is born again into a body then this description of a cord and its connection to the spirit world again takes effect. But remember this is only a description, it is not an actual cord. During your lifetime whilst your body is alive the cord or the connection to the spirit world cannot be broken.

Could some bad entities travel with me or take me against my will?

You as a body or you as a spirit? But you are not a body or a mind, you travel only as a spirit. As such you are in control of all you do. Bad entities are only bad to themselves or do things to people when they are on your earth as a body.

In the spirit world spirits are in clusters as to their advancement. So you, or bad spirits as you call them, are being segregated to an extent. In any case the only thing that can harm your spirit is your spirit itself.

What about realms of lower entities? Will I be taken there and have to act out their wishes?

At some point you may view other lower spirits but only as a viewer, not as a participant of how they are with their advancement of what they do. All spirit entities have a rating of how they are progressing and the lower entities you refer to are nothing more than spirits who have not learnt much and subsequently not advanced. But there is no world or place for these lower advanced entities and although all spirits are integrated with others, the lower ones are not all together in a place of hell as you visualize in your world.

I am scared of the dark so will I be able to successfully astral travel?

You may need to clear your mind of this fear in order to meditate properly. But I have to say that when you travel involuntarily then this does not apply. When you meditate and then travel it should be that you are in a spiritual state and have no fears.

Is it possible that I have some kind of fear I don't know about that is preventing me from leaving my body?

Maybe, but it is up to you to identify the fear and then ask again if you are still not successful.

How do I return to my body?

That happens involuntarily whatever the outset of the travelling. Spirit will decide when you return.

I always fall asleep whenever I try to relax to do astral travelling? How can I prevent this?

You can't unless you try at different times of the day or perfect the meditation technique.

If I go off astral travelling at night won't I be tired in the morning?

No. Your spirit is never tired or has any other sensation. Your body will not be affected.

Is it possible to meet a loved one who has recently passed away?

Yes you may sense them and communicate if that is the right description, but you will not remember. But the decision for this will rest with whether the other entity wants to communicate with you.

When my spirit is travelling can I visit people in the real world and talk to their subconscious?

No not when you as astral travelling. You can observe them that is all.

Is my astral guide different from my main guide? I thought my main guide never left me.

Your main guide is always with you whatever your spirit is doing. Let us say they are attached to you during your life on earth. But when your spirit leaves your body and comes home during your sleep or meditation, does your guide go with you? Yes it does because that is a time for interim analysis of how you are doing in your life. So what is an astral guide? I have no idea. I can only say it is the same.

Is it true that only healthy people can achieve success in trying to astral travel?

No it makes no difference. I can only say that the spirit has to be advanced in order for you to do this yourselves. If your mind makes up travelling then we could say it was sick in order to do this thing. Everyone, don't forget, does travel when they sleep, whether they are healthy of body or not.

Do alcohol or drugs affect my ability to astral travel?

Yes definitely. They will always bring on hallucinations, even of a small kind.

Why don't most people remember their spirit travelling experiences?

Because it is not allowed by spirit. Usually if people say they remember, it is invariably their mind playing tricks on them.

How can I remember my astral experiences?

You can't.

What is the difference between astral travelling and lucid dreaming?

Astral travelling is where your spirit leaves your body and either returns to this plane of existence whilst you sleep or travels to other places, directed by spirit in order to observe. The spirit moves around. Lucid dreaming is where your mind intentionally conjures up a picture and then moves into it during a dream.

Is it possible to feel myself in my sleeping body at the same time as I feel my spirit astral travelling?

Yes if your spirit wants to do this thing. You do not actually feel yourself astral travelling because your spirit is not a thing of substance so therefore it does not move, it is projected. But not as speed; it projects as an instant of your time. You can view your sleeping or meditative body, that is all.

If I try to astral travel I see only darkness. Is this what people call astral blindness?

There is no such thing as astral blindness. How could that be? Your spirit has no form so it has no eyes. But spirit can sense and do all the things a body does by sense alone. What I think you describe is the darkness that immediately precedes the spirit leaving the body. Very momentarily this will happen and you should not even notice it happening. However if you are trying to meditate to the shift then the darkness is something that you may experience whilst you are trying.

Chapter Seven

Illnesses & Disabilities

"Who learns the most?
You, your family, your friends or the doctors"

Why do people have to suffer horrific illnesses? Why can't they just die when their time is up?

I will say to you that those that suffer invariably have chosen to do so and those which have horrific things happen to them are the same. If they died before the end of the duration of the condition then the lesson to their spirit may not be the same. I say may not because if a life is prolonged past its intended date of termination then this is also wrong and is why suicide is not permitted. You could ask me why is it that people who are suffering have not learnt their lesson early on and therefore do not need more weeks and weeks of agony to undergo? I will say that perhaps that is not the case. Many bodies die early and others die very much later. It depends on the spirit, whether it is chosen or how it was meant to have impact.

Are transplants of body parts acceptable by spirit?

Life should not and cannot be prolonged longer than the soul of the body intends, either in life or as planned previously.

144

The transplanting of an organ into the body is sometimes not good because it is going against the will of the spirit. Transplants are done with good intentions and it is good that experiments are being made in the world of medicine. The doctors and the scientists of the world are evolving in their research well. If you compare them with other worlds they are slow and very far behind, but they are progressing world wide and well. It all depends where you start from, and they started not too long ago. So transplants are a good thing in that respect but they are not good to prolong the life of a person who is destined to die anyway. If the person is destined to die and does die then it means that science has somehow failed. The doctors and the scientists have not proved that they can do this thing. And that is bad. So I say to you that it is necessary that transplants happen for the evolvement of science but it is not good for the prolonged life of souls or spirits who are ready to pass into this world. I know that you will ask if the person who needs the transplant is placed on your earth in that position so that they can be cured by the doctors, or does it just happen for the paths of the people that cross them? It is a little of each. But if a person is destined to die they will do so anyway whether the doctors tried a transplant or not. The taking of a piece of a body of someone who has died is irrelevant. The person is dead and the organ may certainly be given to someone else. It is when it is planned to take the life of a person who is dying too early so that the organ can be used to transplant that this is wrong. In these cases, and it happens very often, the body is not dead and the spirit may not have left the body when this sudden planned death occurs. The spirit must be allowed to leave the body at the time that it needs. It must not be hurried. It must not be given the horror of not going as planned. The spirit will then go into shock, so to speak, and the transition back to this world is not as smooth and as easy as is necessary. The spirit may take a time to adjust. So you see transplants are sometimes necessary for science and for the people who have spirits who planned to live or die in that way, but for the most it is wrong. It would be very difficult for your doctors or the families of the person who is ill to know or choose which type of body and spirit they are dealing with in order to make the right decision.

Why do some people imagine they are ill when they are not? Is it to get attention?

I will say to you with illness there are very many reasons for the fact that there are defects with the human body. I have told you previously in detail how a person can imagine that their body is ill for very many reasons. Some conscious and some not. If a person is requiring attention, or maybe are depressed they will suddenly have an illness that they did not choose from spirit. The illness may be real because they have created it with their anxiety, or it can be fabricated by their mind giving actual pain. This type of illness or condition is of the mind only. Is it to get attention? Yes of course even though the person may not be conscious of creating it for that effect. The imagined illness can have actual symptoms to the person only. An illness chosen from spirit cannot be changed. An illness caused for other reasons can be changed. If I say to you that if you push yourself to extremes, mentally or physically, then you will be ill, it will be so. There is no question. If you choose to be ill, it will be so.

It seemed that when I made up my mind that I was not going to have an illness or problem, it went away. Do I have the power in me to do this thing?

Of course, proving that the illness or problem is not part of your lessons or is chosen. Then it becomes something which can be altered by your own free will. You can always ask spirit or your guide to help you overcome this thing and to assist in making it go away. You have the power to change all things you want. For you to be aware of all things as they happen is the most supreme understanding of all your lessons. If you say you knew that it was going to go away, then your belief alone would make it do so. Provided it was not in your lessons as set by yourself, that is.

But how did it go away? I could not have just willed it away. I must have had help from spirit.

You wanted it away. You believed that spirit could take it away. You believed too that you could send it away. So that is what happened.

Is it possible to do that at all times with all illnesses?

Quite definitely not. Some are to be. Others are tests at a particular time, as were these. Some are just there to see how you cope. Do you deal with them in the correct way? Have you learnt your lessons and can you apply the answers to the real problems?

How did it go away against all odds and even though I accepted the illness to be really bad?

You dealt with the situation and by doing so you overcame it. Belief is the key. If you do not believe how can things happen? They will not just happen whilst you are turned away looking at other situations or other reasons why they are there. So I say to you all, face your problems and when you see the reason or the test, then you will have an answer given, and not before. You do not need to imagine an easy answer, you must see the true root of the problem not the superficial one. When you dig deep enough you will uncover the solution.

Why was I given so many illnesses all together? Surely you could have got your answer to my strength with just one case scenario, not so many.

Probably, but you would not have seen the significance of the results, would you? In only one case you would have thought it just a one-off easy solution that it was not your own thoughts and connections but just coincidence that it was not what it seemed. So there had to a significant few.

What can I do for my father who is suffering badly with his illness?

You must understand that many things, which are related to him or affect him in health or illness, are chosen. Strange as it may seem you needed these aspects to learn. It is not good to watch, however large or small, but that is from your perspective, not his. He may seem to suffer, but in the long term he is not. If he appears not to suffer, as he sometimes does, then he is strong and good. However with regard to spirituality, you need to say nothing if you feel it best and merely send the spiritual thoughts and love – lots of love – to him so that he absorbs these things without necessarily having to deal with the words. That is all.

I suffered from agoraphobia some 20 years ago and still feel I dislike leaving home on my own. If I ask for healing for this specific condition, will I get help and get over it?

If you truly believe that spirit can help you and you ask for help through a good healing channel, then you will receive it and bathe in the warmth of the love and help that this will bring to you. But I ask you to think more about the spirit connection and what it can do for you before you ask for healing. You must believe that this is possible. If you do not then it will not happen. I know that you want this to happen and you will now need the courage to walk the path to achieve this thing. You must be strong and build up that strength of belief in yourself before you make the steps, which could change your life. You should see ways to use your new knowledge of spirituality to help others learn also. By doing this you will forget your fears, for the gift to others of these words will be healing to you in themselves in overcoming this problem which you see as more enormous than you really need.

Is disease or illness brought on by the person who receives it or can it be cured by the person also?

I will say to you that in most cases the illness and suffering which the person is to suffer in their lives has mostly been chosen in advance. In other cases the person finds that for various reasons they cannot face their lessons or their life on earth in however small or large a way, and then they can invent illnesses or feeling ill and then this in itself will bring on the illness because they have actually asked spirit for help in giving them that illness. In other cases you see people with illness or diseases that they are determined to overcome even though they chose to have them and they fight and fight for them not to be there. In these cases the illnesses can be demised to a very small degree and it is of no consequence to them that they are having to suffer and they smile through and try to ignore them. They will not let them happen. Their spirit is strong and they actually tell spirit to take it away. Have you not heard of cases that are miraculously cured against all odds? They have healed themselves with probably lots of prayers from people who care. But if people pray to the Great Spirit for help for another person it does not always get answered because it is not the ill person who is praying. It is their illness, their lesson. Unless they decide in the right way, and this is important - it must be the person deciding in the right way, to banish this illness then all the prayers of others will not do any good. Higher spirits will not remove the illness or stop them from suffering or dying. Dying if it is ordained cannot be stopped. If it is not ordained sometimes it can be stopped if the person dying wants this to happen and the lessons left to learn have not yet been learnt.

Would we be doing wrong if we used substances such as drugs, cigarettes or alcohol to abuse our bodies? After all it is our body not our spirituality, isn't it?

Life is the most precious of gifts from our spiritual leaders and even though there are times when you feel that life on your world is purgatory because of its hard lessons, you must never forget the gift. To be given life in a body and to abuse that life as many do, is a waste and it is upsetting for spirit to see this happen. I will not say to you that we expect a large proportion of you to be perfect in your love and tolerance of other beings, but it is such a waste of your lessons to abuse your body with various things and substances which bring on ill health because of the way that they have made the body deteriorate in various ways.

Always remember your body and the life in it are a gift from the Holy Spirit, and tell others who are using abusive substances that this is the case. Your gift was given with love, the purest and simplest love and no person or spirit wants to give love and not have it received and recognized. All love should be taken spontaneously and then returned three fold to its sender. That is a law of karma.

Some people say they hear voices that tell them to do bad things. What are these voices? If spirit is good, where do they come from?

I would say to you that these people have an illness of the mind. This is the same as any other illness, which attacks the body. Whereas illnesses of the body can be self-inflicted to a point, so can sometimes diseases of the mind. But this is not the case with many people who hear voices. These illnesses are physical in the same sense. The voices are part of the illness of the mind. The mind makes the voices happen. They are not from spirit. They are nothing more than a trick of the mind that is part of the illness.

What about genetic illnesses? Can they be healed? What are they?

You choose your parents. So you see the genes and the illnesses you could inherit if you choose to do so. All is clear before you return to earth. To suffer an illness is a lesson, especially if you know beforehand what pain and suffering you will have to endure. Your family and friends also learn. Can they be healed? Yes they can to some degree; it depends on the purpose of the experience. If you ask for things to be taken away, sometimes they will be. So this category is still the same.

With regard to transplants, can the spirituality of the organ donor transfer to the reciprocant?

If someone has a transplant of an organ there is no way that this organ can bring with it the spirituality of the previous owner and affect the new recipient. You must believe that you are spirit which is renting a body for use in your life on earth. When the life is over and you die you discard the body like a butterfly sheds its chrysalis and you fly home like the beautiful butterfly that is the true spirituality of yourself everlasting. The chrysalis is on the ground and some animal will come along and eat it or it will degrade and become part of the earth by becoming compost, so to speak. The butterfly has gone, what is left behind is garbage. It was a vessel to add to the progression of the evolution of the butterfly. The body part which is reused is done so by two things. The doctors have been given the process to advance and use this technology in order to help other people. The body which is receiving the part has chosen to allow this thing to happen and to not have the spirit leave that person and the body used at the time when apparently they should have died. It is not wrong for this technology to happen if the spirit was not ready or had not chosen to return home. That is permissible because that is what was chosen. If, however, the person was being kept alive by machines after the spirit had left the body and returned home, then this is wrong. Spirit chooses when to leave, not man and certainly not doctors. So I will say that the body must be looked at only as a vessel to carry the soul.

What about hypochondriacs? Why would people want to imagine they are ill all the time?

Some people have minds which make them fragile and sensitive in many things. They may feel inadequate and want more attention or they may purely be interested in medicine and transfer that interest to themselves. In any case I have to say that this is a problem of the mind which must be dealt with by your doctors the same as any others in the mind category. It is not a normal healthy thing to imagine and perhaps you would recognize it as a cry for help or more attention. In any case someone should take the time to make them better.

What is your opinion of medicines or treatments being taken to stop death? By this I mean, if I am diagnosed with a bad disease or condition that could be terminal, should I take medicines or treatments to help it or should I let it just take its course? If we choose our death and that is why I have got the condition, is it wrong to want to change this?

Maybe you had chosen to take medicines. How do you know? Not all medicines can cure. Some are useless and some are only partially effective. But in your world man has found cures for many things. The fact that you have an illness may be a form of him finding the right procedure for you and in fact makes you better because this was not the chosen death. How do you know? You do not. For what seems to be terminal is not always the case. If you do not take the treatment, then you may have made the wrong decision. As with all decisions, you must act as you want. Having said that you may pre-empt death by choosing to not take the medicine and die when this was not the time and it only appeared to be the time. So my answer is sometimes yes and sometimes no. It depends on each case.

May I ask you about people who have phobias? Let us say someone that is terrified of spiders. Did they reincarnate with that fear or how does it happen to some and not others?

You are asking if that particular person had such a fear in other lives and this is a reason why it is so strong now. No, I will say to you that this is generally not the case. There is a fear for no other reason than something happened in their past that caused the reaction and it has done nothing more than multiply and multiply in their mind so that the thing becomes a trauma beyond understanding. I will say to you that if in the beginning the person was put in a position to look and understand that ugly is not necessary a threat, then they would think differently. But the spider frightens them by its appearance, not by its way of life. So let us say that the person, in the beginning, was frightened by a spider. If she had taken time to see that it would not harm her, then the thing would not have multiplied. In so many cases if the person is faced with their trauma then it will go away. To some extent, that is. If it was brought over from a previous life then it would not go away. Anyway that is not the kind of thing that is brought over with you. Fear is not transmitted. Love goes with you.

So you are saying that if a person had say a death by being murdered or assaulted by a wild animal, then they would not bring that feeling over with them to this life?

Yes I am. You can bring hatred or loathing or other things of that type, but that is merely that your karma is such that you do not have the learning to be otherwise. You can bring over love, which is nothing more that a wise spiritual persona. But acts that are committed to you are left behind on this side. Problems you have not yet conquered you will bring with you in a small degree of understanding. But the love of a spider or a wild animal will not be amongst them.

Are severely disabled children the most pure of all souls and are all of us born as such at some stage?

To be born of a body with a disability is the supreme test of understanding and it could be said that to do so the spirit has to have reached a certain level of progression to be allowed this privilege. The spirit must be advanced. The spirit is nearly pure in its realm of progression within this level of consciousness. So it could be called a pure soul or to be exact a nearly pure soul or spirit. It still has to live that life with all its hardships to progress to the pure stage. But all these children are very spiritual and it is obvious in their appearance to all that see them. They are wise in spirit and lame in body. You ask if all spirits have to come to earth in such a body. I will say to you that this is not the case. There are many ways of learning your lessons and these are different for each spirit. Some may choose to come back that way, others may choose a different path that gives the same results and tests.

Is it possible for the power of love, positive thought and faith to overcome any illness or disability?

Not all illnesses or disabilities. It depends if they were chosen by the person as part of their lesson or of a dying process. But I will say to you that love will conquer most things and positive thought by the person will often times make an illness go away. Many illnesses can be self inflicted and others can be sent purely to see how a person deals with them. If you are strong and say, go away I don't want you, then many times it will. To be a lover of an illness for the attention that this illness gets you, is very, very wrong. Sometimes man will have a mind that is sick and this cannot help his body, it makes the body weak even though it is not obvious. If an illness or a disability is part of a lesson or dying then what can you do? You can't make it go away, can you? But you can give it a positive attitude and be in power of what is happening to you. You fight it and add determination and courage. You may still die but you didn't just take it and not give out your passion.

When sending healing thoughts to someone should they be done directly, or through the Great White Spirit or the Holy Spirit?

They should be done directly. But if you want to ask for help for that person, then you ask your guide, or the higher spirits to intervene and do something.

Do different diseases or illnesses take different amounts of love or healing to overcome them?

Each situation must be taken on its own. No two are the same. It is not so much the difference in the disease but more the circumstances surrounding the person at the time. If the person is weak and accepting the illness it will be harder to send healing and therefore to bring about a cure. If the person is strong and positive then the healing will be easier and the flow of energy from spirit will be strong as a healing force. Just do it all the same and hope that the illness will allow a cure and the person will accept it. Where possible talk to the person and explain what is happening. By this you may make them more receptive. In lots of cases fear is a great grounder and this must be overcome, however bad the symptoms. Never forget that the ultimate in life is to return home to live with spirit. Not to live on earth for as long as possible with a body that is hurting and decaying.

What are your views on schizophrenia? Is it more that another spirit is trying to take over a body and is it curable?

There is only ever one spirit in a body at any one time. There are cases when bad spirits may try and influence the reason of a person but that is rare. The disease you mention has many causes. Environmental, hereditary and so on. Not yet known to your scientists. But basically it is a disorder that a person has like any other disease. It is controllable now thanks to your doctors, but it will never be curable. The reason for this is because it is like a maiming of the body. If you have a scar from an accident to your skin and it is so bad it required stitches, you will always have the scar. As so with this disease.

I have many and various types of medical conditions which I am coping with. Are there any words of advice you are able to offer to assist me in dealing with these and their subsequent related issues?

You must all try and cope with all that is happening to you. Try to become aware of your own spirituality and live by that alone and you will see that by distancing yourself from your body and outside worries you become at one with yourself and this gives you a barrier if you like to protect you from the other issues. Perhaps protect you will take in the wrong context, so I will say that by learning more about the spirituality which is you, you diminish the body which is only part of you and not the whole. You will never stop learning and by befriending your spirit guide who is with you ever second of every day, you will see that you do have an ally who is part of you and always, always by your side to help in times of trouble or despair which I know are many. Know your guide, know your own spirituality. For that is the key.

I have seen an interesting program about spiritual healing and the mere fact that people get better only because of the placebo effect. That is because their mind believes they are being healed or will get better, so they do. What are your comments on that please?

What is the placebo effect other than the person themselves believing that they can get better? Whether it be by taking a pill or by them merely thinking the pill will work, it is the same. They have the belief that somehow they can be cured. What they have is not life threatening or something they just have to learn to live with. All things are curable in the mind. I do not mean that some things will not result in death, they will if they are chosen to do so, but all others are curable to some or all degrees. You do not have to believe in spiritual healing for it to work, but you do have to have a genuine illness or condition in the first place.

A certain healer says to her patients as they leave, "Do not invite your condition back". Is this your advice too?

Generally yes, but there are times when the illness will not go however much healing you give or however much the person does not want it. This is because the illness is pre-planned and there is nothing that can be done about it. The person may say now that they don't want it, but in some cases, not all, there is nothing they can do, they have it anyway. Healing will not make the illness go away however much the person believes that it will. Healing will help the person to cope with the illness and that is all.

I do not have an attractive body shape which distresses me greatly. Could you please tell me if there is a physical or perhaps mental reason for this?

Your body shape or type is not you. You are your spirit. Maybe you chose a body that is not fashionable in its shape, to learn how people react to you, or how you react to other people with that body. There are many reasons. Learn to love your spirit self not your body self. To be vain about your body is to be without spiritual understanding. So cry not. If your spirit was overweight with wrongs or hatred or scorn, then you have a problem. When you are happy again, your body will be happy too.

Chapter Eight

Colours & Auras

"Learn to recognise the difference".

Please could you give me a synopsis of auras and colours?
An aura is what is attached to, or should we say surrounds, every person in your world. It does not need to be a colour it can be more of something that you pick up as a feeling. You all know that often when you meet a person for the first time you immediately have a feeling about them – that they are kind – are moody – are aggressive and various stages in between. These could be called auras – they are vibrations that you pick up with your own spiritual advancement. Some people are able to feel and sense a person's aura much more easily than another who is not so spiritually mature and therefore does not have the advancement to be able to do so from instinct. These aura colours change frequently and no person has a particular colour that is with them all the time. Colours change as does the mood of the person. Perhaps a person may be green, which is growing and in harmony with nature, but then someone upsets them and they become angry so their aura colour changes to grey. Then when they calm down the colour changes again to maybe blue, which is tranquil.

The spiritual colour on the other hand is determined by your spiritual advancement. Every baby has a colour when it is born and that is determined by the cluster it was in before birth. As you progress through your spiritual path you go forward from one colour to the other. These are called spiritual colours and are different from aura colours. Your spiritual colour is your progression colour but when you are reborn to your world that underlying colour can change on a daily or hourly basis dependant on how you think and behave, as do changes to your aura colours. For example if your spiritual colour is mellow but your aura colour is mostly negative then this will have an effect on your spiritual colour. But it is unlikely that a highly evolved spirit would behave in a black or negative way, so in some way they are connected.

So let us look at this scenario. We have a spirit that is not too advanced in its learning but it has not done really bad things either. It returns to your world say as a blue which is calm, peaceful and tranquil. It is a calm baby but as it grows older it is influenced by other people's negative actions and does not have the maturity of spirit to act in a knowing way. So it goes along with its peers and takes on a coat of aggression or self pity. The spiritual colour over its life gradually changes because of these outside influences which it has encompassed. You could say that its own spirituality has taken a tumble to a lower level. The aura of the body is changed too and on a daily basis it goes from good and calm to aggression. The aura colour is controlled by the spiritual colour. The spirituality of the person can become anything it wants. It has to be strong to overcome temptations and tribulations which spirit has put in its way. You are reborn on earth to deal with things, not to take these blows into your being and wallow in self pity or become something other than that of your spiritual self. However, many of you are not spiritually mature enough to do this.

When you return to the spiritual world your colour status is assessed. I have talked to you before about clusters. You are in clusters in the spiritual world according to your progression in your spiritual advancement. These clusters are colour coded too. There are seven main clusters with seven main colours but within each colour there are seven layers or shades of colours.

So let us go back to the baby who was born from the blue cluster. Blue is let us say in the middle of the cluster progression. It is neither the starting cluster nor the ultimate high cluster. The spirit of the baby has progressed through its own spiritual advancement to the blue cluster but after returning to earth as a blue spiritual colour it did not do so well with resisting temptation and dealing with life in a spiritual way. So after an analysis in the spirit world it goes back to a darker shade of blue, whereas before it was a pale blue. There is no divide between the colours or within the shades inside that particular colour. No chasm to leap over to get to be a member of the next colour, it is merely a gradual progression from one shade or colour to the next.

Every action of every day is shown as an aura colour. There is no way you can avoid this by being something other than who you are. For example you cannot be unkind to someone and put on a false smile or tell lies and expect your aura to go from the bad colour to the good colour just because you appear to be acting in a nice way. It is the spirit in you that puts out the colour of the aura. As I said at the beginning if you are a spiritually evolved person then you will be able to instinctively pick up the positive or negative aura of a person however they are behaving. Many people in your world are false to themselves and others, but as you learn you will be able to see and feel the reality of the way they are not the way they seem.

As the spirit progresses, does the aura colour change?

Yes it does, but during one life or another, the colour can change. You could progress through many lives and then take on the colour of something previous. That is because of your free will. If you progress say to spiritual colour yellow, then you may have some blue days so your aura will appear to be a darker shade of yellow instead of lighter

We don't understand. Please explain in more detail.

You progress to a spiritual colour, or shall we say a glow of your spiritual learning. That colour is your progression. The ultimate is white and to that you strive to be as perfection. But whatever colour you have spiritually achieved in your birth into your world, it can be changed by your actions. Let us say that you are born from a green cluster and you are gliding through life pretty good as a green, but then you do something which is bad against all laws of karma, then this will manifest itself on your spirituality by making not only your aura a different colour but it will have an effect on your spiritual colour too. This will stay with you until you either do something good to change it or you return home to have your colour assessed. I am not saying right or wrong, only trying to give an example. Let us say you are a work in progress. You are in a costume which must stay with you. If you decide to cast off that costume and go naked, then you will change colour without your coloured coat until you put it on again.

Please tell us about the meaning of colours seen during healing.

Various aura colours have different meanings dependant on the circumstances of the person at any particular time. If I say to you that for example, blue is peace and purple is spiritual, I would also say that blue is cold and purple is life. Black is death, it is not? Black is somber and black is also the meaning of solidarity. There are certain teachings on your world with regard to techniques for healing which have an emphasis on certain colours for various parts of a body. For you to follow this certain teaching for healing, you are also taught that certain colours are associated with certain areas of the body. This is the formula for working within the theories of that particular group who teach that a particular colour is associated with a body part. Theoretically when you mediate or open yourself up to being a healing channel you ask spirit for a sign to what is wrong with the person, and spirit sends you a colour. But this is one way of communicating with spirit when healing and this group thinks it is essential to know what part is sick and they ask for a colour. They have their chart showing that they have allocated a colour to various parts of the body so they ask for a colour sign which they then attribute to the body and then they have their answer as to where the patient needs healing. Of course to do spiritual healing you do not need to ask for spirit to send healing to a particular part of the body because it will happen anyway and heal whatever part needs it. You could look into a crystal and get one set of colours. You could say see yellow on the person when you are healing and then go to a crystal again and see green. So on your world there is a lot of mystery about colours. From our world each circumstance has an aura colour. The auras of people when you see their colour can also change with the mood or circumstances of the person. So no one person has the same colored aura all the time. They may vary from one to another.

Do really bad people have black auras?

Yes from grey to black but not all the time. They could give out another colour, which is showing their falseness, but the somber colour is there all the same.

Tell us more about how we can learn to see auras?

The question of auras is not easy because not many people can see an aura around another person and those that say they can, do not necessarily do so. But you cannot see through their eyes so you can never know what they see. An aura is a spiritual surrounding of the body with a light and this can be picked up by your observation in many ways. Every person has in his aura a definition of his spirituality and his advancement and a sense of the spiritual state of his being at the particular time of a particular day when you observe him and his aura. You could say meet a person on the street and you will know instinctively whether he is good or bad or kind or pompous, do you not? You are picking up part of his aura. Auras are not just colour, they are a set of details about that person that you can tune into if you have the gift and the power. But mostly auras are associated with a colour surrounding a person and this is what all people have. Colour coding, if you like. Spiritual people who are advanced usually have purple or white and these colors go down the spectrum of people to dark browns or blacks for morbid or evil minded personalities. I will not at this stage be more definite about what each color means because you can't see them fully yet anyway and it would be confusing for your group. But remember that the color that surrounds a person is a visual sign of the instincts or details that your guides tell you to pick up from the person. The aura too can change as a person gets emotionally upset or furious with rage, or very loving. So you see maybe an elderly person who has no anger, and loves continually small children and animals and is kind to all he meets will have a much more pastel color than an aggressive terrorist who plans to kill and abuse people. He will have a dense dark color. White is pure spirit and you will not see that. If anyone tells you that they see pure white around a person, do not believe them. You can see spirit, say like myself or the Holy Spirit or the Great White Spirit, but you will not see it around a person in your world in a body. That is not possible.

When I am healing I always get red, green purple not the colours associated with the teachings of Reiki.

You know yourself that perhaps you have moved further than the teachings of Reiki. You have a knowledge that is superior. Red is the underlying colour in Reiki, green is the heart which you now know is the tool for opening the spirituality – love for another word, and purple is spirituality itself. So in your healing you are applying the laws of karma and the acceptance of spiritual help together with the knowledge that it is the heart of love of the patient that is the key to their recovery asking spirit to work with you in performing a healing miracle. This is all you need. Spirit does the rest. You are not the healer, spirit is. For your fellow Reiki healers, they concentrate on the areas of the body and then ask for help using that colour as a tool. You must do no more than open yourself as a channel, already having the beliefs that this is the way that spirit will work with you. You do not need to associate with individual colours.

Please explain being green and its association to spring?

Green means growth, not death. Green is the sign of spring and all things new. Some of you have seen green before as a colour during meditation and some of you have not. If you see green be not at static peace for it is a time of doing things, not basking in the sunshine. I say to you that with the spring and seeing the colour green you will grow as well. It is a time of rejoicing because the chrysalis has emerged and flies the skies on gossamer wings. So be that butterfly and make the flight. You will not regret the decision. The flight will give you strength and even more knowledge from the powers of observation. For it is with the powers of observing people that you learn and grow in your wisdom and understanding. Is that not true? I will say to you all that until you have mastered the powers of observing people and their ways, then you are not understanding many things.

You have told me that my spirit's colour is pink. Where does pink fit in the colour progression?

Your colours often change from day to day depending on your mood and what you are getting angry or pleased about. On the day you asked the question, you were pink. That means you were positive and determined but also mellow. That is all.

The author of a book I have read describes and interprets our schools of learning in spirit as clusters or groups. What can you tell us about these, if they exist?

You are in clusters in the spirit world only pertaining to your own spiritual advancement. Yellow sticks with yellow, white with white and so on. Yellow advises white and white advises grey. Clusters you could call them, but huge groupings or one or two depending on the need. You are still part of a whole. Small clusters within a whole cluster and so on. You are not separate entities, although you are. It is difficult to understand I know.

This author supposes that a neutral white or grey is the starting point of development. Would you agree?

You must think of black to grey and grey to white. That is the progression. You start black to dark grey, mid grey, light grey and then gradually to white through all colours of the spectrum.

Can you clarify the corresponding relationship of colour coding to guides status? What level stage colour can we become guides.

Yellow is the starting point. I am yellow.

Talking about the seven levels within seven levels and so on, how come you as yellow are in the same level as me although we are different colours? Surely each level within the 7 levels has its own particular colour?

I clarified spiritual colours to you as levels which you have achieved as progression. You do not go from one level to another, you progress and merge and take on the other colour and then turn into another colour. I cannot say there is a divide that you hop over. It is not like that. There are seven colours but there are seven stages of density within each colour. That is the difference. What I said to you was that I, as being higher to you in particular, am still close to you in our level. I am ready to take on another density and move away from you. But you are progressing too and not too far behind. You will catch up maybe.

In your teachings regarding the aura/colour coding, can you explain what each colour means more fully?

This is difficult because it depends on the density and hue of the colour. For example you can have a yellow red or a blue red. There is a big difference. But I will say to you that for spirituality we have white, purple, yellow and blue. But not necessarily in that order. For these spiritual colours there are purposes and it is not just that if you see white it is high spirit, or if you see yellow it is not so high. For various reasons, there are various colours. Blue is tranquil and green is growing. Red is positive and orange is peaceful but progressive. Pink is harmony and pale blue is tranquil. Black is negative as well as not very spiritual. Black is on the other side of the colour wheel from white. But for all things, if you say I see green about a certain person and that means growth, you may see them the next day and they are yellow which is mellow and spiritual. People change by the hour or by the day.

Regarding colours and auras, what is the spiritual significance of synaesthesia?

I would not say that by seeing a particular colour around a person that this would influence your attitude to that person, it doesn't quite work like that. However a person can show an aura and you can pick up on that and know their spiritual attitude at that time. I must point out that auras change depending on the circumstances that the person finds themselves at the time. Their aura is not the same all the time. It changes. So although your question is not exactly correct, you can see and feel auras with colours and that could change how you perceive the person at the time you are seeing them. But it is only for the moment, not forever. That is the difference.

You have said that purple and white are spiritual colours - are there any colours that are negative spiritually?

The darker the colour the more towards the negative side it becomes. For example light grey/white is more towards the positive whereas dark grey and black are definitely the opposite to white in all spectrums.

Could, say, a book with a black cover give off more bad vibrations than one with a purple or white colour?

Quite definitely. Black is sombre and negative so although the words on the pages may not be so, they can be perceived by the reader to have those inclinations.

If white is a spiritual colour, are people that live in places where there is snow on the ground for most of the year affected by the white of the snow?

Yes if they were isolated with nothing else but snow, it would be a very spiritual place. But people who live in those areas also have towns, houses, other people etc to contend with. Those things may give off harmful vibrations so it is impossible to generalise. But these snow covered lands are usually very sunny and that in itself is a positive thing to see. But isolation is bad and that should not be considered. Helping and meeting people through your life's journey is what life is all about.

Are people affected by the interior or exterior colour of say their cars?

Yes, we are back to positive and negative colour influences. If a person lived in a room with black walls, then they take on the gloom of this negative colour and become part of it too. With regards to cars, it depends on the internal colour of the car, not the exterior.

Is there any spiritual significance as to whether a person is white, black or something else?

I am presuming you mean the colour of their skin. If so, then no it doesn't matter. There are spiritual and non spiritual people in all walks of life.

Would there be any affect on our spirits from the kind of colour of light thrown off by electric light bulbs?

No, these would not affect your spirituality as such. But they may affect your demeanour.

When spirit looks at our earth, what is the overall colour you see?

Unfortunately at this time I see grey.

Could you give us some insight on aura colours we may see around people and why they have them?

An aura is an essence that every person has around them at any given moment. Shall we call it a glow which surrounds the body. This is a colour going from soft to stronger but never, ever and a bold colour. You can learn to pick up on a person's aura or glow. You can tell if they are cross or saintly even if they don't say a word to you. Auras colours range right across the colour spectrum. For example a very spiritually person who is praying may have a pale pinkish whitish aura, whereas a person about to kill another may have a dark grey or black aura. You must remember too that the colour of auras change from any given moment to another. The person who is about to kill may have been another colour than black the day before the happening. The person themselves brings about the colour of their aura, but the more spiritual person is unlikely to do bad things so their colour will be more consistently light in shade, or it should be at least.

Is there a direct correlation between a person's aura and their spiritual colour?

Any spirit from any colour cluster in the spirit world can do things in your world which could influence the spiritual colour when they come home to the spiritual plane. Day to day living on your world gives off various aura colours depending on how the person is behaving at the time. However it is unlikely that a person who is spiritually advanced will do anything or behave in a way that is detrimental to his spiritual development. The more spiritual you are the better you behave to others. But there are always exceptions of course, although unlikely in this instance.

Would a person's aura or colour change if they for example were in love, broken hearted, pregnant, laughing, in pain?

Quite definitely. All these things are relevant to the body which in turn affects their spiritual understanding and as thus brings about a change in their aura colour.

I have seen the colour pink when treating a patient who believed totally in another healer who has passed away. I don't feel she has the same confidence with me but she keeps coming back. Please explain why and what was the pink light.

This person has many problems, some which she chooses to have, some she does not. To say that the particular healer was wonderful and you are not is not correct for this reason. When you heal you open yourself up to spirit as a channel to come through and heal. The person wants to be healed and so the transformation will take place. Pink is the colour of warm acceptance. This may seem strange to see this when she is not accepting your help in one respect, but is true all the same. This lady is sad and does not understand. She is using her illnesses to gain pity so that is why she had not the faith and understanding to look at being healed. She does not want to be healed, but her mind will change, you will see.

Could you please describe the shades of light/brightness associated with the speed of travel as an entity?

When the soul leaves the body, there is not light. As souls travel home, there is no light. As souls enter the cluster there is light around them depending on how they fared in their life on earth. Bright lights are the pure souls, and dim lights are around those who need lots of help and guidance. To see a spirit in this world which has a glow as a bright light is nothing more than a pure soul.

You say it is not possible to see pure white light around someone. But could I have seen it in astral travel?

Pure white light is pure spirit. From your perspective it is unlikely that you have seen this in its entirety. For to have done so you would yourself be surrounded by the light. It would have transformed you into the light. But this is what happens when you return to this plane of existence. However you may see a fragmentation of the light. You have seen it also. If you see a circle or a spot of white light it is possible and does happen. What I said was that no living person on your earth will be able to remember having experienced this whilst visiting this plane of existence, because you do not remember when you return to earth. I also said that it is impossible for this to happen in your lifetime on earth. It is of course possible to see a part of this white light.

We all have colours that we like; are these colours in anyway related to our spiritual colour?
You will not for example like blue because your cluster is blue if that is what you are asking. But you will know whether you like pale or dark colours best. And that has relevance.

What does it mean if you like bright colours?
That you are a vibrant person.

What if you like pastel colours?
Then you are at a pastel shade in your cluster. What I mean by that is that if you are at a pastel stage in your cluster it is unlikely that you would have the temperament to be a dark colour when acting your life out on earth.

Why are some people drawn to certain colours?
It is no more than your choices in life. In this life you may like one colour best and the next life you will like another, yet you are more or less at the same stage of your development and in the same colour cluster.

What is the order of the cluster colours?
The same as the natural colours of a rainbow which are seen as a prism of light and the reflections of such. Red to purple.

Red, orange, yellow, green,, blue, indigo (a more advanced colour blue), and violet which is purple.

Is it as simple as that?

No because we have red more as a burgundy or dark red going to pink and then it changes to orange with the inclusion of some yellow. There is no yellow as such at this stage. Then next is green and blue and then comes yellow which is the additive to get to purple. So yellow is the essential colour to be to get to purple.

Chapter Nine

Other Worlds

"There are too many for your understanding.
They are like pebbles on a beach"

Are there many other inhabited worlds?

Look at the moon and you will see the vastness of the universe in miniature. Then you will see beyond the moon and beyond still, and then you can lose yourself in the endlessness of it all and perhaps you can imagine just a little of the concept of the universe, ad infinitum. I try to explain but you will never comprehend the extent of all the vastness and endlessness of everything. The stars are thousands and thousands and thousands. The planets are millions. There are worlds you would not dream of many light years away from your world. And they have inhabitants too.

Please describe one of these worlds so that we will have a better understanding of how the people live.

I will only say that of the millions of worlds, some are as you know it with a similar to human life form. Many are not. Many are with more like animals and some are more like beings

172

that you do not understand. For the beings, they may be more advanced spiritually than yourselves.

Are the other worlds that spirit inhabits of the same level as ours?

No they are all at different levels. But to be exact, as you know each level has several levels, so you could say that some of them do overlap slightly.

If we had the technology, would it be possible to communicate with them or even to visit them?

If you were on a spiritual plane you could communicate, depending of how advanced you are in your spiritual progress, but you cannot do so from your world. Even with technology you may travel to other planets and see living creatures, but you are many years from being that advanced. But you will never be able to communicate with those that are more advanced than yourselves. The spectrum of the distances is way beyond even your advanced understanding. For the other worlds who are only inhabited with animal types, then you could not of course begin communications. But in reverse, some advanced spheres can observe and try to communicate with you. However, they do not choose to correspond with lower life forms any more than your men will want to communicate with animals on lands which have lower spiritual advancement.

Would there be any harm in doing so?

If you could, which you can't, then yes there would be absolutely no need to do so and the whole exercise would be pointless. It would be like peasants who have only ever lived in an isolated village trying to communicate with sophisticated business executives.

Do we get to choose which world we go to at our level when we have to return to a life?

No, it depends on where you are in your spiritual advancement. That determines where you go to learn your lessons.

*Does the world we return to depend on the lessons we
need to learn in that life?*

Yes, but as I have said before, it is connected to which
spiritual level you are on.

*Because there is no such thing as time for spirit, could
my spirit be learning one set of lessons here on this earth,
and another set on another world at the same time?*

No because you are only allocated to go to one world for
that purpose. If you could dissect yourself into various worlds
this would be confusing, so the rules are one world at a time.

*Are there spiritually advanced beings who have evolved
from humans?*

Yes there are but not in a time span you would comprehend.
They are in a plane of learning that is spiritually advanced to
yourselves. They had to achieve lessons of understanding and
karma to reach where they are now. The process was gradual.
But from this perspective, as I have described before, all things
happen at the same time. We see yourselves and these beings
as happening together. You advanced to where you are and
so did they at the same time. They are not ahead of you, yet
they are more learned and advanced in their understanding.
The same as you are more advanced than those lowly beings
that are in other worlds, but you are advancing at the same
rate. Do you understand? I think not. For it is beyond your
comprehension.

*Do the beings that inhabit other planets have the same
code of conduct and spiritual karma as us?*

The question shows some confusion and lack of understanding,
so I will explain. Karma is your record, your file, your data
base of you yourself. Living by the laws of karma means that
you are doing things, which will make your progress good and
easy. Your file will be good to anyone who looks and you will
have an impeccable record for moving on. Beings who inhabit

other worlds are the same as you. We are not talking about their bodies; we are talking about their spirituality. Spirit is spirit, not a body. Whether spirit is evolving from an ant to your body or to a being in another world, the spirit is the same. It is just another extension of the same path. So for a spirit to be in the body of another world for the journey of understanding and progression it is the same as another rung of the ladder inside a being in your world.

When they die, assuming that they do, do their souls go home to where you are now?
No they go to another level of spiritual consciousness. I have told you that there are many levels and that is the point of the desire to progress within these levels. You always aim to go on higher to another level. That is why you wish to learn the lessons and evolve higher.

Do the forms that spirits take on other planes evolve as man has done on earth?
Let us take man on your earth. Spirituality of one spirit will go to your earth to learn, and learn in many lives and then when educated in all aspects that this plane of existence requires will then graduate as passing all the exams, and pass onto the next plane of existence going through the whole process again and again. In all worlds that spirit goes to, the process is the same. Not all in bodies which are the same. Not always in bodies, sometimes as observers sometimes in forms of bodies such as man. It is difficult to explain other worlds because you cannot perceive other worlds. But to answer the question I will say sometimes, not always.

Scientists talk about travel through time - Black holes and worm holes - what is your perception of this.
I would say to you that the words of scientists are not the words of spirit. I have already told you that you may travel through time and space within the realms of your own spirituality. You

may say that you can do this anyway whatever the name given to this by others. The scientists of your world generally do not believe in spirituality because it is contrary to their own scientific world, yet they make up new names for traveling in time which is in fact a spiritual thing anyway. Now who is being controversial - the scientists of course.

When this planet started there were only a few souls about. Now there are many millions. Where did all the new spirits come from and how do they appear to keep multiplying?

You must not look at things as if your world is the beginning and the end. For the life of a spirit - which is in itself a perpetual progression ad infinitum - your world is merely a grain of salt. I have told you many times in my teachings that your world grows from dust to flower and flourish to be ruined by man, destroyed and returned again to dust. This has happened many times with many civilizations over a long period of your time. The spirits, which inhabit your earth, even at its most populated, are but a very mere proportion of spirits which are evolving. They too are like a grain of salt in a pillar of salt. Spirits, which are evolving, are in many places for many lessons. Your world is just one of them. There are many other places equal to your world. Many are higher and many are lower. It depends on the lesson of the spirit's path. You ask how they appear to be multiplying. I say to you that they are not. It is merely that more spirits visit earth at this time, that is all.

Is there such a thing as mass consciousness? Does it have anything to do with the fact that this planet seems to be dying?

Your life on earth or anywhere else is a level of consciousness. In the spirit world it is a level too. For the planet of your world to die, there is a strong possibility that it will for that is the spiral of continuing life and death of all things. There are other worlds and other classrooms of learning.

For the purpose of progression, do we inhabit other bodies/vessels on any of the planets involved in astrology? e.g. Jupiter, Saturn?

No, you visit them from the spiritual plane. These do not have lives as such in your spiritual journeys. But they are areas of learning nonetheless. There are millions of such places that are important in your makeup and advancement. For these places you visit many at some times. By your standards the visit may only be a split second of your time although it is many lifetimes of understanding. So time is not relevant, only that you experienced them all the same.

Outside this physical realm, is there a structure and form which does not change?

Outside your physical realm is spirituality and other physical realms as well. For the spiritual realm, as you call it, there is no structure and form. For the others there is at the time that entities are in those realms to learn, experience and advance. Their structure and form varies as do the experiences. It is difficult to define in one short question.

How many planes are there?

There are many, many planes, ad infinitum. There is no beginning and there is no end. From the spiritual plane you can see back but you cannot see forward too far. Spirit only knows that it has to proceed from plane to plane for that is its purpose. Our ultimate ambition is to learn and advance.

What limitations lie within each of the more common planes? For example - boundaries, time?

For boundaries on each level, you must achieve all that is required to advance in each segment within each level to finally achieve graduation so that you can advance to the bottom rung, so to speak, of the next level. It is like being an infant in school and leaving as a senior only to go to university and start again as a freshman. There is no time. We have no sense of time. Time is an earthly thing. From the spiritual plane all that happens in your world now, in the past and to some extent in the future, can be viewed simultaneously. Also we can see and feel two people on different sides of your world and experience what we see and feel at the same time. We can absorb many things at the same time. For example you may ask how can a person asking for help in Australia be heard if there are a million people in American asking for help as well. It is easy, that is all.

Should we try to prepare for leaving the physical plane?

Every day of your lives. You must face your lessons, overcome them and learn, for that is your purpose. You must develop your own spirituality, which has been advancing with you through many lives and experiences. You must face the things in life which are against the laws of Karma and know that they are not accepted. You must respect and understand, or try to understand by your own spirituality, all other persons on your world regardless of their culture, colour or their own wrong doings. For that is why you are on your earth. That is your purpose. You must prepare from your birth to leave your world. For you do not know how long you have to learn your lesson. You cannot wait. It may be too late if you lead the wrong kind of life and then try and put everything right at the last minute before you die. Spirit, you see, is the constant observer.

You have also stated that there were previous races to humankind on earth, who evolved to a particular point and then destroyed themselves. I have heard this idea from other sources but have always completely discounted it since I have never heard of any physical evidence of their existence - no fossils, no archaeological discoveries. If there were civilizations before humans, why is there nothing to show for them?

Man destroyed completely the world and then it rose again from the ashes after having been 'cleansed' shall we say by the power of spirit. This has happened many times. All evidence of its former occupation in different ways was removed. To dig down in your earth for such a short way and see relics from a by gone era is only very superficial and easily removed. From the charred remains of a world a small shoot of plant life is given and from that the world will grow again to a land of beauty. The seed was not in the earth, the seed was put on the earth to start life again.

Do space aliens have souls?
Every living being, wherever they live, has a soul. But the term aliens is not always correct.

Man has sent space ships to every planet in our solar system. They have ruled out all, except perhaps Mars and Jupiter, as being able to sustain life.
They have not even touched the tip of the iceberg. They have seen nothing compared to the vastness of the whole. Yes there is life elsewhere. Not all bad as you imagine. All are at different stages of spiritual development on different levels of consciousness.

Could you comment on the alien bodies supposedly found in 1947 near Roswell, New Mexico and the one who was said to have survived until 1952?
Aliens, as you call them, will self dispose of their worldly litter so no bodies would have remained, dead or alive.

Is it true that the US government made a pact with aliens that they could take humans and animals in exchange for information about their advanced technology?
None whatsoever. The other worlds know enough about your primitive lifestyles to satisfy their curiosity. If they travel to your world they are more advanced than yourselves and often have previously, a long way back in their spiritual advancement, been on your level of consciousness too. All experiences that

the spirit entities have during its long voyage of discovery are remembered and documented within its own karma.

Many people believe they can hear voices in their head. Some obviously have mental problems but others seem fairly sensible. Sometimes they blame these voices for telling them to do things which they would not otherwise do. Can aliens talk to people this way?

No, there is no communications from aliens or beings from other worlds. But guides can talk to people if they listen. It is not such as words but more ideas they plant although that sounds too contrite. Guides talk to you in answer to your questions only. Guides give you instinct to do or not do something that would harm you or a decision you may need to make. Some of you call it instinct or a gut instinct. But to that which you are referring, it is more that someone has a mental problem or just has a high imagination which is extremely possible. The person imagines they hear the words and in fact they may do so, but it is from themselves. It is the same with pain. If someone told you that say you had an ulcer and you did not, you may in fact create a pain to act out the theory. You are in charge and you can in fact materialize anything you like.

You have said that there are many other worlds - do they each have a specific purpose, more specific than just to be a place where spirits can evolve?

Each world has a purpose in its own spiritual level of consciousness. They are extremely complex sometimes if the world is more advanced than your own. There are also primitive worlds too. But each is parallel to the progression of the spirit entity. For example people in your world are at one stage of development and would not therefore be put into a sphere that is more spiritually advanced. If you look at your world and the purpose of the lessons you will see that the lessons are in fact limited to just a few categories in which everything else will be encompassed that you do and feel whilst on your earth. In other worlds it is the same.

What is earth's specific purpose?

It is nothing more than a classroom for you all to experience and hopefully learn from your lessons. Let us say it is a stage on which you can improvise and perform with the higher spirit entities watching.

Are there UFOs with people from other worlds, or are they from somewhere else completely different?

I think, for simplicity, we can call all other places that have life forms, other worlds. But UFO's are only your description. Unidentified Flying Objects. They don't actually fly. They are what you could call visions being projected from another place. The projected vision will observe the same as your time travelling or viewing during a meditative state.

Can people in other worlds affect us on earth?

Not at all

Can other beings travel from planet to planet across the universe?

Quite definitely and they do.

Are we watched by these higher beings from other planets?

Yes you are. They are curious and they are learning from you as you would do with your own scientific research of your times gone by. You are curious to know how the peoples lived centuries ago and how they built structures with crude tools, do you not?

Did a UFO crash in 1947 in Roswell New Mexico?

There was fall out from a craft but it came from the atmosphere and fell to earth in pieces. It has been grossly imagined by your peoples and is not what it appeared at all. Definitely no beings on board, it was debris nothing else. Beings were transported back via light.

If these beings were transported back home via light, why did they need a spaceship to visit and observe our world?

Firstly it was a vessel but not as you know it as a space ship, although you can call it that for your own reference point. The craft that I describe was used for scientific purposes and was actually disintegrated purposely so that it fell to earth. The occupants were observing your world and testing many things too. They were let us say historians, fact finding for their own thesis on world and its inhabitants. But it was used and the data taken back to base and then the ship, which was shall we say an illusion of nothing taking form to be a ship, was not needed. So it was disintegrated so that debris purposely fell and man then observed and gave out various ideas as to why it had happened. It made man think that there could be life elsewhere did it not? However what happened expanded on this idea and man made a being as an alien to go with this happening.

What are the purposes of lives on other worlds?

The same purposes as you have life on your world. Each classroom is set for a specific set of lessons. Other worlds have other lessons although they are mostly more advanced than your world.

Is Earth the only planet where you learn lessons?

No, as you advance in your spiritual progress then you go to different levels. From these you go to other worlds.

Are there planets for spirits without form?

No, that would be the spiritual plane. We learn here too.

Does time exist on other planets?

Not as on your world, but time does exist. It is more a set space of time in which to be there but some of them they are not born or they do not die, they just arrive for a specific time and then leave.

In physics there are laws of certain things on Earth, do these laws apply in other worlds?
Yes, but in other ways not yet known to man

Do life forms on other planets have a carbon base and live on water and oxygen?
Some do and others are more advanced in that these are not necessary.

How far is the closest planet with life of spirit? Is it in this galaxy?
Yes.

Do flying rods exist and what exactly are they?
Yes. They are a communication device. You have telephone waves, other beings have rods of light.

Are you describing the same rods as people are capturing on film?
Yes, I will explain better. I describe them as rods of light because that is what they are. But they appear black because if they glowed as light they would not absorb the surroundings. Black does absorb atmospheric conditions whereas light is pure in substance. So let us say then that a light rod appears from nowhere and shoots across space and then disappears. It is materialized for a short space of time and the nearest I can describe it for your understanding is that it is capturing pictures and actions and in one flash of movement has more data than thousands and thousands of rolls of your films. They pick up energy from the sources from where they materialize and that makes them work from nothing to being highly charged and then to die out, having sent back to base all the information that is captured in the flash of movement.

What is the phenomenon of dying animals in freak accidents, such as 1000's of crows falling from the sky?

The crows were used as vessels. When their task was complete they died. I will explain in simple terms. Spirits from other worlds, advanced spirits who can take over life forms of animals, take over birds for example and then mass and then build up energy to visualise from the sky many things. When finished the birds fall to earth and the beings move on. They do not have spiritual sight, not all of them that is, for your world, so in their lessons of observation of you they come up with various ways to look at you all. Do not be alarmed they are not dangerous to you.

Do boats and people really go missing in a place called the Bermuda Triangle? What happens in this area?

Ley-lines merge, energies are high, and vibrations affect boats' navigation equipment or interfere with the simple aids like the placement of stars etc. Everything is seen differently for a short time and this causes the boats to become disorientated in some cases. In others people will report this happening when it has no meaning at all.

What makes Stonehenge such a spiritual place?

It is not actually a spiritual place. Years ago there was a belief system in many countries in which they worshipped Gods by the erection of stone temples or statutes. In the case of Stonehenge it was a site where many thousands of people worshipped and because it was set at the crossing of ley-lines it made the vibrations somewhat better. It was situated because of the ley-lines but that is the only point. In fact this site did not become a spiritual place because the prayers and sacrifices were to false Gods and it was not spiritually based. However, it was used by primitive people who did in fact believe that there was a god that governed them all. But their interpretation of what that God required was totally not right. They did some horrific things there such as sacrificing small children and offering them to the gods or beheading men or pulling out entrails of others all in the name of worship. The very acts then desecrated the site from any spiritual sanctions.

Do spiritual beings from other planets try to contact any of us personally?

Rarely, they do not need to at this time. They cannot merge with your life forms and they have no more interest in you other than scientific.

Why do spiritual beings leave things for us to see like crop circles?

Not all crop circles are the work of other beings. Some are man made. But yes some leave signs for you. They are interested to see if you earthmen can work out the meanings. It is a test from them.

Has anyone living on Earth ever lived on another world?

Yes you all have at some time. There are worlds higher in vibrations but there are ones lower too. To get to live on your world you would have already had to have lived on other worlds too.

Why do spiritual beings come to visit?

Just to observe you as I have described before.

Is there any way for us to connect to other spiritual beings on another world?

Not with your level of ability, no

How many other inhabited worlds are out there?

Hundreds.

When people say they have been abducted by aliens, does that kind of thing actually happen?

No. a man made illusion, that is all.

Are there other planets similar to Earth?
Several similar, but not the same.

Do other spiritual beings reproduce in ways we do on this planet?
No, the bodies are made and then the entities are put in them. That sounds similar to your world. But I mean that the bodies are scientifically made not by a male or female. There are no genders on most of the worlds similar to your own.

Is there a number amount on how many planets we reside on during our spiritual journey?
No. It is as many as necessary.

Can you describe what a world would be like after I have completed my journey on planet Earth, and am ready for the next one?
It is a gradual progress. You will stay on the world levels until you get to the time when you spiritually evolve to the next level. Then you will go to a world similar to your own, but that is way more scientifically advanced. But the people live as you do without elements, reproduction etc. It is just that they have a different environment because they live underground or underwater. They do not need the scenery or fresh air that you do. However it is advanced and more pleasant.

Can you skip learning on earth's plane to advance spiritually?
You could learn on other planes and not come to your world, but those of you who are on your world are now in a sequence of lessons so you have to finish those before you are spiritually richer and can move higher to other planes. Maybe you could have started this level on another world and in that case you would have had to stay on that world until you had finished the sequence there too.

You talk of dimensions, what is your explanation of this?

Dimensions are levels. I talk to you of levels because that is one way I was taught to teach you so that you would understand one level against another level with a definite division from your perspective. But in fact all levels are dimensions, because they are the same thing; they merge into the next and there are no definite boundaries. However, you in the early days of my teachings could not comprehend that one level did not end and another did not begin, so hence we called them levels. So let us look at dimensions. What are they if not described as levels? They could be planes if that works for you, or they could be areas of learning, which of course they are. If I said to you in your current development you are at say dimension 6 in a series of 7 dimensions then perhaps this would explain. Dimension is a classroom; it is a theatre set; it is a period of timescale if we had it. It is a classroom which has many grades of students all trying to pass the exam to move up to the next dimension or level. But there is no up or down because the levels are all around you. Spirit surrounds you and you move parallel.

Is there a way to connect to the other dimensions/levels?

You can view them from the spiritual level which you call home, where I am now. You can see the levels below you and one level or dimension above you in learning but nothing else. You cannot view from your world.

If some crop circles are meant to be interpreted and we eventually understand it, how would the spirits from the other planets know if we understood them and what would they do?

The other beings are observing you as does your scientist look at the behaviours of rats or mice. They see the pattern of understanding and intelligence. So they send a math question and watch to see if you can solve it. Not a math question of course, but a puzzle for you to solve. What would they do with the information? It would only be stored in a data base of things they are trying to understand. For example if a man in your ancient Rome built a building for a specific purpose but you didn't know now that purpose, your historians would try and understand the mind set of the person who built it. The same is with you and the beings observing. Nothing would be done as such, but lots would be recorded.

Who built the pyramids in Egypt and other similar ancient structures? Were they made by beings from other worlds?

Each one had a different purpose but they were bases for what you call aliens who visited at that time. I said to you that aliens will not visit your world now and land on your earth but they did many centuries ago and they did build structures as scientific experiments using your earth's materials and their own powers of construction and strength. They left behind mysteries similar to the crop circles to see what man made of them as an explanation.

Were they built with mans' help and/or presence?

The stereotype of each type of structure, including a type of pyramid, were built only by the beings from other world. Then your men copied these structures because at the time they thought that they had a spiritual significance, which of course they did. Then man used the structure and observed the construction and copied them in order to make their area more spiritual within the understanding of gods and higher spirits that they had at that specific time. They had the blueprint, so to speak, to build copies, which they did. Originally it was only the beings from other worlds on their own who built the stereotype. Man was not in those areas at that time. Your historians are dating the copies not the original, which explains why you think that man and beings worked together which I tell you they did not. Man and beings from other worlds at any time have not interacted on your world.

What is the difference between other worlds and other dimensions?

Other worlds are classrooms which your spirit travels and lives on in order to have lessons. Dimensions are levels of spirituality which relate to how you have progressed. However from different levels you go to different worlds to learn. For example from one particular level of achievement you will go to several corresponding worlds. The worlds are not for all levels but more specific.

Chapter Ten

Psychic Phenomena

"All higher spirit entities can do this with ease"

If ghosts are souls who have not come to terms with dying, why is this so if every person chooses when they die?

A ghost is your earthly term, not ours. I will try and explain by saying that a ghost is an appearance of spirit in its last life form. For to say to you that a ghost is a figuration of the body before it reaches this plane of existence is not perhaps quite true. So we will start with the death of the body of a person when death is not expected. The spirit always knows, at the point of death, when it is to die. But as I have told you before, if that act of death is so fast that the body was not expecting it, then there is a problem. Most people dying know so and prepare for the passing of the soul or spirit back home to this level of existence. But in some cases of death this awareness is not necessarily apparent. So the spirit you could say is not ready. In another scenario perhaps the spirit does not want to leave the body because it has great loves on your earth or concerns for people it leaves behind and this creates a problem with its journey home. In both cases and several others, the spirit is fighting death and it tries to cling to earth when it should have a straight passage back home. In these cases then the apparition of the spirit trying to cling to its dead body will occur. In time the spirit will be helped back whether with words from your world or whether from its own guide or spiritual leaders from here.

I have heard of a disruptive spirit entity which would not leave a home until a religious relic was placed in the basement of the house. Why was this if religion is not important to a spirit?

A blessing will not remove a spirit unless it is done in the correct way. A spirit will not linger in a place after its person's body is dead, unless that person died in bad circumstances and the spirit does not have the power to cut ties with the place. I could say to you that the spirit is confused because it is in shock. That is not the case in this instance but it will show you the scenario. So the spirit is tied to the basement. Being now completely spiritual it will not agree that a blessing frees it from the person connected with its death. This is because the circumstances of the death is more powerful than the spirit that has passed on. It is not the spirit that is lingering that is the problem. It is the person, or shall we say the spirit of the person who caused the horror that made the death happen to the person who died that is still lingering and therefore making the spirit of the dead person linger too. So the lingering spirit is not affected by the blessing because it doesn't see it as doing any good. The lingering spirit is not at fault, but the person/spirit that caused the horror of which the effect is happening is causing the spirit not to pass over because it is in shock and cannot move on. Eventually a religious item is put in the basement and because of the legend about the power of this object is believed by everyone in your world as having the power to remove the spirit. The vibrations because of the beliefs of many people raised the vibrations in the house and the lingering spirit moved on because of this. So you see it was not the object that made this happen, but merely the beliefs of the people that this could in fact happen. I have said to you many times, the power of belief will make something happen.

Can you tell me if God protected me from the demon when he wanted my soul?

There is no such thing as a demon or Satan. It is all in your mind. The concept, that is. God is pure and is total love. Love cannot be Satan. It is higher than all things. Satan as you call it, even if it was fact, would be nothing in comparison to love. Love is the essence of all things. If you do not have love you lack spiritual growth. So your question was that Satan wanted your soul. Not possible I'm afraid. But you could say that you as a person were led to an imagination that a demon force was in existence and wanted you to be bad rather than good. That is blunt. I would say to you that if you have spiritual growth then you do not have any way that you can be put down by any other force. The force of good is far superior to anything bad. Man is bad. Spirit is good. God is good. There is no heaven and hell. Heaven is in fact the spirit world, but you are not punished or sent to a devil if you do wrong with the laws of Karma. You live by the rules of Karma, you experience your tests which will include temptation by your so-called devil, and you then become richer in spirit. Never think of evil forces because they do not exist. Man can make you think this, but that is all.

Please tell us about miracles at shrines or religious places?

Miracles can always occur anywhere because the Great White Spirit is everywhere. Miracles at shrines are more symbolic because of where they are happening, that is all. There are always lots of miracles, some in the church environment with people who are spiritually evolved and some at other places which have no significance at all. Let yourself think that miracles are not repeated in any one place usually. A miracle will occur because of a set of circumstances and those people who go to the place hoping for another are usually disappointed or are cured because of the connection of their own spirit wanting for the miracle to happen. It goes back to my lesson about the spirit healing the body. But the Great White Spirit does not have to prove his power by lifting stones or doing other things. These do not usually happen. As for statutes of idols weeping, this is in the eye of the beholder. Those, and there can be many, who look on this idol can see what they want if they believe strongly enough that they can. You do not think this can happen, but it can. You look into the face of a trance medium and you see their face alter. This happens only because you see it to happen. Some people in the room do not see it happen. This is because the face itself does not alter, only the person looking's perception of the face. If the spirit takes over the body and has a definite image then several people looking can see the same thing. They all see the same thing because spirit has told them what to see. But the face of the medium does not suddenly grow a bigger nose or have a bad scar on his cheek. No, this is physical and what they see is spiritual. The same thing is with the statues of idols. Spirit tells some people that they are seeing tears and that is what those people, and those people only, see.

Please explain a natural happening like an earthquake? Do those come from God?

This refers to an event where many people are killed and their spirits return home. Many are distressed. Others are injured. Why is it allowed to happen if spirit is love and the Great White Spirit protects you all? I will say to you that these trials and tribulations are to be part of a living on earth that is neither perfectly pristine nor terribly ugly. There must be good and bad things which happen to people otherwise they would not learn the lesson. From the cause of the earthquake, for those people left on earth the effect is enormous to many of them. From each effect they learn and can change path as a result of the cause. The ones who return home planned to do so and their time on earth was finished. I know that people have asked you what happens when there is a plane crash or a war and so many people die at one time. How do they all return to the spirit world together? If the world population was totally destroyed would there not be overcrowding in the spirit world? My answer is purely this. The world of spirit totally and individually on each plane is far, far greater than you can ever imagine within the realms of your present understanding. For the whole of the world's population to return home at the same time is as a one speck of rice in a bowl of rice, it is so small by comparison.

What are crop circles? If they are communications from other life forms, why do they do so that way?

These things are not from the world of spirit. Spirit can talk to spirit, as you know. Other civilizations are more advanced than yourselves, but they can therefore speak to you also. But the problem lies in that not all people on your world are as advanced as others. So some people will be curious, some will understand the meaning of the circles and some will be afraid. For the people from other planets to speak to you, bearing in mind that your population is split into groups as I have just said, it would be hard. I would say to you that many beings have spoken and acted and many people in your world have understood. Not all have been understood when they tell their stories by others in your world, and that is the problem. So I will say to you that these are games of observation. These beings observe your reactions, thoughts and deeds. That is all. I have told you that all can be learnt by the powers of observation. They understand this more than yourselves.

Why did the pyramids have lines which connected from the sun to a spot in their land? What was the purpose?

It was a connection that was visible from the earth to the sun and vice versa. The purpose was merely that from out of your world these lines were visible to fan out from the sun to certain directions on your world where man had shown that he had the knowledge and understanding that these lines could connect other beings to their world.

Did we evolve from Adam and Eve? If so how was the event ever recorded?

I have told you many times that the messages from the spirit world to make you understand things are often symbolic. This is the way that stories are told for you to understand the simplicity of them. But in the story telling the simplicity has been replaced by many people with a complexity that is not real. It is thought that the message is too simple and the people have therefore misinterpreted what was said. So for the fact that Adam and Eve were told by your spirits or God to be the start of man on earth is not in fact correct. What was said was that from two people the world started. Still not in fact correct. Life evolved as your scientists know, but the human form did so gradually and not with just two people. What was said was that life got to a certain standard and then man emerged as just that, a thinking human, and life then became as we know it. To have started from Adam and Eve was perhaps right for the cycle that was being explained. They were not just suddenly put on earth in order to start the human beings as you know them. This did not happen. But symbolically they did. Do you understand? It was a message of learning, nothing more.

Is there such a thing as Electronic Voice Phenomena or is it just made by the recording media used?

This is rare but sometimes, and I say sometimes, it is possible. If there is a noise made by a spirit entity then if the recording equipment is sophisticated enough some of that sound can be heard. But in other cases it is a vibration of the equipment that is recorded so in fact is not totally true. I am sorry if I am being evasive on this answer, but it depends on many factors. If you ask me individually about each situation I would be better equipped to tell you.

How does levitation happen?

The spirit can leave the body and hover above it. That is no problem and easy for all of you to do. But for the body to levitate that is a different matter. That is caused merely by static electricity from the body itself and nothing to do with spirituality.

I am curious about how telepathy works.

Telepathy is easy. All higher spirit entities can do this with ease. It is nothing more than tapping into another person or situation. But the higher you are evolved the easier the process. Let us say that baby spirit entities cannot achieve this at all. Telepathy is nothing more than picking up the vibrations of another spirit entity and virtually being part of their vision and experience. I am not saying that this is in any way intrusive to the other person or spirit, it is more superficial and is done without malice. You could say that two people on the opposite sides of the world are able to connect by telepathy, which they choose to do. It is virtually very easy.

Please could you explain the actions and identical lifestyle choices of some twins even if they were separated from birth and do not know each other?

In all cases of twins or multiple births, these individuals are connected in some way through the spirituality and their experience of being together in the womb. This is chosen before they return to earth. They had decided that although each had a separate and individual spirit entity within them, they are connected with let us say a thread which would connect them through their life on earth. This thread is in no way intrusive to how each of them leads their life and does not incur rules or togetherness which cannot be broken. But it does connect them spiritually in a very unique way. If these children are separated from birth in any way, then they can connect spiritually always. They will invariably like the same things and act in similar ways, whether or not they are aware of the other person during their life on earth. Hence in twins that are separated at birth, both will feel that they are somehow missing a part of themselves and may spend a lifetime unconsciously searching for something which they know not what it can be. Seemingly too the twin will perhaps have similarities to the other. Say for example a love of art, or a gift of music or a love of a particular colour.

Are Ouija boards dangerous tools?

I have to say, probably yes. These games, if we call them such, use the unconscious thoughts of the people playing. If for example, you were to ask the board what spirit was in the room with it, the people themselves may say an Egyptian princess and thus one of them would push the pointer to show this, the other people would just follow and push too. One person is the strong force and the others will submit to this too. This of course is an extreme example. But if the board is used by, say, people of a spiritual group, you ask for spiritual help, and each person is made aware beforehand that it is not possible for them to move the pointer, although of course it is, then there can be some advantages. In either case it should not be prudent to use such a tool which could have fallible answers. These false answers may give you false information which you could take as truth.

Do dowsing rods and pendulums really work or is it the unconscious behaviour of the person using them?

They can and do work. It is more that the person using the rod believes that it can work. They ask spirit to help them find the water. Whether this is conscious or unconscious it has the same results. The rod or pendulum will therefore move as and when necessary.

Is the Bermuda Triangle for real or just superstition?

There is no substance to this belief other than the fact of repetition of accidents in the area which are nothing more than coincidence. But you will say to me that I said there is no such thing as coincidence. Yes I did, but in this case I should say that as things happen with seemingly repetition, then man will try and put another meaning on it. It has no spiritual meaning.

The phenomena such as Big Foot or the Loch Ness Monster, do they really exist?

There are animals in such locations and some of them are of prehistoric descent although in no way still of that type. Some live in the depths of deep water, some do not. They are not necessarily large and definitely not of a type that is not known to you. Are they unique, no they are not? How does man photograph them? Many ways. By seeing something that is not there. By enlarging something that is small, and by imagination.

I have heard that spirits will cause electrical equipment failures or interference. Do they try and communicate with us that way?

Yes they do. There are very few ways in your world that spirit can communicate or make themselves noticed where man will know that it is not the normal thing to see. If we use a breeze or a sound, it could be interpreted as being something else. If we make the lights turn on and off, then this is pretty obvious that it is not a thing which usually happens. Why does spirit want to communicate? Lots of reasons. Just take it as a sign that they are around you. Nothing sinister, just to notice them. Try and understand why they would want to communicate with you. Is it someone who has just passed over? Or are you in trouble etc.? Whatever the reason, take comfort that you are not alone and someone else, your fellow spirits, want to help.

There is a phenomenon of the mind we call psychokinesis by which a person can bend spoons, metal rods and other things just by using his mind without actually touching the object. How is this done?

Yes, with the mind. Very advanced things to do. It is no different than a person using their mind, or should I say their spiritual advancement, to cure and illness or make a thing happen which they visualise. No difference.

Some ghost hunters talk about enigmatic odours. Why would ghosts need to send out smells?

Sometimes if spirit decides not to materialize for various reasons they will adopt a less 'frightening' approach such as an odour just to let the person know they are there. But I say to you that these smells are usually pleasant and never, ever strong. Sometimes people will interpret them lots of different ways to what they were.

How do people have precognition (seeing things before they happen)?

In a person who has a high degree of spiritual awareness they may also have the ability to put themselves instantaneously ahead of time whilst at the same time being where they were. A person may stand in a park and look at children playing and then see a football come and hit them before it actually happens. All done in a split second of awareness.

Spontaneous combustion is a scientifically disputed form of human death. However, scientifically, there are plants that deliberately set themselves alight, such as a plant, similar to Dittany or Burning Bush. Is there any truth that these may have inspired the Bible story of Moses and the Burning Bush?

The burning bush was known to the people but they could not explain why it happened. It was a miracle to them. So it was used. Other plants do the same, you are correct. It is part of their lifespan so to speak. Their purpose is done with so they die. With man it is not quite the same thing. Man does not combust in the same way. There is always some other reason. Sometimes the life must end and it is done that way. Man does not do it. End of life as chosen does it. But this is rare. It is the effect of another cause. It is not possible for man to ignite himself with thoughts only in order to die. Man can do anything with thoughts, except die. So I say that man cannot inflict death in this way. It would not be possible. Man can kill himself, which is of course not allowed by any other way, but not this way.

Will a spirit entity play tricks on us?

There are many levels of spirits on this plane of existence and even the new spirits have a different way of contacting people on your world than do the advanced spirits. The new spirits who advance to being able to contact those in your world are inexperienced and although they think they are giving our comments, visions of our world and advice through mediums they are not yet experienced enough to be able to do this with clarity and perfection. I am a very advanced spirit yet I have to get help constantly as to how to teach you various aspects of the things that you must learn. So you see that spirit entities lesser in their development than myself will perhaps pass messages through that are not true, or at least are distorted. Spirits playing games is not quite the case. But spirits not quite getting messages right is often the case. Many of your mediums or channels who receive spirits to pass messages onto their loved ones or friends have two things to deal with which will make the message itself perhaps not quite accurate. They have the experience of the spirit entity and they have their own capability to interpret the message. Many, many mediums are not such as ordained by spirit; they have gifts of communication with our world at various levels of psychic and mediumistic phenomenon, but they are not true mediums. Many are, but more so are not. If they are communicating or picking up spirit on a poor phone line, so to speak, because they are hard of hearing or the spirit or person on the other end of the phone is not talking clearly or coherently, then they will guess at the message and retell it in the incorrect way. And this incorrect message will have different connotations and meanings. So really these links are best left alone and not done. True mediums are ordained by spirit and those who have this gift, and I say a gift because that is what it is, are exceptionally good and accurate at how they work for spirit. Ordained mediums are given this gift at some stage of their learning to work with spirit and there is absolutely no question of the distinction of those who are ordained and those who play at being ordained and call themselves the same.

Can you be helped in your working lives by people who were good in that profession and have passed over to the other side?

This is a good question because I know that you have asked before about a gifted child who plays extraordinary pieces of music at a young age. Well, I will say to you that from the spirit perspective all spirits can help all people if they choose to pass on information. That is one respect. Your guides daily tell you what is right and what is wrong. But for a person who has died to tell you how to do something, that is another thing. I think you already know that if you ask for the answer to a problem then it is given. I need say no more. What a person is good at on your earth, we are all good at from spirit. It is a mere nothing here. So you see that if a person is good in your world then that is unique, but for a spirit to be knowledgeable of that subject here, that is ordinary. All of your life is very simply ordinary to all of us on this plane of existence. None of you will be special when you return, only your spirituality will set you apart. We do not say that a Queen is special in our level of spirituality. She is the same as a poor man who died on a street. There is no difference. Now if the Queen was exceptionally spiritual then there would be a difference, but only different from the poor man if he was not.

What is an apport?

Apports are the gifts from us to you, but they always have a meaning. Sometimes they are to get your attention when you are not listening to us or are not aware of us. Apports are given to you at certain times for certain reasons. It would be silly of me to say to you that some are genuine and some are not because you are tired of me always having an out to every question, are you not? But I will say to you that many people who want to appear that they are working with spirit will invent an object as being an apport. In other cases many people receive apports and do not recognize them as being such. They will suddenly find an article, say, that they lost some time ago or left in another place at another time, and will say how wonderful it was that they found this thing quite by chance. So let us take the concept only. From spirit we have very few ways to attract your attention when you are not listening and by sending something to you that you know you did not have before is one way. Usually, and I must say in nearly every case, there is a connection between the object and the message from spirit. But as I have told you before there

201

are always inexperienced spirits which play games or try to do things which they are not really capable of doing well. So let us take an apport that has been sent to a person, how does it arrive there? Spirit has the power to materialize an object when there was nothing in its place before. It is complex to tell you all how this is done, but I will say to you that it can be done. It usually takes advanced spirits to do this. It is not possible for one of you humans to materialize an object like that, so the thing only comes from spirit. Usually if you cannot see a connection with spirit on the things that a person calls an apport, then it is not one. If, say, a person has many things the same and thinks they are apports because of the way that they appear, then you need to help them look at the message in several ways. What is the connection? What is spirit trying to tell him? Why was it sent at that time and that place? For spirit to take this difficult route to attract his attention then the message must be important. Usually it will only need one object to be sent, unless the person is not connecting with the right response. If a person says that they have received very many objects of the same type, then this is usually not all true because spirit would not do this. Maybe they sent the first one and the others are made up as having happened by the person concerned. So always look for the connection and it will always be given by spirit. Do not spend time just thinking that this wonderful thing has happened and leave it at that. Then the whole exercise will be wasted.

Tell us about spirit moving objects around?

Theory has it that all things of combustion will combust if alighted. So I say to you that all things spiritual, when awakened will do the same thing. They come to life spontaneously. The spark is there and they become something else. They change. So if things change this way, then so do all things of material as well if the spiritual aspect is applied. For example an object cannot move on its own unless it has some form of fuel that propels it. So how can an innate object move on its own? If spirit applies to it the art of spirituality then it can move. If the body was designed by the spiritual plane of existence, then so can spirit move an object. The body is complex in its design. Moving a solid object is therefore very easy for a spirit entity to do. Let me show you why this happens. I have said many times that all things that spirit does have a purpose. There is no point in it being otherwise. Spirit will not act unless there is a reason. So if an object moves or a light comes on or a sound is heard, yet there is no reason for it to do so, we must look at the action as having come from a spiritual being, in whatever capacity. Now I have said to you in whatever capacity and you will immediately think I am talking about things from outer space, that is not the case. Spirits of humans which travel around when they are asleep is one thing, spirit entities from this side are another, spirit entities of beings from other worlds are also a factor, although they do not visit beings in your world in this way. They have no substance or permission to do so. The beings will appear only as beings first in a material way. Spirit does not move from beings in another world to people in your world by merely transferring by the mind or vision, that does not happen. But for all things that occur that come from a spiritual purpose there is a reason. Why does object A go missing or appear in another place than that where it was left? What would be the purpose of spirit moving object A to location B? None, you would think. Is it a game? No, far from it. There is only one reason why this is done, and that is to get the attention of a person, for them to question the action and come to the conclusion, be it after some time, that this action is not normal and must have spiritual connections. From this assumption then the person will hopefully try and contact spirit through meditation or via a good medium to find out what spirit wants to say to them. So that is the reason for these actions.

What are poltergeists?

We have talked before about earth bound spirits and those spirits which have not reached here for various reasons, and I can only say to you that the phenomenon that you call poltergeists are nothing more than confused spirits which haven't reached home.

What appears to your eyes in your world is not necessarily what is meant by what the spirit is trying to convey when it incorrectly tries to attract your attention. I know that there are horror stories about people in, say, their own homes, being haunted by ghosts or poltergeists from a spirit entity that has a reason of its own to have lingered in that house. I cannot say to you that there are such things as evil spirits that manifest themselves in the garb of a poltergeist or ghost. These spirits are confused, that is all. You ask if certain people on earth, such as teenagers of a certain age can attract these earth bound spirits more than say an adult in the same house. This is not the fact unless the spirit entity can connect or cannot shed the link with the teenager themselves or a similar entity in a body which it knew on earth. Sometimes small children can see the spirit more quickly or even at all over their adults, and this is something that children can do when they are small and have not had earthly things taking away their gift. And for a spirit to move things around a room is not difficult and I will say to you that with only a few exceptions, the spirit is trying to attract your attention. That is why when a person such as a spiritual or religious person speaks to the spirit and explains that this behavior is not acceptable and that the spirit must try and return to a spiritual plane of existence, the spirit itself usually understands and leaves. There are always spirits, inexperienced spirits, which will do what appears to be playing games although this is not a true definition of what they are doing. They have a reason, but it is because they are inexperienced and need to learn.

Could a place or a house have vibrations of other people, which we can feel and possibly make us upset or uneasy? Does the same thing happen with objects such as jewellery or stones? Can they give us bad vibrations too? It is said that a ring keeps the aura of the person who first wore it. Is that true?

In theory, yes. For all things around you there is a part of your aura which stays. The more spiritually advanced you are, then the more peaceful the aura. The younger the spirit entity, then the more aggression or disharmony will remain. With regard to possessions of that person, then yes they do have this aura, but in a much less degree. This is because they do not wear the article all the time, they take it on and off and break the pattern. The aura of the person in a place is consistent; it is not fragmented and thus has more effect. You ask about a ring. My answer is yes and no, it all depends of the owner, even though it is possible to have strong vibrations, in extremely bad cases.

Chapter Eleven

Mediums & Psychics

"To work with spirit you must have reached a level in
your spiritual progress approved of by the higher spirits."

What is the difference between Mediums, Clairvoyants and Psychics?

A medium connects to the spirit world and passes on messages from spirit entities there to be given to people in your world. They would also pass on teaching messages or those of general information that the higher spirits want to tell you people on earth. A clairvoyant is a type of medium that is able to see spirit as well, and see into your future by visions given from spirit. A psychic does everything by sense. They take a situation or an object and using their spiritual senses they understand the circumstances or, say, the previous owner of the object, so they can pass on that information. As such they do not actually converse with spirit and spirit does not talk to them in the same way that it would do with a medium. There are many types of mediums. There are those who just hear spirit which is called connecting as a clairaudient, see spirit called clairvoyant, sense spirit called clairsensative and so on.

How do you work through mediums?

It is difficult to be precise about because there are very many different types of mediums or channels, and many more different types and stages of development of the spirits that try to speak through them. The mediums that are good are the ones with higher spiritual developments. These people are chosen to do the work of spirit because of this fact. There are others who have psychic powers who call themselves mediums, but they are not. They pick up the sensitivity of the person they are with and they think they connect with spirit when they do not have the ability to do this thing. These mediums, as they call themselves, are not connecting with spirit, they are reading the person or persons they are conversing with on your earth and they are telling them things which seem true but are not from spirit. They read the person in a psychic way and they attune themselves in to the secrets of that person's mind and existence and in some cases to what they are thinking. This is a very powerful gift but it is not talking to spirit and it is not being a medium. Mediums are chosen by spirit and are ordained at some stage of their spiritual learning to become spirit communicators. Many mediums in training so to speak are not yet ordained but call themselves mediums. There are others who are false and call themselves mediums and these people are neither psychics nor mediums, they are just impostors. These impostors sometimes really believe themselves that they hear voices from spirit. They do not and they pass on false messages to people who usually make them fit to their own circumstances and wait to see if these things will happen. The medium that is false usually does so for one of three reasons. For money or material gain, for self esteem to themselves, or for esteem in the eyes of the people or person they are giving the reading to, who is dependent on making their every word happen.

True mediums have to be ordained you said, how is that done and when?

Firstly, a person has to have the gift or the progression within their own karma, which makes the effect of spiritual advancement on themselves to a certain degree. They have to be evolved within spirituality to a certain level. When this happens and the spirit is in a body on your world, then they usually want to work with spirit. The higher they are evolved the more aware they are. But they are on your world to learn also and in many cases during a lifetime they may advance in their spirituality during that life and come to the level necessary to become a medium. Then, if they achieve this progression, they are ordained from the world of spirit and allowed to act as a medium. People are not born as mediums, they advance to it during their lifetimes. So when they are ready they are given permission to work, so to speak. Spirit entities that enter your world, being higher in their advancement, are already ordained.

All of you have the gift to be a medium. But with most of you this gift is not developed. In some people the gift is somewhat developed and these people are in training so to speak. The problem is that many so-called mediums are not yet ready to call themselves such. They think they are developed when they are not. They hear only a proportion of the conversation and make up the rest. Some hear not at all and make it all up. Some are totally false and some are a little right and some are more right. There is a difference depending on their personal development in this sphere. But there are many who are naturally developing because of their own high spirituality - the progress they are having because of the development of their spirit. These people could be called natural mediums. They do everything with ease. Now you ask how a medium can become ordained. When we think you are advanced you will be ordained, or should we say given permission from spirit to be a medium contact with the spirit world. There are few in proportion that are ordained, because there are many who are not even good enough to be remotely considered to do this work.

There are many books written by mediums on spirituality. I am curious to know why various spirits come through medium channels and say contradictory statements.

They are not necessarily contradictory, although some of course are. These are written in a way by a person who does not necessarily perceive the message in the correct way. But mostly the spirit entity who is trying to speak through the medium is loving and wanting to pass on advice and teachings. They will not all say the same things unless they are explicitly teaching, and I say teaching, about the exact same situation. Mediums that perceive a faintly uncompromised and surface view of a situation, or where they themselves have preconceived ideas from other sources will give different views. Each of you has views of various subjects as Aleisha had early fears that she thought she would be writing only her thoughts, or bring into these writings thoughts which she had read or experienced herself and which were not necessarily the correct ones which I teach her. So you see I do not come from an easy place to describe to you and I can only teach you that which I have been told to teach you. It is not wholly my perception although I do agree with all that I speak to you. Spirits vary in their development in the higher worlds and this has a bearing on the things they reveal if they come back through a channel to your people. I am of a higher plane than many of the spirits that speak to your mediums. You must believe that many on the plane higher than you are now are not necessarily evolving as experienced spirits ready to move higher after more tests and lessons. Many are static so to speak because they are not evolving with continuous learning and education to their entities. Compare writings of all true messages that come from spirit you will see a definite pattern of the truth.

There are a lot of people who trust and believe certain mediums. How do you know which medium is ordained and which is making it up?

Perhaps we can talk about some mediums that the others of your group trust and think that they say the very utmost truth about all things. Maybe they say the truth about some things. Maybe they do not. There are too many of them and their hundreds of books for me to comment on unless you ask a specific question. So generally I would say to you, Ishamcvan tells you the truth about all things. Sometimes it will take a while for you to comprehend what I am saying but I say the truth about all things. For a time, if only all of you would try to trust me and learn anew. Then analyze my answers with your readings and then ask again your specific question. It is essential that you listen to what I tell you and not just say that certain spirits have different perceptions of the spirit world or on what level the spirit entities find themselves. They do not. I tell you they do not. Everything here is clear to all spirit entities. It is not so clear cut to say that one spirit coming through a channel will say one thing and another spirit coming through another channel will perceive differently. They may make out they do but they understand if they are on this plane of existence what is correct. So you see the teachings of other writers, even if they convince you that they come from spirit are best left unread until I have taught you all a great more many things. What better could you have than me here to teach you and to answer directly all your questions? Why do you need to read the perhaps untrue writings of others? Analyze later. In the meantime give me your undivided attention. I can assure you that I have been chosen by the Holy Spirit to teach all of you. I am not a spirit playing games with you. It is only others on the spiritual plane lower than myself that will do this. I am higher and more important a teacher. More important is not true but you understand the expression so I will use it. Do not be alarmed or question how I speak to you, I am trying to speak in your tongue with your understanding.

How can mediums make mistakes at what is being said to them from spirit?

Many spirits who come back and visit some people in your world and talk through mediums will indicate things that are sometimes taken the wrong way. They are mostly eager to make themselves known to relatives and people that they loved on earth. They need to contact these people to tell them that there is an afterlife and that they should not fear death. But they are not in a position of teaching, as is Ishamcvan, so they do not do so in the correct way. I had to spend much, much time in learning how to teach you. Most of the other spirits that come back through your mediums have not done the learning to try and get a lesson of survival after death that can be understood by the people that they are trying to contact. Do you see they have only enough time, if the medium or channel is good, to make known who they were and to show the contact person a sign that they will recognize as being from that spirit. It would take many, many of your time hours to teach more. Either the spirit is incapable of doing this, or in most cases the medium has no capabilities to listen and pass on for such a long time.

Why would a spirit that had passed over want to contact a person in this world? Have they not gone on to better things?

It is not surprising that so many spirits try and contact the people they have left through mediums as channels. They want so desperately to tell them that the world in which we live is far more wonderful than all their expectations and they should not fear death.

If the laws of karma say that people on our earth have to abide by various codes that are acceptable by spirit, how then is it that some so-called mediums, who do not apparently meet these codes, can still be mediums?

I will say to you that this cannot be the case. There are no exceptions to this rule. If a person on your earth is to truly, and I state truly, work in very close connection with spirit as is required by medium channels, they have to have evolved to a certain spiritual level in their past lives and proved also in their life on earth that they are still progressing within the laws of karma as set down by the Great White Spirits. If a person on your earth breaks these laws then he does not work for spirit in that life on earth. He may in future lives when he has overcome the problem or problems which he did not successfully live correctly in his life on earth. It is possible for the person who is not living within the laws laid down by spirit that he might attempt to rectify his wrongs whilst still doing them with his excuses to himself, and he may work with spirit in his attempts to make amends. But spirit will only talk to him and work with him to a certain level; spirit will of course not ignore him or chastise him, spirit is always with the bad people in your world as well as they are with the good and spiritual people. Spirit does not judge whilst the spirit is in a body on earth. While the spirit entity is going through its tests and lessons, spirits from my plane of existence will not interfere. The persons guide or guides are always with them, if the person on earth tries to work with spirit, spirit will work with them. But to work as a channel for spirit, to tell your world about the Holy Spirit and life on our plane of existence, that is not permissible under any circumstances unless the spirit itself is living an existence true to laws of karma. A medium or channel who is ordained has to be to a certain level of spirituality as I have said before. And so you ask why so many so-called mediums do not seem to be living by the rules? As you read my words I have answered your question. They want to work with spirit and spirit will pass messages from entities in our world to people in yours but they are not mediums. The messages are sometimes sent to the person for whom it is intended and the so called medium picks this up with psychic powers. Watch mediums at work and you will soon see the differences. You will get to know those who are truly working with spirit and those who are working on their own. There are many more false mediums than there are those who are ordained. It is difficult to be explicit as to who is and who is not because there are exceptions to the rules that you see should be, but for various reason do not. For example when a person appears to be living against the rules of karma but is not or never has been, or people are perceived to be what they are not, you cannot possibly know, only spirit knows.

Please talk about crystal balls. How do they work? Are they a tool and how can they be misused?

Crystals in all forms are very powerful spiritual tools or devices to ask for and accept help from spirit. They store up energy and that is why a crystal sometimes feels warm from the vibrations of its owner and they transfer their energy which is stored in the crystal. This energy then gives the person who has the crystal the extra vibrations to contact spirit. I will stress though that the possession of a crystal is not a dark, evil thing. The possession of a crystal is just a tool for helping you to connect with spirit. The crystal must be personal and if possible not handled by any other person at any time. There are varying degrees of sizes and shapes of crystals and you should start with one that is small and learn to use it before you transgress to a larger and more powerful size. When you have personalized your energy into the stone then you can send messages to spirit in the same way as you do when you ask for help or talk to your guides. This is not any different. But to receive messages from spirit it is perhaps more concrete in its assistance. You can meditate or use a fixed gaze at the crystal and it will show you images or things that you want to see and cannot do so with your mind. The images can also be achieved by meditation but this crystal is a tool for helping you. To have possession of a crystal ball is better than a rough crystal because if it has a good surface to contemplate things and meditate, the pictures it shows are clearer and finer than with a rough surface. The misuse of crystal ball fortune telling is very widespread and has conjured up a bad name for mediums who use them in a genuine way. We are back to the subject of frauds trying to tell fortunes and making up most or a greater part of what they think their customer wants to hear. There is no other stone than the crystal which has more power from spirit to you and from your energy to spirit. I have told you to smooth your crystal but you have not yet done so. Even so you have connected with it and that is good.

Are tarot cards spiritual, and what can you tell me about the way mediums or psychics use them?

They are a tool, nothing more. For a spiritually enlightened person to use cards their interpretation is instant and by spiritual message, for another person to use them who does not have this instinct, then this could be nothing more than storytelling. With these too you must learn and memorize every single picture on every single card and learn their meaning. You must hold each card, blindfolded so to speak, to hear and feel the message coming through it. When you have perfected this technique, and only then, are you ready to use them as a tool to hear their message. In wise and spiritually enlightened hands they are excellent, in others they are not. It is not good to try and read them to another person without the preparation required. In ancient times a student would learn for many years, privately with their tutor, before they were allowed to read for others. Now they are a fairground game. The cards are used by spirit to give you a message which you would not necessarily receive in any other way, for example through a medium. If you do a reading about a person who wants to know the answer to a question about their future this is not good, but if you use the cards to read about the person and their personality or their problem in order to help them overcome their difficulties, then this is accepted and a message will be given. You know by now that Ishamcvan regards fortune telling as not good, so you must think hard on this one to see that the use of cards as a tool can be interpreted in the wrong way.

What can you tell us about Nostradamus and his book of Prophecies written in 1555?

There have been and still are many people who have vision; mediums, prophets and various types of clairvoyants. Many were good, many were excellent, and some were very new to the methods. Some you all know about such as Nostradamus, and some are obscure. I am not saying that all he said was good, only that he did have vision. Unfortunately his words have not be been translated accurately and many new interpretations have been added which make them now mostly a work of fiction. But at the time the words were true.

Years ago ectoplasm was widely quoted by spiritualists. Can you define what it is?

As you have no knowledge or thoughts on ectoplasm perhaps this would be a good subject to convince you of the closeness of Ishamcvan on this night. The phenomenon is a gift from spirit and is a link between an exceptionally good medium and a spirit entity. When the medium makes the link then the spirit enters the body to emerge through what is called by your world, ectoplasm. This is your word not ours. The spirit entity seems to emerge from the body on this energy force, which is what it is. In other words the medium summons the spirit entity and then gives it enough energy from his body, this thing called ectoplasm, that it can appear to emerge from his body and materialize into a recognizable form. It is similar in a way that a voice medium uses the vocal chords of a person to materialize a voice. Only good channels or mediums can do either of these things. It is very simple. But in the case of ectoplasm the medium must do half of the work. The spirit does not take over the body but merely is given permission to work in this way from the person himself.

Please talk about voodoo?

I have answered this one when you asked me about evil thoughts from one person with the purpose of harming another. Voodoo is the same. It can be practiced in various forms from sacrifice, chanting, witchcraft, spells and many more things which all mean the same. It is evil of badness from one person to another, nothing more. It can be stopped by surrounding yourself in spirituality or a white light. You have the power to stop this thing. You need not be afraid even if you are faced with it head on. Love always overpowers bad. Goodness is supreme over badness. You can turn evil around and send it back. There will always be bad people trying to harm others. If others are weak or confused or without spirituality or understanding then they are prey for the hunters.

Why it is that someone who is murdered of body and returns to your world does he not come back through a medium and talk about his killer?

This is usually because when the spirit leaves the body and returns home it is at peace. It does not want a tie to earth because of its violent death. It is not interested in the problems of earth or its existence there. I have told you before that the ultimate decision in a spirit entity after it leaves its body is to return home. There are some cases that do not fit into this category and that is when the spirit is inexperienced and is bitter about what has happened in respect of the effect the murder is having on the loved ones it has left behind. In these cases then the spirit, which you must remember is inexperienced, tries to contact someone - anyone - to tell them what happened to them. But remember that the spirit is inexperienced and they would have to choose a medium very carefully, in the right place at the right time to be able to converse extremely strongly and with great effort because of the length of their story, and speak through that medium. This happens, but not usually successfully which is the key. A medium could know the description of the man and the circumstances of the killing and deep meditation can give an experienced medium or channel clues. but usually nothing more. These clues are usually right but not enough to make a definite diagnosis of the murderer and his circumstances. It is sad for you on earth but for us in the spirit world it is a pointless exercise because the spirit has returned home which is the ultimate over a life in a body.

Some psychics who talk to the police of our lands about missing people or murders or similar and never seem to get the facts right so that the culprits can be caught. Why is this?

If messages are sent from spirit to these people, why are they not correct so that the psychics can help to capture the guilty people? Well I say to you that not all psychics, or rather people who call themselves psychics, are in fact that. Most do not have any connection to spirit. They make believe they see and hear the voice of spirit. Some of these people are well meaning and just not gifted although they want to think they are, and some are just down right impostors. In either case they do not have the ability to give this information. The remaining small proportion may have the ability, but lack experience to sustain the correct level of information that is required. They may only see fleeting things that are not in the right sequence or giving enough detail. There are of course a very small proportion of these psychics that are good at being psychic but not necessarily good at finding people or seeing situations in this context. The finding of people and what it involves with signals from the spirit world is a specialist gift and not always the same as just being psychic or a channel or a medium. These three things are different as I have explained before. Also even if a psychic or channel has the right information I am afraid that it will be very difficult to get the message across to the right person in the detective team who will listen and act accordingly. I will not say to you that spirit does not give accurate information which would lead to the police finding the person, more that the information is only useful if it is given to a person in your world who would use it in the correct way. Very few are gifted in this respect. But a few chosen people are given the gift of sight and are good. If these people were chosen to find say a child, they could do so. But the opposition is immense. From the spiritual plane it is not so important for these facts to be found, as it is acts which are being performed on your stage with your players calling the tunes. Spirit did not make the murder or the abduction happen; it was part of the actions of people in your world. When the spirit of the body of the persecuted returns to our world we rejoice at its homecoming. We are not sad that this thing has happened to the persecuted spirit. When the persecutor returns home, his actions will be analyzed. The persecuted is on a path, so is the persecutor and all the people who are involved in the incident. For a psychic to find the persecutor may not necessarily be the answer that spirit requires at the time.

What about astrology? How does spirit view this? Is it acceptable or does it go against all the teaching of Ishamcvan?
There are many tools to be used to convey the meanings and laws of the spirit world and spirituality itself, and astrology is one of those. This is a means of using the universe to plot

your life in essence and in its entirety. The universe is a key in lots of ways to spirituality and so therefore the study of the stars and moon patterns is certainly one way in which the readings of spirituality can be used to run parallel to similar teachings of Ishamcvan if used correctly. Yes it is certainly one way of looking at planes of existence, if in perhaps a more basic manner.

Why did one of the greatest mediums of the 19ᵗʰ century invariably get premonitions right but sometimes he was way out and was totally wrong?

Spirit has control totally of all things that are told to you from this plane of existence. If spirit does not think a question is asked for the right reason, no answer will be given. But the channel will think that always a reply will come so will make up unconsciously an answer. There is a great difference, as you know, between that which comes from spirit and that which comes from the mind. With all channels this is a problem to distinguish. It is the same with thought mediums, speech mediums and channels such as Aleisha. A good medium or channel knows instantly which message it is, whether from spirit or imagination. How many times has she ceased to write or on few occasions not started to write because she did not feel Ishamcvan, her teacher, her guide, with her? You know that this is true. So you see this psychic and medium was human too and if under pressure and tired, did not distinguish from where the message came. If he was honest with himself at the time, he would have admitted that this was not from spirit. But then you ask me, if this man was in a trance, as he was with all his psychic visions, how was he to know? I will say to you that he knew.

We would like to ask you many questions about mediums. We are having trouble adjusting to your answers at this time. Will you please explain how the process works and how to detect a fraud or a person who has a vast imagination for the truth?

We have touched on the subject before but I will try again and perhaps you can connect with my comments and your experience. True mediums are gifted from spirit. All persons on your world can connect with spirit as I have explained, if they choose to develop and understand. Not all these people are mediums although many think they are. To say that all of you can meditate or instantly connect with spirit is to say that you can develop that link because you all have the power within you to do this thing. Let us say for example that a person tries really hard and perfects this thing and can pick up spirituality and words or visions from spirit which is relatively easy with practice. Then this person tries to find answers for other people who ask him or her to ask spirit for messages or signs which they can pass on. This person does not have the special gift which is bestowed on mediums, but thinks that they have special powers because they have connected with spirit. They will be very limited on the words from spirit. This may be because they are young, inexperienced or untrained spirits themselves so are not so mature as to be gifted as a medium. But they do not know this thing and they think what they have is a true gift, which it is not because they are not experienced enough to use the gift so it has not been given. Now let us take the true medium. This person is a mature spirit, has perfected through many experiences and lifetimes the components which make up a spirituality which is capable and wise enough to be a medium. This person finds it easy to connect with spirit, as Aleisha does with these writings. There is no effort and no wonder that the connection will not happen. Is this correct? It is pure and simple and completely natural. This person can talk to spirit in a natural way that is easy and spirit will make all the answers in the same way.

Why will you Ishamcvan not foretell the future?

I know that all of you know that I have said many times that I will not fortune tell. By this I mean that I will not give you the answers to your tests and lessons, nor will I tell you when to expect them or try to foretell that anything which is necessary to your spiritual development by these tests, will occur. If I did so you would avoid the tests by your own cunning and wisdom. But what

I and any of the mediums, true mediums, on your earth will do, is to prove to a novice person that there is life after death, that there is spirit who will answer and by doing this initially they always bring in a spirit connection of someone close to them who has died. Let us say that is to get their attention and to give the proof to them that spirit is everlasting and can connect from another plane. Of course this is coupled with the fact that there are many spirits, who having passed over, are perturbed by the problems of their loved ones on earth and although they encircle them always at first, they cannot make the person see them or hear them and they want them to know that they are there. So having made the connection the medium asks the person various points from a spiritual perspective and when these points are recognized, yet another person believes in the realms of spirituality which is the main purpose of the use of a medium for the teaching of others. Next the medium, having such a strong, natural link with spirit, can expand the advice from spirit to a third person and this is given to help and comfort the third person as much as possible. It is no different than my saying to you that situations will get better, you must look after your health, and so on. There is therefore a great difference in the careful messages from spirit through a chosen medium, than those from a person who only thinks that they are capable of doing such things and who repeat things which are without the careful forethought and planning that is natural between a medium and their guides.

There are some people who want to be mediums and try very hard to pretend that they are. Will they be given the ability because they persevere?

They have not progressed to the necessary level of understanding so are not true mediums although they think that they are. These people cause a great deal of misunderstanding. They do not connect to the world of spirit in the fashion that is necessary. They may make links, but these are weak and they themselves are not advanced enough to interpret what is being said. They have to work with the progression of their own spiritual understanding and when they have reached that they will be considered by our elders to be ordained. Until that time they are still people who want to be, rather than actually are, mediums

A medium told me that my mother who had passed to the spirit world would not move on until I passed over too. Where is she going and why must she wait for me?

We have no time. So by saying this effort to wait until another spirit returns is not important. There is no waiting, for here and now and far away in time are the same. For her to say to you that your mother will not return to earth in a body until you have returned home too is irrelevant. The spirit can connect with spirit at any time. It does not matter if one spirit is here and another there in your world. It is of no consequence to spirit. It is of consequence to the mind and feelings of a body. So let us take the scenario. The spirit of your mother has returned home to this plane of existence. The spirit can see all in your world. Sometimes, as is the case, the spirit may remain in this world to assist you in that world. As I am with Aleisha. It is a choice. All the time that you are in that world, then the spirit, who was your mother when in a body, has chosen to remain in this world to be best placed to assist you when required. It is a choice as all guides and spirits in bodies connect. As for where is she going, well that could be many places. She could return to your world in another time and another place, to learn and advance more, or she could remain in the spirit world until she makes that choice. This could be later than you having returned again to your world. You are all free spirits to make choices. But you see if you return to your world again, seemingly before you mother chooses to do so, you will not necessarily be first because there is no time and everything is happening in lives simultaneously.

How can we know the difference between the types of mediums you have mentioned?

For you to detect the difference between a medium who is ordained and a person who is not is by pure instinct, for you will know. Do not doubt your instincts for they are good. If you have a doubt, then there is a reason. It is good for you all to be keen to work for spirit, but in most cases it is a long way to learn and you must never pre-empt that you have arrived when you have not.

When a medium connects to a spirit entity they sometimes refer to an intermediary spirit entity called a doorkeeper. What is the purpose of a doorkeeper? What does he do?

Well I don't know. What is a doorkeeper? Perhaps I should ask you what fantasy you have read about this phrase. Ishamcvan is curious; it is not a concept I understand. How can I tell you? How can I visualize what he is doing? Is he here to let people through who want to communicate with people on your world? Does Ishamcvan have to ask permission from him to open the door to Aleisha? Well, I am lost for words. This is a concept that is strange and I know this was not what you expected me to say. It is written often in your books of fiction that this spirit is there with a queue of spirits waiting for him to let them in to communicate one at a time. The nearest concept I can come to this is that with inexperienced spirits there is usually a higher spirit teaching them how to communicate and giving advice, if that is the correct terminology, as they try and try again initially to make contact with, say, a loved one they have left behind. Wiser and more experienced spirits communicate easily and do not need this help. For several spirits to come to one person at the same time is not uncommon and it does not need organization. We are spiritual entities after all, not school children. So I know you will say that at a séance or a circle of people meditating then is it necessary to control the order of things? I will say to you that this is not quite so. Spirits will come with respect for higher spirits and then with respects to each other. Sometimes higher spirits will take preference, as I do over Aleisha's guides, but this is something which is the law of karma and just happens. I love the terminology and am curious to know where doorkeeper started. It doesn't sound very spiritual. Perhaps the doorkeeper also looks after the hospital and the nursing home too which many people believe are in the world of spirit.

With a voice medium, how does the spirit enter the body to take over to speak?

Spirit connects with your spirit, which sends a message to your brain which sends a message to your vocal cords and then your body speaks as spirit dictates in the manner and dialogue that it requests. For a person to say that they felt the form of spirit take over their body by standing behind them or in front of them or to one side of them and then spirit taking a step into the human body is a gross exaggeration. Spirit is not a form so this cannot happen. Spirit can be with you to such a degree that you feel the presence so strongly that you know that the spirit is with you, but that is all. For a spirit to speak so then the connection has to be very, very intense. Does spirit under these circumstances give off a great deal of heat or energy? Spirit is not energy, spirit is spirituality. This has been called energy but this definition is confusing for the uninitiated because energy is a life force of the living body and spirituality is not. So you are best not to describe it in this way. If you are asked to define spirituality then say it in this way. Spirituality is nothing more than a feeling that is instinct and is intuition. So it cannot be defined. There is nothing to define because it is not matter. The air around you and the forces of the earth's atmosphere can be defined and some people describe spirit the same, it is not. There is no substance so there is no definition.

Is spirit always right when it speaks to a person here through a medium or can it play games and deceive?

It is the newer or less advanced spirits who like to revisit your world with messages and because they are novices they are misinterpreted or hard to understand even sometimes by your more special mediums.

Please explain spirit "Speaking in Tongues". Does it bypass the brain?

All words from spirit to man bypass the brain. The brain is not required. I could speak to a mentally impaired person and

223

they would hear me. Speaking in Tongues is only a form of spirit speaking to man and man speaking as he hears.

But you say that spirit does not have a language so how can man speak as he hears and then interpret it in jumbled speech that no one understands?

You are quite right. There is no language. However man may hear things that he does not understand. So instead of repeating the gist of things he cannot do so because it is alien to that which his brain can interpret, so he says a jumble of words that neither he or anyone else can understand. It is his interpretation or the unexplainable so that is how it comes out of his mouth.

Can spirit from your plane of existence use the vocal chords of a person in our world in order to speak through that person, and how does it work?

Well, you have seen a person in your group speak with spirit, have you not? It is a difficult one to explain because it is a set of circumstances which come together at a particular time to make all the components right, before the action of spirit speaking through a body can take place. I will say to you that the spirit entity doing the task has to be very spiritually evolved, as does the person in the body. The spirit entity has been taught how to do this thing and it is not difficult once the technique has been mastered. You will see that spirit, once it learns the way, will be able to do this very easily and often. However, the initial one or two times it is difficult to sustain for any length of time. Do not think, as you have read, that this is exceptionally difficult for spirit, it is not. But the circumstances have to be right for this to happen. Not only does the person, the subject, have to be in the right frame of mind to accept the spirit, he has to be spiritually aroused by vibrations and energy from other highly spiritual people around him at the time. This builds up the vibrations which are necessary for the voice spirit to accomplish his goal. That is why a spirit will not become a voice spirit when the vessel of the person receiving the spirit is on his own or not surrounded by the right spiritually minded people. These vibrations give him the right protection, the right channel for acceptance of the spirit and the right circumstances for the receiving of messages from the spirit world. That is why it is rare that this thing happens because these circumstances are rarely possible. So back to the question. How are the vocal chords used? Well I will say to you that spirit can do anything with your body if it is given permission to do so from the Great White Spirit. This of course does happen in other ways, but to take over the vocal chords is not difficult. Let us say that the person in the body is put, by us and by himself, into a trance like state where he is taken over by the spirit. The spirit will enter through him and express his spirituality by making the person speak in a way that is not like his own voice, but as the spirit entity chooses to sound. It is not the spirit speaking in actual facts, it is the person speaking with his body parts, but it is the spirit using these body parts to speak whilst they are under his control. Do not fear when I say to you that spirit takes over the body, this is not in a sinister way. It is not like that. But do not think either that the spirit is speaking through the vocal chords, spirit is sending a message to the brain of the person and telling the brain, whilst it is in a trance like state, to speak in tongues and say words that the spirit alone wants to convey. It is as simple as that. The body is alive and must be for the spirit to work that way. The spirit must go through the brain of the body in order for the brain of the body to send a message to the vocal chords to say the words which the spirit has spoken to the brain.

I have read the books about another spirit entity who spoke through a lady voice medium and another person took down notes in longhand as she spoke the words, also using a tape recorder. These notes were transcribed into several books. The dialogue is similar to your own but in some cases considerably different.

I will say to you that the spirit entity was a teacher much the same as me but with all things as I have told you before, the spirit entity speaking and his teachings are not always recorded and passed on accurately. It is essential with all teachings not to alter the words or the context and in a great deal of the words of this teaching entity, this has been done. Man does not realize that by altering one word here and there even will change the whole concept, by making it seem difficult to understand or merely saying the wrong thing. Eventually Aleisha will be asked to make comparisons with the words of Ishamcvan and those of other seemingly similar messengers and it will be interesting for you to do this. But this particular teaching entity was not taught in the same way that I have been and this will be interesting. I have been taught to teach in a way that is perhaps revolutionary compared to what has gone before. It is considered that simplicity must be the key for you to understand and pass on the information and this was not always done before. We have found that whilst spirit realizes the simplicity of the whole realm of spirituality, man does not even begin to comprehend a mere portion of it. Perhaps it is like any person in your world who has knowledge and tries to teach others who are new students. It is difficult for the teacher to understand the vastness of his knowledge compared to the nothingness of that understood or misunderstood by the pupil. So the way that this teaching spirit entity was sent to teach in your world many years ago is different to that which I teach you, although of course lessons will cross over and be with the same eventual meaning. Also from these particular lessons that are written you will see that many connotations have been added and some things which were regarded as being inconsequential have been omitted.

What are white magic and black magic? Are either the voice of spirit?

These are nothing more than an earthy thing and nothing whatsoever to do with spirit. In both cases the persons participating in these things are doing so for power and wrong doing. White witches think they are doing well but they are not following the laws of karma, nor leading spiritual existences so this is not good. Black magic is really using power to conjure up the worst possible things and inflicting these things on other people who are unsuspecting and innocent. It is the same as persecuting people through war or revenge or abuse. Black magic and black witches are doing the same thing. So you see Ishamcvan cannot say to you that either are good. You all have it in your power to be spiritual. If you follow spirituality and the laws of Karma you cannot be touched by the doings of the witches, whether black or white, because you are protected by your own spirituality, even though the persons doing these things may try hard to harm you. If these persons attack, for want of a better word, other non spiritual beings, these people may be taken in and join them or be affected by them because they lack their own straightforwardness in the light of the adverse reaction. You need never fear that this bad thing will happen to you and that you will be affected by witches or similar, but I will say to you that there are many persons in churches in charge of these that are practicing a form of witchcraft upon their congregation although they do so in the name of religion. These normal seeming people in responsible positions with the care of people are a great risk for persecution of others by the use of power.

Aleisha asks: How would you describe our connection?

I have told you from the beginning that you are a channel, not a medium. But I will clarify this by saying that you had to be to a certain level of evolvement before this was possible. Also you had to have an equally strong link for this to happen. Most people on your world who are channels are open vessels for spirit to pass through. You freely and simply let this happen. You wonder why, but it still happens. So you started as a channel and I spoke through you just as spirit will pass through a channel in order to heal. But in the process of passing through you, there was an enormity of learning on your part as well as natural trust and lack of fear. So over the months and years you have matured and so have I. We have grown together and this is as obvious to you as it is to me. Now with yourself we have a situation where you could take a person to you as you write, as you have done, and you could ask me in this natural way for answers to their questions. We could if you wanted to, but I prefer not to at this stage, connect with spirits who want to send a message to the person with you. So you see from being a channel you can mature to be a medium. I will not say we are there yet because I do not choose for you to work in that way, but it could happen as we build our relationship to an even more advanced stage. So you see you will not only have the ability to write as I speak on all things in a fast and comprehensible way, but you can have people ask me questions through yourself in order for them to learn and find peace in my answers. One day we will pass messages from spirit entities through to others, but not yet. The time is not now. For now is the time for advancement and achievement in your work with spirit. All work you do must be for spirit from this day forward. Please recognize this fact and act accordingly. I will write as much as you will connect and this is necessary for there is so much to say and so much for you all to learn. Please I ask all of you, go back to the beginning and learn again the wise and comforting words of your friend and advisor Ishamcvan and fill in the gaps with more questions and I will give you the answers to all things in pure and simple terms that you can relate to yourselves and to others who are desperately waiting for your help and reassurance.

Aleisha asks: You say one day I will be a full medium but at the moment I am only connecting to you not any spirits that are waiting come through. Why am I not yet there?

You are working with passing on the words of spirit and that in itself is making yourself an open channel for the words to flow through. But we are working one to one. A medium will connect with many spirits who are trying to get a message through to be understood by a person in your world. That is not your purpose at this time. But, having said that, you are learning to know my presence and to read my words now with clarity besides writing as I speak. So you are nearly there, but not quite. My words to you are that you are not there so are not ordained, but in comparison with a large number of so-called mediums in your world, you are more advanced.

Is it possible to go to classes to learn how to be a medium?

You can learn how to meditate and certain forms of enriching yourself to a more relaxed state to let the spirituality develop, but no you must have the gift of progression of spiritual understanding to a certain level. Without that you cannot be a true medium as I have just explained. You will only be a person who wants to be one and tells themselves that that is what they are actually doing.

Please tell me if my friend, who is pretty accurate in her readings, is ordained as a medium?

Firstly I must say to you that spirit can see and hear all things so you need not explain to me what I can already see. You can ask that which you do not understand, which is the purpose of trying to help you see things much clearer. But to say to me that your opinion of a person is fact and not just through your eyes is another matter. For you all see and conceive things differently and it is for this reason that it is essential that you step back and observe and not jump to hasty decisions about any person and their actions. So I say to you that a medium who gives a message, by using these powers you have of standing back and observing, then you will see the truth by observation as to whether they are a good medium or just an extremely kind hearted and well meaning person. There is unfortunately a big difference. A medium who is ordained is such a very high spirit that the perfection of the messages is right every time. They are so spiritual that they are accurate as well. There are no wrong shots and no trying. Now let us look at other mediums. These range in varying degrees from fraud to mediums who are very high spirits. Along this line of others, there are many who are good people and many who are not. The person who you refer to is an exceptionally good person and she is so loving to everyone, but she still has much advancement to achieve through her own lessons and is not ready to move on and change levels of consciousness yet. So although high, she is not yet the highest.

Why would what you say be right and what other clairvoyants etc. say be wrong or have a different interpretation?

What I say to you is correct. I cannot say any other things. For your proof is that the words are written and written very quickly. I say the words and Aleisha writes then as per my dictation. Now with a clairvoyant it is different. They hear the words and then pass the words verbally only to the person who asks the questions. Some are very good and are right. Some are very bad and get nothing right for they make up most of the data. Some are in-between. Now let us look at a good clairvoyant. They are very highly spiritual people. They know by intuition and by connecting to various spirits or guides of the person who have made themselves ready to be contacted. She picks up whoever is there because of her gift and then she tells the person what is being said. Now the next type of clairvoyant maybe has some of the spiritual learning but is not so advanced. She listens and thinks she hears some things but the line is not very clear. She passes on what she thinks she heard. That is all. That is the difference. I am a highly developed spiritual guide. My learning is advanced. I am able to communicate one to one and my channel is open and good. You hear what I say. There is no distortion.

When a person is contacted through a medium by the spirit of a person who has died, does that mean that the spirit has not yet reincarnated? Does a piece of the person's spirit remain connected with the spiritual plane when it reincarnates, or does it simply appear to be in two places at once because of our human understanding of space-time?

The few spirits which take longer to return home would not be sending messages back through a medium. They could be contacted by a medium in some cases and given a message from your world, but not the other way around. All spirits who appear to mediums are from the world of spirit and have returned home here. From our plane they observe you all and if one of you goes to a medium or to a place where a medium may recognise you, then they may feel it is important to get you to realise that they are now at peace, or describe the new concept they are in and so forth. They may even give you words of encouragement in your lives for they can see the future as well as the past and the present all at one time.

Please explain transcendental mediumship.

It is merely a type of meditation in which the person who has a gift of connecting to spirit will be able to do so. A truly gifted person will connect anyway and there are many people in your world who use this term to somehow justify a connection with spirit which is not really there. But I say to you that a person who has the maturing of spirit of themselves and who is advanced in the learning of the spirit, not of their body, will be able to connect anyway. So transcendental they do not have to be.

What is the cord of life that some mediums supposedly see?

You have heard that this connects the body from the spirit world as long as the body is living and spirit is within. When the body dies then is the cord cut? I think in this instance you have read the many references to this in your books and I would say to you that this is an explanation to the uninitiated to show how spirit is within the body and then leaves when the body dies. You could see a connection from the spirit world if you had the vision to see and you may see this as a bridge of a connection, but Ishamcvan would not like you to take this too literally. It is not a cord as a definite cord. It is a link, that is all. Whilst the spirit is in a body there is a link between the spirit world and the earth world and the body. When the body dies there is no link to the earth world because the spirit has gone home. Do you see that it is not a physical link, it is a spiritual link and as you cannot see spirit then there is no cord to be seen? It may be said that some psychics or mediums can see the cord. They can see the link, that is all.

We know that psychics work on a type of intuition. How do they differentiate their own thoughts from psychic awareness?

Intuition and psychic awareness are the same thing in how they work. A psychic will know something from a person or an object and through this knowledge, which is in fact their awareness, they form an opinion of the previous ownership of the item, for example. They can take any situation or any object and let us say receive vibrations from that so that they can form an opinion or have knowledge for their own use.

Please explain why a channeled connection is not the same as a mediumship connection?

A channel connection is to one spirit and one only at any one time. It is a pre-arrange liaison between the man and the spirit entity. Sometimes, and this is rare, two entities will come over in the connection. This is because spirit is in fact part of a mass whilst in the spirit world, not a one entity. So if the said entity wanted to show itself to man it would mass with another and call itself by a group name rather than that which it was in a last life. Mediums on the other hand open themselves up to connect to whatever spirits are 'flying' around who want to get their message through. These are usually spirits who have a specific message for man on earth, and whereas a channel is for teaching or information about the spirit world, a mediumship connection is for spirits and the people on your earth to connect and recognize that there is in fact life after death.

What is a clairaudient connection? You said once that Aleisha has that with you.

A clairaudient medium can hear spirit only. A clairsensitive medium can sense spirit, a clairvoyant can see spirit. I talk to

Aleisha through her mind. She hears me and takes dictation writing down what I say.

Can true clairvoyant mediums see everything that is going to happen in the future or only some things?

It depends how good they are and what spirit will allow them to see. If spirit does not allow the vision then it will not happen however good or advanced is the medium.

If a clairvoyant sees into the future why is that allowed? You have told us that knowing that things will happen negates your lessons because you will already know the answers.

That is why our spiritual elders are selective on what they allow the clairvoyant to see.

Is clairvoyance a spiritual thing?

That depends. If the clairvoyant is a truly advanced spirit and is gifted with the ability to see spirit, then yes of course it is a spiritual thing. If the person is a so called amateur and not gifted from spirit, then no it is far from spiritual.

Is it true that there are more bad mediums than good?

It is not whether they are bad or good but more that the ones that are genuine are from spirit and there are those that are not. Unfortunately it is fashionable in your world to read fortunes and say that you are a medium, so there are in fact more bad than good.

How would you advise a person to choose a genuine medium?

The more spiritually advanced the spirit with the body the easier it is for the person to know the good from the bad. An advanced spirit will automatically feel that the medium is genuine. But for most of you it is hard. There are questions you can ask of course, but it will be more by proof of the messages if you are not able to connect through your own instincts.

What is the difference between a clairsensitive medium and a psychic?

They are one of the same in what they do, but the message comes through in a different way. With the clairsensitive, then they sense spirit around them and work with whatever that spirit entity tells them. A psychic will sense a situation and be given an explanation from spirit. They have a much wider scope of feeling because they work with situations, people and objects, whereas a clairsensitive usually works with only one spirit entity at a time, although that is not always the case.

If a clairvoyant can see the future could they give a winner of a horse race?

That is not allowed because the winner of a horse race is not a spiritual aspect or lesson. It doesn't matter to your spiritual advancement whether one horse won or another. Spirit is only concerned with your development and your lessons which in themselves are connected to the laws of karma.

Why couldn't a clairvoyant tell us the winning numbers of a lottery so that we can use the money for our spiritual work establishing the sanctuary of learning?

That would be spiritual work, I give you that. But in fact money is not a spiritual thing and whereas it needs lessons, it will not improve your spiritual advancement even if you master the ground rules. The money for the sanctuary will come but from an unexpected very spiritual source; certainly not from the lottery.

Who reads a crystal ball, a clairvoyant or a psychic and how accurate are they?

The medium and the clairvoyant. The medium will see spirit and receive messages from them. The clairvoyant will see into the future or have answered the questions about a person or object that is required.

You have said that if you have a spiritual gift such as mediumship you are not allowed to put a price on it. If that is the case how is it that most mediums do charge, sometimes large amounts, to venerable people who cannot usually afford anything at all but just want help?

It is wrong for ordained mediums to charge and if they are that very high level it is unlikely that they would do so. But mediums in training will give you lots of excuses why they have to charge although the laws of karma say they should not. It all comes down to a material aspect on something which they look more to as a form of income than purely a means to help people who either are confused or do not have the self confidence to help themselves. All people need help in some way and the teachings from the spirit world are essential in all respects. Some may say that money changing hands keeps the spiritual connection going. I say to you that to help someone without anything in return is the ultimate in self sacrifice and learning.

Chapter Twelve

Prophets & Spiritual Teachers

"Those sent from spirit all have the same message.
That is how you can tell the genuine from the imposters."

**There are many teachers of spirituality the world over,
but why is it that you say not all are true?**

All true teachers of spirituality are the same. I was taught to
teach in a different way that was revolutionary, if you like. But all
teachers from our world have to tune in with their pupils and the
way that the words must be passed on depends on the spirit's ability
to say the words that will be understood by those who hear them.
Jesus taught the people of his time with the words they understood.
It was very simple. But the translation of those words over the years
have been twisted and brought into your modern day. In doing
so the meaning in lots of cases has been lost. Many teachers or
prophets who are the same as myself have the same thing to say
but do so in a slightly different way because the people are different
from yourselves. The problem with the words of all teachers is that
some other person records their words and passes them on, whether
written, or spoken. It is unique for a channel subject to write them
down as I am asking Aleisha with my words. The transcript must have

236

no additions or alterations whatsoever to be true to the words from spirit. So although a channel or medium may be good, his recorded words are not necessarily accurate and may have inaccuracies which are passed on and maybe taken as truth. This is an example of what has happened over the ages with many of your religions.

You mention that other prophets are similar to Jesus but not the same. Is it because he was the Son of God that makes him different from others?

I will say only to you that Jesus was an exceptionally high spirit and a prophet to your world. Now he has progressed and will not re-incarnate to your world. He is a higher spirit in this realm of consciousness as well as being also in the next realm, which is only possible to those who have reached that level of perfection. For you to say that he is the Son of God is somewhat vague. For spirit is part of the whole mass of spirit over which there is a higher spirit and a higher spirit and so on. Spirits in progression on this level are overseen by higher spirits of which Jesus is one, not the only one, but one. Over these higher spirits there is another and another which you call God. It is not one man or one spirit as such. I talk of the Holy Spirit which is Jesus because that is the name he acquired and the Great White Spirit which you call God. God is Great Ordinance Divine. There have been and will be many people sent to your world as prophets. All sent from spirit will be excellent although not all will be recorded correctly as I have told you before. It is like a rumour that started with a truth and was twisted and rephrased by people who heard it and passed it on. As well, you have the self opinionated people who have no knowledge at all and take it upon themselves to prophesize what they think to be true, not what actually is true.

If various prophets really existed does this mean that most of those connected to various religions walked the earth at some point as well?

Yes, many of them. Jesus was a prophet who spoke to the people of his time on earth in a way that they understood. There have been many, many prophets in all nationalities who did the same thing to their people. Their words have gone on to form various religions or belief systems. In fact there is no body of men on earth who have not been visited by such a prophet. All religions you see stem from the same point, spirituality. Religion is an interpretation of spirituality, sometimes manoeuvred in a way that suits that particular church or religion. Many religions or churches did not want to lose power and the words of the prophet were altered or stretched so that the meaning was not quite as it was intended.

Does this make other teachings for different religions real and true as well? If so, which religion should we follow?

It is not necessary for you to follow any religion. You must follow spirituality only. Religions are twisted and not pure and true. You may believe in Christ for that was true, you may believe in the Buddha, the Great White Spirit who came to the native Indians and many, many others because they are true. But these prophets are only messengers of the word of spirituality, as I am.

Please tell us about Jesus, because so many religions follow his life and teachings.

I will say to you that Jesus was one of the highest of teachers and was sent to your earth as a spirit entity of the purest and most holy, so that he could make an impact on the people and try to teach them about spirituality and how they should live their lives in the way that was required by the Great Spirit. There have been other great teachers who we have sent before and after Jesus. Some have been as great, some more mellow in their methods. To become a teacher in this plane of consciousness for souls is not only a great honour to be chosen to teach, but it requires a great deal of study and hard work to do this thing. Once we are chosen by the Higher Spirits to be given the powers to teach, we embark upon what you would only understand me to say as a long course of education into the way people on earth such as yourselves would welcome the aspect of spirit teachings, and then how to make you understand something which is really past your comprehension. Do you not remember how Jesus and others of his time spoke to the people in parables, using stories as examples? In this way he was trying to teach the people in their own language - their own comprehension. Today you are all more aware of things because of education and learning, but the problems for us are just the same. I try to talk to you in words that you can relate to as being understandable. You already have knowledge because of your inquisitive mind over the years so you do not find what I say to you as being unbelievable.

We are curious to know what you think of the various teachings, channeled writings or spoken words from other spirit teachers

I will say that some are good and true and honest, others are the figment of the imagination of the person who heard them. Not necessarily the medium who spoke them, but the person who recorded them or edited them into the printed form. Many mediums have uttered many profound words but they have been lost because they were not interpreted properly. It is the same as when you meditate and we send you perhaps a single picture and then you discuss this with others in your group, as you do. Everyone has a different reaction to that picture and there are many interpretations of why it was sent. The same thing happens with the interpretations of the voice mediums. If you could read a true record of what was actually uttered then you could form a more accurate interpretation of the meaning we sent to your world. It is the same with the words of Jesus, Moses and many others. You do not hear now from your books what was actually said at the time. Several of the writings you read are very good and the teachers are the best for many, many years. You ask of Silver Birch and White Eagle. Both did actually teach and they were the best and most accurate. Read them again and ask me the questions that they were asked. I look forward to answering them directly with you so that you can compare the answer. Then you will see the meaning of Ishamcvan's words today about the way that there are two views to everything.

Will Jesus return to our world?

I will say to you that this will not happen. Yes there will be other saviors but Jesus will not return as a spirit entity. He had evolved higher and it will not be necessary for the spirit to do this. There will be other saviors or teachers or prophets of the spirit world and there have been lots since the life of Jesus. For your people to wait in expectation of another Jesus they are ignoring the prophets and teachers already amongst you. There are many. There will be many more. A higher spirit may return. There may be more than one but I do not know when or how or where. The time must be right for this to happen. The people of your world are blind to that which is before their eyes. They are stubborn and they do not wish to see the wise men amongst them. If they would only listen to the spiritual people on your world and discard the prophets of religion who shout from the highest pulpits about how wonderful and pure they are themselves, then things may improve. Men generally are too busy being powerful and putting up a front for all other men to see about how wonderful spirituality is and what wonderful work they do to even have the smallest part of spirituality coming through. Religion must change. Religion is an arch old thing of the past. There are many types of people in many places all around your world who believe in the power of the spirit, everlasting life of the spirit and reincarnation. Many religions all have the same underlying beliefs along this vein which is good. It is the manipulation by the power seekers and the bigots that have spoilt and changed religion out of recognition by spirit.

So you see that my lessons to you are essential as they are with other spirits working in the same way or similarly with other channels. It is all a plan. That plan cannot and will not be stopped. It is essential that the word of this spirit plane and my lessons to you and the lessons of other spirits to their pupils be known to your world.

We are still afraid of the influence of various people who are not with spirituality although they boast religion citing various prophecies.

I have told you before that any problem that is of another person is not your problem so it must not be taken on board by you. People demonstrate themselves in many ways that are not necessarily what they are thinking or feeling. They put on a good front and act in a way that if it were analyzed then it would not be seen as true. By acting falsely they are sometimes moving against their own spirituality. Jealousy is a very bad thing but so many people in your world have this and must be seen to be better than the person next to them. Most things and reactions stem only from this reason or that of greed. It is usually of one thing or another. You must stand back and be remote from these situations, especially if they are directed at you. By doing this you not only put yourself in a superior position to gain control of your feelings, but it puts the other person at a disadvantage by turning the tables on them so to speak. Watch and you will see how they react.

What else should we read to know about the interpretation of the World of Spirituality by other prophets?

Follow the Book of the Dead now and you will learn all that there is to know about those comparisons. Later as you progress you will see the same base beliefs in all religions and it is important that you know and remember these for future reference. You will find the comparisons interesting. The further you go back in time the more connected various belief systems will be seen. What was very simple to simple people has now become so complex that even the educated people have a hard time seeing the true meaning. Read on and you will see. Ishamcvan will guide you all in your learning and discovery. I never said that my lessons would be easy. I said they would be simple because spirit and the evolvement of spirit are easy and uncomplicated, but the lessons about your world and its complexities are hard lessons to learn.

How and why are saints sainted and are saints a type of prophet?

Saints are nothing more than spirits in a bodily form who do exceptional spiritual things in their lives and touch many people in different ways. They work with spirit. They do things which are out of the ordinary and they are seen to perform miracles; sometimes once but usually many, many times. There are saints, if you wish to call them that, in all civilizations and countries of the world. A quiet person tending the sick in the jungle could be a saint as well. There are no values but it is an earthly term. From spirit we would call these people merely high spiritual beings who are aware of the true meaning of spirit and the word of the Holy Spirit and live their lives accordingly and work as a channel through us.

Were the ten commandments rules of karma told direct from spirit to Moses?

I have told you before that many prophets tried to teach the people of the day in simple words which they could understand. To say things in simple terms sometimes adds to confusion when read or listened to by intelligent humans because they read things into the sayings and make them out to have deeper meanings than they actually did. Prophets tried to set out codes of behaviour to the people of the day and some of these were later known as the ten commandments. Read these again and you will see the simplicity of reason, which they have and will understand in what sense they were told to the people. They knew that if they said for example do not covet thy neighbours wife that the people of the day would not have loose sex or immoral behaviour to one another. Or if a prophet said that they must love one God, meaning the Holy Spirit, that they would not spend time worshipping idols or stars or moons or animals as they did at the time.

Is the spirit world planning a further revelation by sending another teacher like Jesus?

I suppose you mean a teacher who will be hailed by man to be equal to Jesus. I have told you before that there have been many teachers since Jesus, but none have been acclaimed as being equal to Jesus and most have not even been recognized. Until man can stop and listen to what is being said from its messengers from spirit, then how can they possibly know a similar teacher to Jesus when they see one? Yes, I will say to you that there have been and there will be more teachers like Jesus, but at the same time I will say to you that no, man will not listen for some time yet.

Are the mystics who shut themselves off in isolation better at getting closer to spirituality than those of us who lead normal lives on earth?

I would say to you that the only thing that they make better, possibly, is their own spirituality, because they have taken time to study and perfect the teachings from spirit. But even though they learn through meditation and contemplation, it is not the same as putting these laws to the test in lives connected to other people and the problems which this brings. So even though they are perhaps enriching their own learning they are not practicing what they have learnt so in a way the lessons are wasted. They may as well have stayed on this plane of existence and studied from this perspective. All spirits do this but they have to experience and live the lessons in order for them to become true lessons, and your mystics must do the same.

So I will say to you it is much better that you live normally and teach, than it is to go to a mountain top and contemplate for the rest of your life.

Do most of the prophets say the same things?

Do not confuse the words of Ishamcvan with the words of others, because they are not the same. I have told you many times that although the words of other prophets may have been correctly said at the time of their lessons, the interpretation of most of them have been changed in their translation, so to speak. So it is very important that the words of Ishamcvan do not get changed and remain exactly as spoken. Then there will be no doubt as to their meaning and when considered by skeptics they cannot be taken in two ways.

Are you different from all the other teachers?

No, I am not to be considered one of the first and only teachers that has ever existed. There are many everywhere. All teach and pass the message of spirituality on in different ways. And yes it has been going on for many years, hundreds and hundreds since time began. As soon as man was on your earth then spirit from here communicated with him. In the more simple minds it is easier. It is only those of you who are more intelligent with questioning minds that it becomes more difficult to communicate initially. But to question and ask for a different opinion to your own is good. That is why I have been taught in a completely new way how to approach the subject with you and teach you why it is so new that it may not be approved of by your so called experts, because they will question its simplicity. But it is the very essence of the spirituality simplicity that makes sense, does it not? For to make it complex is to make the whole thing out of proportion to the truth. So you see for me to come through to you is not in itself unique. It is done many times every day to many people in your world. But I know that you question whether others are taught in the same way as yourself and I will say to you that this is so. It is a new way of teaching but whilst I say that I was taught a new way I do not mean to infer that others of spirits were not taught so also. But what I must say is that this is a recent way not an old way. For the progress in the spirit level of consciousness is progressing forward also. Is that not true?

Why was Jesus sent to earth?

Jesus was sent as a prophet to help the people understand the laws of spirituality. Jesus was not sent to help the life on earth become wonderful and enlightening in an artistic or scientific way. He was of the people for the people, nothing more. It is of no interest to spirit whether life on earth is advanced or not. It is the way that man treads his path that is important. That may be in a remote mountain village where all he learnt was humility and understanding. Earth is a playground for the development of the spiritual understanding, and man as a body is used for the purposed. All things that you enjoy in your world, such as historical figures of art and culture and learning are good for you, but not to the spiritual leaders. It is the people around you today and your actions with them that has the importance. That is all.

I have read the words of another channeller who works with a teaching guide' by writing words in a way which appears to be almost identical to your own. Is this a fact?

Yes I told you many times ago that there were people all over the world writing and speaking just as you do. They have their own teacher guides as I am with you. We all have different relationships and past karmas with our subjects on earth, but the teaching outcome is the same. In the case of ourselves our lives have been interwoven for many existences; in other cases this may not be so strong. But you see our togetherness is good and our understanding and acceptance from you, is richer for the bond. But yes there are many people with a similar purpose. The man in America is good and he writes similar, that is true.

How should we know which prophet to believe and follow?

I find it very hard to try and explain to you all my words on the subject of reading others prophecies whilst at the same reading my own. It is very simple. You must choose who you want to learn the world of spirituality through. Is it to be me or is it to be another prophet or teacher? Many teachers are there to pass on the word and many are wrong in what they say. A few are right in all aspects and some are only right in some aspects. It is like the telling of a story. Some people in human form will elaborate the story and some will miss parts out. Only the trained and true will keep explaining the same thing over and over again from as many different perspectives as is necessary for the person to understand. I say to you for all the things I have tried to explain to you that you do not understand, I have many more ways to tell you the same thing. I know that you will ask me why I do not know the correct way to tell you so that you understand first time, but I will say to you that you have freedom of choice to accept or to question further the answer, and I cannot know which way you will go. So I know you will question again and say how is that so if your lives are chosen, which is another aspect you do not understand. Your life is chosen only in some aspects. The rest of it is tests and problem solving. For those aspects you have free choice. I can see, but not to the extent that I will know which way you will go. For this reason your guide will always try to show you the way. If everything was preordained that would not be necessary for the plan would be set. So I say to you all again, if you wish to learn and understand the words of Ishamcvan, then learn them before you read elsewhere. If not you will get them muddled. If you wish just to look at all spiritual writings, of which mine are one of many, then read away.

There are many famous legendary people that are known to have done a lot of good for mankind. For example, Mother Theresa and Florence Nightingale. How have their spirits progressed now? Have they progressed to a higher level than yours, or have they re-incarnated to the earth plane again, or a higher learning plane?

There are and there have been many teachers on your earth. You do not necessarily see saintly people as teachers, but that is what they are. You look at their lives and their work and you should take an example from what you see. They deal with life on a level that shows understanding of spirituality and a maturity of their own spiritual being which enables them to live and react to situations the way they do. Some of these people will come back to your world, not necessarily because they haven't matured enough to move on within the world of spirit, but because they may be instrumental in helping certain spirits that need to return and they help this spirit or spirits with their lessons. Others move on and don't return. The level of myself is to teach spirituality to your world and was an option given to me rather than to return for one last time. So my level may be higher than some of the ones you mention and lower than others. If that is how you look at the levels to help you to understand.

Chapter Thirteen

God

"God is the name for the Great Ordinance Divine.
The one, the whole, the source and the infinity"

Please tell us how the Great Spirit or overall God in your terms can see every single person in our world and answer their prayers and requests.

He has divine love and that is what gives him the power to do this. It is difficult for you to understand but it happens. Love is the secret to everything. Love is supreme and I cannot tell you exactly how important this is. Of course every person in your world has a guide or guides and our purpose is to look after you and many times when you pray it is us that answers your prayers. Sometimes though, we want you to do one thing and that is not what you have asked, so it cannot be done. We are one in this plane. One of the Holy Spirit. We work as one to a lesser degree. I am evolved but not yet mature. Do you understand? We can progress further from where I am now.

The Holy Spirit or the Great White Spirit, are these God?

Well this is difficult to be precise about too. I feel that you on earth have a comprehension of one man sitting up here controlling everything and you call him God. This is very far in fantasy from the truth. There is no man. There is a spirit which is over every other spirit to be the nearest terminology in your understanding and this you could call God. But it is a spirit, not a being. Let's get this right. You must listen carefully and not write what you think is correct. Listen to Ishamcvan and get it right.

The highest of spirits that is within my realm of comprehension from my level of development is the Great White Spirit. This spirit is the highest of high to my spiritual realm. It is not the highest of all and my spirit will not see higher than the Great White Spirit until I have evolved to many more planes of existences. Every so many planes of existence there is a higher spirit in control. You could call the Great White Spirit, which is supreme in your and my evolvement, a god. A god really is an idol by people in your world, which is worshipped by many religious orders. A god is a person or an idol. It is not a spirit. You will not hear me refer to a god. You hear me refer to the Great White Spirit as the highest of high in my realm of consciousness and you will hear me refer to a Holy Spirit which is a level below the Great White Spirit in my realm of consciousness. The Holy Spirit is of course an exceptional high spirit and near to the Great White Spirit, but not as close. And then there are various levels of spiritual powers between the Holy Spirit and my spirit, if you understand. The Great White Spirit is called as such because white is the greatest level of power in the spirit world. I am not aware yet of any spirit entities higher than the Great White Spirit, but I know that they are there. I have to evolve higher before I know of them. So I hope that I have answered your question about God. I think that you all think in terms of a god because of religions that you have learnt since you were tiny children. Religions are not the same as spirituality. To be spiritual you do not have to follow a religious order or thinking. You just have to follow the laws of cause and effect, your own karma and the laws which the spirit world asks you to follow to make possible the cleansing of your spirit or soul and your evolvement higher. You will notice that I said the cleansing of your spirit, not the learning of lessons. You do have to learn lessons as I tell you repeatedly. But these lessons in fact cleanse the spirit, not make it more knowledgeable. Do you understand? If you go back to the stories about Jesus, who was a very high spiritual person on your earth, and his teachings, you will see that he refers continually to his father in heaven which is the Great White Spirit or the lesser high spirit the Holy Spirit, and these in fact are correct. He did not refer to God. It was the interpretations of the sayings of Jesus when they were written by man that the mention of God was included. God was the writer's interpretation of what was being said, not factual. But to pray to Great White Spirit is the same as praying to an almighty God. It is of no difference in the praying, it means the same. But I have just told you the facts. Do not be alarmed. Spirituality is the importance and you must remember that. There is no heaven and hell. No one is judged when they return home to this next plane of existence from earth. You are not punished if you do wrong or do not lead a good and merciful life. Everything you do must be for your own spiritual development and this development is in your hands only. If you do not want to develop to a higher plane and learn all the lessons that are necessary you stay at the same plane of existence and do not move forward, so to speak. It is up to your spirit to decide. The choice is yours. It is as simple as that. Many people in your world are frightened of dying because they fear the wrath of God and how they will be dealt with on the day of judgment. There is no day of judgment when you are told you have been good or you have done harm to many people. You are analyzing yourself and your past life and if you desire, you ask the Holy Spirit or the Great White Spirit for help in telling you how you can plan to learn more lessons or redo the lessons which you failed to learn. It is up to you. There is no judgment from any other spirit here. Your spirit may judge your spirit, that is all.

What is Holy?

You are confused because you relate that word to your bible. Holy Spirit is older than the bible. Jesus referred to the Holy

Spirit. I have told you previously the identity, so to speak, of the Holy Spirit. Holy means on high, or highest. The Holy Spirit is on high. It is the highest on your next plane of existence. It is not the overall highest, that is the Great White Spirit. Many words in your bible and that of other religions and groups of religious people are taken from the words we use in this plane of existence. Read the words of Jesus and you will see how spiritual they are. Read who he refers to in heaven (heaven is this plane of existence, whether the next plane or the next plane or the next plane, it is the realm of the Holy Spirit and the Great White Spirit). Jesus says, "My father in heaven". Jesus says, "I am the son of my father put on earth to be a prophet." Keep reading, you will learn much.

Why do you sometimes refer to the Great White Spirit, The Higher Spirits, The Holy Spirit, but not always God?

I refer to a Holy Spirit or a Great White Spirit. I had previously mentioned God to you and why did I contradict myself? In the early days of my teachings to you I had to talk in your comprehension. Now you have advanced. Now I tell you a more detailed description of all things. You may call it the Great White Spirit, the Great Spirit or God. It is up to you. The difference is the same. You kept thinking of a god. I knew this so I spoke to you of a god. It was of no consequence. As spirit we do not think of God. As man you may think of God. Spiritually we think and use terms a little different to you. It is good that you have asked this question still knowing that I have not proved myself to be false and contradictory. As a teacher I must try and get my message over to you in words that you will understand, in words that you will relate to by your comprehension. Gradually as we progress I will teach you little by little our words and our ways. It will be a long lesson.

When did the Great White Spirit start and grow to what he is today?

This is the ultimate question. Ishamcvan must phrase it so that you do not feel rejected by his reply. I can only say that from your perspective, spirit and spiritual leaders, so to speak, have always been. You cannot possibly even begin to understand a small degree until you experience the vastness and timelessness of the spirit world. I cannot say to you that it was several millions of years ago, it was millions times millions times millions and even then that was not the start. Do not forget that I have already explained to you that there are various high spirits in charge of each level of spirituality or plane of existence, so if you take that concept for the Great White Spirit over several or many of these levels of consciousness then you are beginning to see how vast a concept it is. The Great White Spirit is over all you can comprehend and more, but the whole vastness of planes and levels goes on and on and there are other Great White Spirits eventually which go higher. Poor Ishamcvan is very frustrated to get you to even touch on learning how to understand. Here it is a simple concept of a shepherd and his flock and then another shepherd in another field and with another flock and each not aware of the other until they know each other as they do here.

Are the highest spirits responsible for earthquakes and natural phenomenon which result in death and destruction?

These things are caused by natural conditions of your earth's structure and weather patterns. The Holy Spirit made the world and all that goes with it. But the world is a place for man to learn lessons. Not all lessons can be learnt in a good way, some must experience hard or difficult things too. Earthquakes are part of that structure. But I must say to you that it is part of the effect of the cause of man's destruction of the world by pollution and disregard of natural environments which could give you some problems which are not natural. Or I would say that the natural problems are accelerated by the wrong doings of man to his environment. It is good that your mankind is now more aware of what former generations have done to destroy not only the earth's surrounding atmosphere but also the earth's crust and the natural vegetation that grows on the surface of your earth. You all know that the destroying of the natural vegetation causes difference to the weather patterns, as does space travel and aircraft polluting the atmosphere. It is again cause and effect. You cannot blame the Holy Spirit or the Great White Spirit for this. They are responsible for natural phenomenon which is within the mixture of things used to give man a work experience for his lessons.

When the Holy Spirit sees atrocities in our world, why doesn't it intervene and stop them from happening?

Well I must say to you that things that happen in your world are by the making of man, not of the Holy Spirit, so it is the effect of these actions that must be reaped by man and not by spirit. I will also say that it is not that the Holy Spirit will not intervene, more that it is your laws and not ours. It sounds not very kind but that is as it must be. The atrocities are man to man, not spirit to man. Spirit did not send atrocities. Man sent them. So man must pay for these actions.

Are all prayers answered?

Unfortunately no they are not. This is because of many reasons, some of which I have discussed before with you. Prayers that are genuine, asked with passions and with beliefs that they will be granted are certainly considered and usually granted. The only exception is when you have chosen from spirit that you want to experience a certain thing and it is for this thing that the prayers are asked. The Holy Spirit will not take this thing away under these circumstances. If this is not the case and the prayers are genuine then they are granted. Prayers should always be for happenings, not for money or possessions, or violence or death. This will not happen. Every prayer is different and every prayer is looked at in a different way from spirit. So why, you ask, do some people live through many hardships and their prayers are in vain? Genuine people who believe in prayer. I would say to you that these prayers may not be as they wanted granted from spirit when they chose their path. Do not pity these people, it is their choice. If it is not their choice and they are aware of the Holy Spirit and the power of prayer then spirit is here to assist and comfort. Many prayers are for others, this is different. If you pray for another person, that person must be willing from their own spirituality to accept the answer to the prayer or it will not be given.

Why do we have to wait, sometimes for a long time, for prayers to be answered?

I know this is frustrating and you see gloom and despair while you wait, but maybe the time is not right. The answer to a prayer may not be as simple as one action, it may be a whole chain of events that bring about the answer. Look back on some of the things you have prayed for and see how the answer was given. Sometimes it is in disguise.

Is there only one God?

Now I will say to you about the question of the spirit and the powers of spirit which you call God. I have mentioned to you before that one God is only within the realms of your existence on your plane and was to be understood only in that context. There is only one God or overall spirit that is over your lifetime on earth and this is correct, but with the whole then there are many Gods or overall spirits. As to the overall spirits, there are many ad infinitum. God is Great Ordinance Divine as I have told you, and this was man's comprehension of God being one man or one overall being in your own image. The image of your spirituality, not the image of your body. There have been many misunderstandings on this aspect. God is spirit. Overall spirit, Great Spirit, Great White Spirit (White is pure spirit) or Holy Spirit (Spirit ordained as the most Holy in that realm of consciousness or plane of existence). All are the same. The Great White Spirit to your understanding is higher than the Holy Spirit. It is all a chain reaction of things that are as one as spirit is as one. You are not one in your spirituality when you are here. When you are there you are on your own, so to speak, for the period of your life. Not on your own that you cannot connect with the spirituality as a whole of which you are a part, but on your own during your lifetime on earth when you are not one with the other spirits living in bodies of man. So you see you can be one with us but not one with fellow man. Your journey is a lonely one, in as much as others you meet are also on a journey of their own. That is why man has a problem understanding that when you return to this plane of existence you become one. You do not carry one being what you were in a body. That is a different aspect.

What is the difference between the Great White Spirit and the Holy Spirit and why white?

There are very many spirits. For higher spirits are ruled, if that is the right word, by higher spirits ad infinitum. The spirit over your realm of consciousness on this level of consciousness as its base is called by you as the Holy Spirit. This is man's word. It comes from ancient records of the spirituality of this, my world. Above the Holy Spirit, next in line, is the Great White Spirit, also a word belonging to man. But it is good that you see the difference. So shall we say that the Great White Spirit is an advisor to the Holy Spirit who is the same in turn to higher spirits like myself who are advisors to you and your spirituality. Look at it as a chain of spirits and teachers if you like. So if you pray to me I may help, if you pray to the Holy Spirit you may get greater and more definite help and to the Great White Spirit you ask for more important matters. It is not exactly like that but I think you may understand if I tell you in this way. You can call them what you like. We have no names. We do not need names. We know by instinct if you like what happens.

As for white, white is pure light and spirit is pure is it not? So the white light is therefore considered pure spirit. If you meditate and see a pure white light you will be in harmony with spirit on a higher level of understanding than if you do not see the light as white. You may say that you are advanced in understanding and that by seeing the pure white light you are rewarded with the vision as recognition of your understanding. So the two spiritual names you have questioned are so because of these reasons. Holy because Jesus told many stories about his father in heaven and the Holy Spirit who assisted him. Father being the Great White Spirit and Holy Spirit because holy is a church word that people recognize and is supreme in power. He also referred to father and he in the masculine. But we have neither sex nor gender so the reference is only for your worldly understanding that is all.

It is said that God is omnipresent. If this is so, then how could it be possible that all we do, think, feel, experience, is not dictated ultimately by God? Are we just supposed to think that we have free will in this life on earth in order to somehow aid in our learning?

If we look at the high spirit as being supreme and the assisting high spirits as being your teachers, then you must be living a life in which you should be aware always of heeding their laws. But your conceptuality of God is more of paying homage, which has been turned by the churches as more a dictatorship instead of a spiritual love between a father spirit and a child spirit. There is a big difference. If the father is loving and the child wants to learn, then the child will learn faster and without the barriers of fear or domination. The child knows the rules and the child wants to mimic the father. He does not live his spiritual life in fear that if he does not do everything right the father will be angry. The father may be sad at seeing the child fall over and over again because it does not listen to his words of wisdom, but he loves the child all the same for his faults. But your churches have made their God a golden idol that has to be worshiped and adored. Your spiritual father asks none of that. But he does ask that you listen, learn and follow his laws. You must read my words and learn too.

Are we all tiny particles of the Great Ordinance Divine going through a learning process in order to ultimately merge again with our creator as an even greater miraculous entity?

The spirit world is one as molecules of a cloud are one. There is a whole yet there are separate particles of the whole, which are being a separate entity in their own right. Let us say that the higher the spirit entities within that cloud the more divine are they in their presence. These higher or denser spirit molecules are therefore the teachers and guides of the other lesser-educated or smaller pieces, which are yourselves. The molecule of the cloud which is you, does not leave the whole in order to return to a life on earth but is more suspended by a thread which still links it to the spirit world until the life on earth is finished and it returns home without its lifeline or thread of earthly existence. It is no longer suspended but again a firm part of the cloud, which is the whole level of spirituality to which it lives, or is a part of at that stage of its development. When it is in itself a richer spirit, a larger or more educated spirit, then it must move to the next level of existence and make way for the other particles or spirits to grow themselves. So you see it is an existence of continual progression, unless of course you fail to learn and have to keep yo-yoing back and forwards to earth or another planet sphere, to learn before you grow and progress.

Does anything exist that is not of the Great Ordinance Divine?

Yes. The Great Ordinance Divine are the higher spirits of the whole. The Great Ordinance. Lesser spirits are lesser spirits in the divine ordinance, which is spirit as a whole. They are part of you but you are not yet mature enough to be part of them. I do not contradict myself when I say that you are all one. Yes you are. But in the one there are those who are the Holy Spirits and the Great White Spirits, of which you are not. They are the governing spirits if you like. The Great Ordinance Divine is the whole being governed by these higher spirits. The God as you call them.

I believe that the only sin or evil is a wilful turning away from our connection to God but if the connection to God is not understood, then any act that may be interpreted as sinful is simply not knowing any better. I believe that negative acts are a manifestation of a need to belong or feel loved. Is this just naivety?

In some respects you are right. But I will say to you that everyone on your world is in progression to reach the almightily level which is inspired by that which you call God. So to be perfection in the eyes of God, as you have been taught. is in fact being able to reach the level of perfection that is God. In order to reach that level the spirit entity which is yourself has to go through various stages which are tests. Not really tests, more so experiences and tests of your own spiritual evolution. With all sets of circumstances in your world, there is an element to test your own learning and spiritual advancement. So to do wrong is to interpret that situation in a particular way. There is no right nor wrong by spiritual standards, so there is no test in that respect. But to handle a situation must represent your knowledge and growth. So to be like God is the essence. You need to be loved by God. It is not quite that simple. For God is love. There is not justification. God will love whether you do right or wrong. But you yourselves will be wrong to yourself by doing what is not in the eyes of God, the right thing to do for your advancement higher in the realms of spirituality which is yours alone.

Could you talk to us about God please?

It is said that God, which we will call the highest spirit, was alone. In order to make observations of itself it had to become more than it was. It had to see itself, which it could not do, as a one. A high cluster of one. So it made hundreds of thousands of spirits as little versions of itself so that these spirits could see spirituality and the high spirit for what it was and what it represented. These tiny spirit entities, which were made at various times, had the irresistible urge to purify and make themselves as good as the highest spirit entity. So each was put on a journey and during its path of discovery it was presented with many tests and challenges, which it had to pass to be able to call itself more spiritual and have the full understanding of spirituality itself.

We ask whether God is one God over all other spirits, the Holy Spirit and the Great White Spirit?

All levels have an overall spirit which is higher, who has another overall spirit which is higher and so on. Is there a God? I have told you of this terminology. Overall, I must say no. There are always higher spirits, that is all. I suppose if you restrict yourself to the next plane of existence and your world only, you could say that the Holy Spirit is the "God" but when you return to the next plane of existence you will know that this is not the case because there are other planes of existence after the next and after the next. So Jesus taught of his father, God in heaven. This was the Holy Spirit, in charge so to speak of the next level of consciousness, the next level of existence.

If Jesus referred to his father in heaven and said he was made in his image, how can this not be God as one man?

As with many things that have been recorded, this is not as in the context it was originally said. Man is in the image of spirit for man is spirit. The body of a spirit in your world can be the same in this world too. For you to understand that spirit can be materialized into any form - a human form - an animal form - that of another world. For spirit has the power, if you like to do these things. For people to understand the power of spirit, it was told to them that the god or the power of spirit being the overall power to their world was in their image. They were the same image as God, which of course you all are. So let us look at the word God. Is there a God as such? Yes, there is. Is it how you all perceive? No it is not. For there is one God yes over the world of spirit, but there is a God or higher spirit above that higher spirit and so on. So yes there is one God from your perception, but no there is not one God in the overall range of spirituality, there are a vast many. But the God that is directly responsible to your own spirituality at this level of your progress is in your image. Of course. For spirituality is the same in every entity, it is just that the progression of each entity is at different levels. The higher spirit or God over you now is the same, just very much more advanced.

In the bible it keeps referring to the wrath of God. Does God get angry?

You need not fear the wrath of God because that will not happen. We want you to question the bible. God is love, not fear.

God is the Holy Spirit and the Holy Spirit is the Great White Spirit and the Great White Spirit is part of another spirit ad infinitum. So God as is referred to in the bible is only part of the spirit complex and that you know by my teachings is not as is written in the bible. I have told you it is simply love and goodness to fellow men and fellow spirits within men. So to fear God was not preached as that. It was preached to fear the spirits within themselves. Not as bad spirits but to question every move they make in their lives and how they treat other people and other things and this alone will open the way to the higher universe. If Jesus had not named certain spiritual aspects in terms the people could relate to then the people would not have understood as I have said before. Please do not get confused. You are analyzing the similes, not necessarily believing what is written just because it is written. Say, as you were reading today, Jesus walked on water. His spirit was seen to leave his body and walk on water, that is all. Jesus said that if you believe you can do something it will be done. You prove this. But you must want to believe or it will not happen. Everything is possible if you believe it will happen. Jesus said that you could move a mountain if you believe it is possible. Another simile of course.

What about the people who believe that Jesus is healing them, if in fact you say that Jesus is now on a different level. How can that be?

It is not that Jesus ever did the healing. He does not now because he is at a different level. Healing is done through spirit as a mass of spirit or individually dependant on the level of the spirit doing the healing. If I said to you that I could heal you would not find that strange, yet you do not ask me to heal you ask spirit to heal and that happens. The people of your Christian church think of Jesus and Mary and Joseph and many other people who were connected at the time as having the power to be elevated on this level. I can agree that they were of a higher level than perhaps yourselves when they returned home, but they are not Gods in any respect. They were a prophet and his helpers that is all. A good and high prophet but that is all. You could pray to an unknown spirit called anything you like but someone here would answer your calling and know what you wanted. Names mean nothing in the spirit world. Jesus lives in your world but not here.

If there is a high spirit on your level in the spirit world does he not evolve and go to the next level or does he stay in charge where he is?

No when he reaches supremacy in our level after he has gained perfection he will go to the next level and become as one as happened with Jesus. Then another spirit in this level will have progressed to be superior in his spirituality above others in this level and he will take over as a high spirit and then one other high spirit will eventually be the Holy Spirit and the Great White Spirit in our level. So let us look at the highest, the Great White Spirit. He also moves on. Another spirit will be elected to fill his place, as a description you will understand, so to speak.

Chapter Fourteen

Religions & Faiths

"There is a vast difference between the world of spirit and the interpretations that the various religions have put on this basic truth"

How, when and where did man lose track with spirituality and change it from what we were originally taught to the way religions see it today?

You must believe that all religions have a spiritual basis and the majority of them go back to the same source as each other. Over time, a long time, many religions and faiths have put their thoughts, extended beliefs and personal understanding and interpretation on these basic principles. It is an easy thing to do. They take a word here and an action there and then say not only to themselves but also other people, that the thing is something different or an exaggeration of the original. Also remember that some churches seek power over the people and as such they interject their laws to keep the people paying homage to them in order to control. Once this is done then they become little idols themselves who man must worship or, as they say, the person will perish in hell or some such horror. Today, many hundreds of years later the belief systems of your religions are so apart from each other that it is even hard to recognise the similarity and certainly the source. How could a religious man say to you that it is permitted for you to kill in the name of God, that God said it was ok and man will be rewarded if he kills men who believe or act with a different religion? Ask yourselves.

What is the best way to deal with friends who try to 'push' religion onto me, no matter how respectfully they do so?

Firstly you must try and understand why they are clinging to their particular version of spirituality. You notice I say spirituality and not religion. In fact religion is the interpretation by one body of people about spirituality itself. Unfortunately these people do not have the ability to go back to the basis of all spiritual understanding but instead they cling to a version that someone somewhere said about it. That is a big difference. Most religions have their own saints and prophets which they say said or did something in the name of that religion and these people expect everyone else to follow them. I talk about prophets and saints in jest of course, because most of these leaders are only thinking this about themselves, there is not justification. They become little Gods within their special religion and as they realise themselves as one of two things they educate others to believe in them too. Firstly, they are totally ignorant of all the basic rules and as such they are as unsecure as any other scholar who has not learnt his lessons yet tries to lecture about them anyway without correct knowledge. Or, they are charlatans and are living a dream of power. In either case the leaders are wrong, yet they are powerful enough to make their followers believe in them too. So in answer to your question about what should you say to these followers who try and convert you, I would say to them, very simply, "I respect your beliefs and know that you have the wisdom to dissect them for the truth, but I prefer to follow my own understanding even if eventually it comes to the same conclusion as your own. We are all on a journey of understanding and as such I believe that we have to make our own decisions based on our own heartfelt convictions which may take us time. I am pleased that you have the comfort of having found your own answers."

I understand that religion has nothing to do with spirituality, but why is it that most people on earth belong to a particular religion.

There is a vast difference to the world of spirit and the interpretations that the various religions have put on this basic truth. Whatever religions you belong to you are, if it is true to the basis of that religion, believing in spirituality. Christianity is the word of Jesus and the things that are recorded and made to be fact as to his teachings and idealisms. What is wrong with all religions is that the facts have been distorted and additions to the truth have been added. The basic spirituality has not been allowed to remain pure. For many reasons the facts have been engineered for the purpose of the church.

Are there so many different religions in order for man to learn the lesson of finding their own spirituality?

If man was that interested in learning about the true one and only basis of spirituality then they would question the religions as many of you have done and many more will do over the years. But religions were made by man, not by spirit to give man the lessons of observation. That is the difference. Man has a brain and that could be used to question religious belief systems, could it not? But to be at one with a true spiritual understanding you must learn and learn and ask questions until you are clear in your own minds that this is right for you. You cannot use your brains necessarily, you use your instinct and spiritual perception initially and then you go on to learn and as you learn then you understand.

Why does it seem natural for man to think of themselves as lower than religious elders or lower than spirit, especially as taught by most churches?

The essence of spirituality is that all souls or spirits are equal. None is superior to the other. None should be in awe of a higher spirit even though they are in fact superior in their level of spiritual experience. What is happening with religions is that

264

they have to have the population or their congregation in their control, and in order to do so they make the person in charge of that particular church as being a superior being because of his connection to God, rather than the congregation who are perceived to be lesser mortals and having a lesser understanding of that same God. By raising God and his workers in the church to a higher elevation than the people gives control and control is power, and in many cases this is exploited with the priests and the people being servile to the higher beings of the church. I would not say to you ever that a priest is higher than a poor man in the pew or that God, which you call the higher spiritual power, is in any way superior to myself or similar spirit workers. Do you learn lessons of observation on this point, yes of course you do.

If you were to pick a religion that would be of the most benefit to the average person, which one would it be?

All religions go back to a central point and that is spirituality. Many religions have the basics as correct but they have not brought them to the modern world. I would say all are now wrong, but many have lots of aspects which are correct, although not necessarily being interpreted correctly by their clergy or advocates.

Are we living in hell as humans? That is, with all the awful things that happen in the world today and throughout history, this life must surely be some form of hell that we are put on to live, make mistakes and learn from them?

You could put it like that, but it is a bit extreme. There is one purpose for your existence on earth and that is to learn. But you must understand that the status of each spirit of each body are not at the same stage of learning. Some are infants and some are university graduates. There is a big difference as to how a senior will tackle a problem because of his wisdom and understanding of the problem than would an infant who goes in with all guns blazing. Life is a melting pot of many types of learning and lessons must be given in order to make a situation for the spirit to learn. But there are also horrors which have to be experienced, usually made by spirits which are not yet in tune with their environment. You must read all my words as you must learn in order to pass the message on to others.

What religions were there before Christianity and others of that time period? Were the beliefs of the people the world over very similar before religion and its diversities came into being?

Most ancient religions were once the same wherever in the world they began. Tribes in the jungles who had no other contact with humans could believe the spirit because they had experienced it. This still happens today. The other side of the world another uneducated civilization would believe the same. The Egyptians believed the same as the aborigines but with various connotations as the years passed. But they all believed the same once. Do you not find it strange that once the whole of human occupation on your earth wherever they were had the same beliefs in spirit? Then, as they became educated, they lost these beliefs or they were changed in various ways to suit the living experiences and interpretations of the various nationalities and tribes. It is the same as a newborn baby who has spirit with him and accepts spirit as part of his life, but as he gets older and more educated and more influenced by elders, he loses the connection with spirit, sometimes altogether.

I have a question about a man of a certain religion or church that dies of body and returns home. He may have preached many wrong thoughts or misunderstandings of spirituality and the ways of God. Why does he not try and come back through a medium and tell the error of his ways so that the people know he was wrong in his thoughts and preaching?

Well I will say to you that many do. But the power of the medium telling everything not only correctly but in the connotation and intensity that is required, often are not quite so powerful as is necessary. The message is there but many would not listen, especially church members who tend to disbelieve spirituality. Spirituality is the only way of the light. Religion came from spirituality. It is only a different way of believing the same thing. But man has put onto spirituality his own embroideries so that the God is worshipped and spirituality is lost in a sea of confusion. The bible is the power, not the spirituality. The bible is only a recording of spirituality and the voice of the great spirits telling the people of the ways of life and life everlasting. But this has been altered and changed for the benefit and understanding of man and in doing so the spirituality aspect has been pushed back in the line of acceptance. Back to basics and the message will be clear.

How is it that there are millions of people who will follow one religion and believe literally in every single thing written in their 'book', when those things may have been said and recorded symbolically not factually?

I will say to you that it is not the masses that are necessarily right. It can be only one man who is right and a million people who are wrong. You wonder how. I will tell you. It is because they have been told what to think. People think what the next person thinks just because the next person thinks so and so does everyone around him; so he thinks this must be true. He doesn't stop and use his brain and analyze what are the other perspectives. If he did and remained alone whilst he did this perhaps he would be a wiser man.

Many religious doctrines talk about each coming from different levels of consciousness. Please explain?

The words from the development and understanding of various so called consciousnesses on your world are not necessarily words from spirit. I know that all words I use when talking to you are your words formed into your figures of speech in your understanding, but when you give me words for explanation that are neither your vocabulary, nor the words referring to the world of spirit, this is more difficult to explain. The Akashic files are the files I presume of ancient records made by various forms of consciousness of people in your world and I would dispute that they are of any importance to you to take any notice of and I certainly would not from this form of consciousness. I have told you before that it will confuse you if you or any of your group try to read the words of others, until I say that it is within your learning to do so. As I have said, it is correct to read about Jesus and the bible. The Akashic records I do not know. Elemental spirits are nothing more than the spirits that pass between your consciousness and mine and this is the simplest form of explanation I can give you. Do not concern yourself either with this description. It is not from spirit.

Are really old religions from pre-biblical times true because of their age, or have they been changed over the years?

Much of them are basically true but have had a great deal of fancy work done to expand it and make it sound more fancy. The world of spirituality then, as now, is simplicity. The life of the people then was very simple, although many, many people were able to contact spirit through meditation and by thoughts.

Baptism, is it good or a waste of time?

I will say to you that it does no harm but it does no good either. Spirit does not bless the water, neither does it bless particularly the baby at the time of its baptism. This is an act of a church, not of spirituality. Spirit blesses the child with birth and it blesses it again when it comes home. The development of the spirituality of the child will not be increased if it is baptized. Then you ask about holy water and the fact that it appears to heal. There is no such thing as holy water either. But there are miracles perhaps that come from spirit or from a healer channel that can be linked to holy water and its ritual.

Why do some people feel the need to be so forward and outgoing about their religious faith? What do they think it will do for them?

Unfortunately many think they become more spiritual in the eyes of God if they project their faith in everything they do and say so with the exclusion of all else, including compassion to their fellow men. It is not a requirement to shout faith from the rooftops or pester people who are not yet converted to that particular way of thinking, but it should be more the way that man acts to others which is of the supreme importance. You cannot be of a particular religion, devout and true and then go and rape someone and expect to be forgiven just because you have the faith. Faith will not protect you, because your actions are the only importance. If you have a belief in a spiritual existence and know the laws of karma, your own spiritual development, then you will understand to respect and love your fellow men.

We are curious to know about how the bible was written and how long did it take to put it in its present form?

The bible was not started for many tens of years after the death of Jesus and it was added to for many centuries and even today is being continually altered with different emphasis being put on words, sentences and events. If you take some of the work of your great authors of say several hundred years ago like your Shakespeare, think how there are modern versions of his plays in a different style and tongue or speech and think how Shakespeare would feel if he heard them as we hear the bible's stories of Jesus. He would say that that was not as was written, or as we would, not what happened. So whilst there is evolving life on earth you will have different interpretations and variations of what people think happened. You can see this happening also in all the new religious orders that have started in, say, the last one hundred years on your earth. Each religion says that it is right and has a different interpretation of the bible or God or its idol's interpretation of religion as they think it should be. They all think they are right, but they differ. The same is true of the different people who wrote the bible or any other religious book, they all had different opinions and teachings. But the text of some of these writers has been altered or obligated over the years by the church to fit in with what they wanted the religious version of the book to be.

If you take spirituality as being the only truth then you should compare it to the ancient civilizations and the way that they believed in simple evolution to a higher plane, and this comparison is much more enlightening than reading the bible. I have asked you to read the bible because I want to make you realize the teachings of Jesus, who was one of the highest prophets to return to your world. Once you have read the hidden meanings within the text you will be well on the way to being enlightened and you will see how much they reflect the teachings of Ishamcvan. When you have learnt this lesson you will have to go on to compare the beliefs and writings of other religious orders throughout the world. But think too of the native Indians in your country and how they took only from the land that what was needed to feed themselves and keep an existence. They killed only to feed and clothe themselves in warm skins and they never did so without this reason. They believed wholly and positively about spirit and they talked, saw and felt spirit every day of their lives. It was pure and simple, just as spirituality is in fact. There were many, many ancient civilizations too that lived by basic, simple ways with spirit always with them. You have heard of people who were religious frightening these simple people and trying to convert them to believe in the bible, sometimes threatening them if they did not do so. These people often said that they had changed just because they were frightened of their persecutors who they feared when they told them that they were savage heathens. It was not them that were bad, it was the persecutors. Today religion is the same. The people who shout with the strength and voice of a religion are often telling other spiritual people that they are heathens and witches. It is the same. The persecutors of the spiritually evolved people are the same.

Is there a heaven and a hell as set out in the Bible, or is this simply a fantasy that has been developed by man to give him hope and some sort of salvation?

This is a difficult question for you to understand the answer. I will start with hell. It is not a matter of choosing the good people from the bad and then sending them to different places where the bad people have no hope of redemption. It is the same with the so-called good people. There is one place not two, and that is what you may call home base. Now, whereas we say from spirit that there is no right and wrong because man has free will and does always what he thinks is right or wrong at the time that he does it, he has justification to himself for all his deeds at the moment they occur, or they would just not happen. The Holy Spirit or the Great White Spirit (your God) does not judge. But there are laws of karma - a code for living which must be learnt and understood. When a spirit returns home it evaluates its life on earth and let us say is awarded points which enable it to progress, return to learn again, or remain static because it just hasn't got the message at all. In very rare cases it will go back, but it cannot be destroyed. So you could say that hell is going back to your world, and you could say that heaven is moving on.

You say that Jesus was right when he said that if man believed in him, that man would have eternal life, and you have explained why. I assume you do not mean that man would become immortal - but you have already said that souls don't die, so in that respect our souls live forever anyway, whether we believe in Jesus or not.

You will only have eternal life if you progress. To do this you have to know and experience the laws and lessons of spiritual learning which is itself perpetual. If you believe in Jesus, who was a prophet of spirituality, then you will understand spirituality and have the desire to achieve eternal life. You will not be immortal for you still have to learn and still learn, but you will be on the path of eternal life. Those who do not believe or turn away from the prophet and his words are doomed to fight

271

time and lessons until they take the first step on the ladder of understanding.

Could my religious upbringing be partially to blame for the conflict with my physical and spiritual self?

Quite definitely. At an impressionable age you were given a set of rules of the church which in many ways were in conflict with the very essence of spirituality. Any church is materialistic and demands a lot from its followers. Spirituality is pure love which has no strings or rules. The churches of your world all go back to spirituality but have been changed by man, to suit man. They instil a fear of the devil, in doing wrong, in confessing sins and then being able to do that sin again. Spirituality is a continual path of learning. Examples of tests are shown to you in many ways. I say to you that a beggar on your streets, a poor man with no worldly wealth who never goes to church, is richer in spirituality than any of your cardinals or bishops. Yes it did affect you, but now you must see for yourself the right and wrong of the situation. Do not live by past values. They are the past. Learn and move on.

I have read recently about the theory that there was no historical Jesus, that the stories in the New Testament were originally simply allegories used by a mystery school to explain or help explore our own divinity. These stories were misunderstood and later interpreted to be historical. What is the truth?

Jesus was merely a prophet. He was one of many. There was no difference to him than many of the prophets in your world today, although he was a high spirit. But he made an impression on the people of your world at the time, and as such was remembered. Unfortunately the religions, or followings of the day made them more than they were, his words that is. But yes, to say that it was a group trying to find out more about their own divinity was also perhaps true, because it made people look more to the laws of karma, the world of spirituality and what it means to man himself. But no, it was not merely for that purpose.

Always there have been people trying to explain to others about spirit and the world beyond that which you now live.

You must try and imagine the times in which Jesus lived and the mentality of the people at that time. Most were uneducated and lived by very simple terms. They were quite spiritual in that they lived by natural laws of the best way to behave that actually stemmed from the spiritual laws, although they did not realize this. Many people were in fear of the laws of the land and those who ruled and they would do anything not to offend them. They did not question what miracles they saw as you do today and this was good. But I say to you that because of this fact the people were easier to control by the persecutors and by the time that the bible was started many years later, the people could not read what had been written and even if they had there was no way that they would have questioned its contents. Jesus did have his friends and followers, the disciples, and he worked closely with them as they learnt also how to teach about spirituality and the power of the Holy Spirit. But as people are, some of the disciples were true to him and some were not. There were many more than twelve but these were the main ones. The people were taught by teaching and by their seeing various healings and miracles. This was the only way.

When Jesus was killed it was simply the only way to get rid of a person who was trying to set down the church with tales of his spirituality. But as you know it is the same today in your world. People choose not to believe and they get angry when anyone questions that which is written in the name of religion. Jesus said many profound statements about spirituality, especially when he was to be killed and if you read these you will see exactly what he meant in relation to the lessons I have given to you. Use your own intelligence to do this and then ask me again the questions you do not understand.

There are many figures of worship from various cultures and religions, so how can it be that they have so many different beliefs and teachings, all of them believing they are correct?

There were and are many prophets. Each follower or religion, stemming from the words of each prophet, has its followers believing that the words of that particular prophet were true, as was no other. This is far from the case. All the original words of the prophets were the same. But unfortunately some prophets were not clear in their message and some listening did not understand the words. The words of the disciples of Jesus are a good example. Read all of them and compare the differences of their accounts of the same words, the same parables or the same miracles of healing. They are not the same. Man has a brain and a fantasy for weaving and altering the truth to make it sound more attractive. That is all.

The code we are asked to live by is all about love and tolerance, is this the same as the Ten Commandments?

The laws of spirituality are much deeper than just these two aspects. A law covers every aspect of your lives as I have tried to explain to you all in so many ways. The Ten Commandments were ten items of these laws that Moses gave to the people of his times to try and make them see that they must live with spirit and lead lives that reflected that. The people were simple and so therefore were the laws. They are very basic and understandable. But that does not mean to say that there are not many, many more. But love is the key to all things. The various churches all required different aspects of importance from their followers. They focus on very many different things for many reasons which have nothing at all to do with spirituality. So I say to you whilst observing various religions do not take any of them as being true, for they are not. The only true laws are those of spirit. The churches all have their purpose to make people believe in the overall power of spirit or God as they call it, but the churches will one day crumble and be no more. There will be no need. But this will not happen until people themselves find within their hearts the true belief of spirit.

Am I right in believing in one Holy Spirit? Therefore all terrorists who want to die in the Holy War will in fact go home to the same paradise as everyone on this planet?

Firstly it is not paradise. It is the level of spiritual consciousness above where you are now. Your wrong doings must be analyzed and you must learn what you have done wrong. Yes there is only one level where all spirits from your world return. To go to another level you would have to be that much more spiritually evolved and that does not happen in your world to that greater degree. So the Muslims return here also. You are all the same in that respect.

Is Christmas or any other religious occasion a more spiritual time?

That is the time of year when all normality has gone and it would appear that many people have false values as to the season of goodwill. This season is not what it appears. If man was good to man on a daily basis, then this season would not be necessary. The celebration of Jesus' birth is good in one way and bad in another. The celebration is now nothing to do with spirituality. That is something which is gone. People think that if they are good and understand another person because it is Christmas, then this is good. I will say to you that it is worse to be good for only a short time than it is never to be good. The meaning is just the same. If you are good to each other each and every day, this is good. If you are bad or indifferent most days and good on one, it is bad altogether. There is no difference. So think as you watch, and watch as you think. And see as you watch and hear as you listen to the merriment and the rejoicing. But of what do they rejoice? Of only themselves and their vanity, I am afraid. The poor man is not rejoicing. He does not need to rejoice. He is with himself every day. This is all that is needed.

Many religions believe that if we have not lived good lives we can slip into a pit of hell when we pass over. Is this true?

Just look at the basic principles of these beliefs and you will see that they mention, with variations of their own beliefs, that the soul leaves the body at death and goes to the next plane of existence and then higher if it strives to do so.

Chapter Fifteen

Fairies, Angels & Demons

"For all things that are good you would expect
there to be opposites"

Tell us about fairies?

Fairies come to help you. They are spirits. I have told you
that your guides are with you and that others come in to help
for various purposes when required. Your main guide is with
you all the time. There may be one or two secondary guides,
who may or may not change during the course of your life.
Then there are the fairies. They are always there when required.
They are helpers. The little helpers of the guides would be a
good description. They do little helpful things. They are guides
in training. You have to learn to become a guide. They are not
without learning in the ways of karma and spirituality. Imagine
a spirit who was allowed to be your guide, a helpful presence
through your life on earth, not being experienced and knowing
all the answers. They would not be very good at assisting you
would they? These guides have to have training too, if that is
the right description. So they start way back as fairies and learn.
Fairies are not always with you; they come and go as required.

There are many around you. They gather and they observe whilst they help. I hope this is the answer that is clear in your understanding.

Why do some people have angels for guides and some don't?

Mostly you have angels at times of trouble. Always an angel will try and help you. However, some people on your earth are higher in levels than others and for this reason a high angel or guide will be with them at specific times.

Do leprechauns exist and what are they?

Of course they do. So do fairies and elves and imps and all sorts of little people. The folklore of various countries and areas call them different names but basically they are little spirits, usually of children in last lives. However they are fairly mature spirits and are guides in training. To do so they have to mix with the people to see how they live and to observe them. They are allowed to visit earth to do this instead of observing them from the spiritual plain. These little people are spirits. As such they are nothing of substance. They are a puff of smoke, a curl of fog, a vision that is not there. It is the person who will put them in a category of their own imagination. No two people will see a leprechaun or a fairy at the same time. Only one person per imp at any one time.

Are leprechauns/fairies/elves the same type of entity but just with different names? What is their purpose? Do they come into our lives very often?

Yes they are the same thing and their job is to help you spiritually. Most often when you are young you will see this type of spirit and they will comfort you and give you pleasure so that you are happy. They are playful and full of love and this is what a young child wants to see. The children are more connected to spirit anyway, as you know. It is only as they grow that their parents and other adults persuade them that to see fairies is silly and train them not to do this thing. It is sad.

When I was small I had an imaginary friend; was it a spirit I was connecting with or was it my imagination?

Yes a spirit. You must remember that all children from birth will see spirit. They get a lot of comfort in their early years by having this friend. Some see many things that are spirit and some see one and make it their own for many years. Sometimes it is their own main guide, sometimes it is another guide who is there to guide them through the early years. One day the friend leaves and the child cries for a while. Sometimes the friend will appear to visit less and less until the child sees nothing at all. No it was not your imagination, it was real. Or should I say spirit.

I know it seems a silly question but do fairies and pixies exist?

In your minds, yes. In reality they are spirits. To talk to fairies is to talk to spirit. The same with any fantasy form. You have to have a communication person when you are small, and the spirits talking to a child will take on a form, usually something that is pleasing to a child, like a beautiful fairy. The connection to these forms is remembered as you grow older but by then you feel it is silly, as you said, so you refuse to admit that they are in fact real.

Please explain about angels.

These are specific messengers from the high spirits. They perform miracles and are sent to deal with problems of a serious nature. They herald and they prophesize. They work with your guide when you are distressed. Angels touch you with spirit. Just as in biblical times the people could identify with angels and a god. Many had seen angels or spirits when they meditated and their culture had told them that there was a god or type of god. So I hope that you now understand an angel. All your guides, to have reached that level of progression, could be called angels whether they are male or female in their last life. A spirit who returned home with his last life as say a burly warrior could manifest to you as a cherub type angel, because that is what he thought you needed to see. So I know that you are again confused and tired and this is not something which is easily going to go away quickly. It is difficult but it must be for a reason and a time. Do not despair.

Are angels male or female?

Spirit does not ever have a gender. Sometimes spirit will take on a name or description of one of their past lives in order to identify themselves. Sometimes one of you will give the spirit a name or imagine a gender. But we definitely do not have them. Therefore angels do not have gender either.

But our guides touch us with spirit do they not?

Yes, but your guides are with you all the time and teach you and help you on a daily basis. When things get really bad, then you may be sent an angel to clarify a point or touch you with spirit when you are in a time of suffering. They touch too your guide. He takes strength too from angels. I am taught by angels. Angels are my guides, if you understand.

What is the purpose of angels?

They are spirits of course. They are very highly evolved spirits. I could have been an angel but I chose not to be. Spirits have to have reached a certain level to be an angel. Angels are also guides, but guides are not necessarily angels. Visions of angels are not always the same. Sometimes they manifest themselves as small children or cherubs. Spirits that spent their last existences on earth briefly and passed over as small children will take on the purpose of showing themselves as angels, as will very highly spiritually evolved souls who wish to heal or be guardians to people generally. Sometimes they are such only for a brief time. But all angels are very highly achieved souls. Do you see them? Not maybe now, but you did as a child as most children do. They are always around you at certain times of trouble or when you need them as guides or just guardian helpers.

Tell us about angels' wings. Do they really have wings or is this an earthly concept?

Angels have no form. They are spirit. They are not people. Many years ago your artists painted angels with wings and the concept that they flew. They were beautiful and they were also like butterflies. They drew them as ladies with wings. Beautiful and ethereal. So their wings are purely man-made and not real. Angels are spirit. Spirit has no form.

Are there such things as "national" guardian angels such as one angel who would guard a country or city?

This is a difficult question because I have to make it clear so that you understand my answer. Spirit, as you know, is not a person and is in fact part of a whole which we will also call spirit in its collective state too. Now if spirit is a whole which is made up of lots of spirits then there are in fact many spirits within that whole that we could say work together. More like a cloud of spirits over a particular place to help. On the other hand we have individual spirits which act as spirit guides or angels, who work one to one with their partner on earth. Not joined partners but soul mates all the same. One in the world of spirituality and one on earth. Never any other way. So if I said to you that for all people in a city there is a one to one with their guide, or guides if they need more at any particular time and that a mass of spirit is connected to floating cloud-like over and through a troubled city that may perhaps enable you to see what happens. One spirit would not take over a mass of people. We are good but not that good. Our elders or higher spirits would be helping and in charge if you like, but not on their own.

What is the difference between our spirit guides and an angel?

All angels can be spirit guides but not all guides can be angels. I would not say to you that angels are messengers of God but more that they are on a higher vibrational plane than most of us. I am a higher level guide but there are higher level angels, who would work in the same way. I am on the next level of existence although I do travel backwards and forwards to the next level again. Angels on the other hand are on the next level again but choose to spend some time on our level of existence. By that I mean the one that you came from and will return to also. The angels are higher spirits or guides. They are special helpers. Rarely are they main guides. They are helper guides who come in for specific purposes.

We hear of babies dying young in our world and becoming angels. Is this true?

Babies that die young are usually a spirit entity which is nearing its time of graduation, so to speak. They need only a few points to proceed to a higher level. So the spirit will choose a short journey in your world, just to complete its education so that it can pass the final test. It may not need much to experience in your world to do this. Sometimes a spirit will choose much suffering in your world rather than many idyllic lives without much learning or reward of progression within this level of spirituality. So the baby is sick or ill treated or has a short life and then dies so much the richer in spirit. Now you will understand that the spirit which has taken this route is of course a spirit entity that is advanced to completion in this level of consciousness and ready to move on to the next level of consciousness. So the spirit leaves the body of the baby and comes home. It has nearly graduated. But it is not so much that the spirit leaves this sphere and steps into another. There is no beginning and no end and no distinct groups in between. But of course there are groups in between. It is difficult for you to understand. So let us look at the transition between one level of spirituality and the next, which is as I have said, continuous. The spirits who are graduated and no longer babies come back to us and become angels. They are wise in their learning and their spirituality. They are the highest in the spirit level over life on earth and the spirits who act as guides. Those spirits who act as guides have not completed their education. They too still learn. As with myself I was not quite ready to move on. I had to learn one more aspect, that of patience and understanding. So I chose not to return to earth to learn that lesson, but to teach from this side instead. So myself as a guide to Aleisha also has an angel only when really necessary. That angel may have been the spirit of a baby who died having completed all the lessons with flying colours and was ready to move on. During the transition to the next level the spirit became an angel.

What is an arch angel?

Man's description of a chief angel.

Do we have guardian angels?

This is man's description of a guide, usually a main guide. As spirits become angels when they evolve high enough in our spectrum, then angels too can help main guides.

Can angels reincarnate back onto the earth or do they go onto another plane?

They can go back to your world and live in a human form if it is their purpose to do so for a specific reason. In your world you could call them living angels as was the question you didn't ask me. But mostly angels are highly evolved spirits and therefore the majority move on without returning. But some have specific jobs to do with your people and it takes a spirit that is mature to do so. If I had come back to your world in a life I would have been an angel.

You recently said that an abused person we know who passed away recently was now an angel. Do you mean that she has progressed spiritually to being an angel or was that just a metaphorical description?

The more that a person genuinely suffers in their life on earth and even against all odds seems to be able to overcome those difficulties and still love their enemies shows that they have great spiritual understanding. She only suffered with her health in the way that she did because she was there being so as a test for her family and for those around her. It was a planned existence, for herself and her persecutors. As such she was rewarded because of her spiritual understanding and the way she acted. She had already risen to a higher mature spirit because of things before which were enriched by the trials of that last life. So yes she is an angel.

Please explain what those termed earth angels are and how do you know if you come across one?

I am not sure what you are referring to because this is not a spiritual term. However we will presume that you mean angels within your lives on earth. There are many amongst you who do such a lot for other people that you could call them angels. They are high spirits and have the aura of near perfection in love and humility. They are angels. Also there are guides which may be called angels because they help you. You could say for example that a guide who lives a life with you could be classed as an earth angel whereas ones who reside on the spiritual plane are 'heavenly' angels, although that terminology is not quite correct.

A well known psychic often mentions 'light workers'. Are these souls the same as earth angels?

No they are not. She is referring to the 'workers' who assist mediums in connecting with spirit entities who want to speak to others in your world. The connection between the medium and the spirit world which has the presence of light will often be known as the spirit of the light workers. They assist the spirits in the spirit world and the medium or people in your world.

If all spirits are good, then what is a demon?

A demon is nothing more than a terminology of something that is man-made. The world of spirit is pure love and although many of your students are still learning, there is nothing in the spirit world to be called a demon. But religions in your world have invented this term to describe an evil or bad spirit. There is no such thing.

If we do wrong in this life, do demons punish us either here or when we return home?

The other thing is to be more explicit about good and evil. Some wonder if evil can reach them. There is no such thing as evil but there are some baby spirits who will act in unpleasant ways or be harmful to people because they are still learning and know no better. Let us call them small children who like to play rough. In your world they are demons, here they are nothing more than new spirits. There is such a thing as evil repercussions from other sources on your world but you have to be receptive to let them affect you. As you observe certain and most situations that you are faced with on a daily basis, it is essential that you look on them as an observer and not as a participant.

What is voodoo and if you accept it will bad things happen?

It stems from ancient people. In days gone by people would sing chants or give out spells and they believed that these things would happen. I have told you many times that if you want and believe something badly enough then this will happen. However I do not let you want bad things to happen. If you ask for bad things to happen they won't. But the reciprocant of the evil deeds does not know that spirit will not let this happen. So the person is afraid and in being so will believe that this thing is happening to them. That is all.

If there are no demons why do we have to protect ourselves, say when giving healing?

There are spirit entities which are raised or mature and there are those which are new or young. When you open yourselves up to a channel, be it for healing or for clairvoyance, then you could be open to allowing the young spirits to have their say. You will see this lots with so called mediums. The young spirits are lively and not very accurate. Their vibrations are not too good. So you say to yourself, I am a mature spirit, I want to do this work in the best way possible, so I do not want interference from other spirits, even though they may be just playful. That is why you protect yourselves.

A person I know claims to be clairvoyant, seeing lower energy entities, from what she describes as the dark side, further warning me to be aware of them also. What truth if anything does she speak or in fact connect to any lower energy entities?

This person has very little gift. She is playing at pretending to be what she is not. If I say to you that to be a true gifted and ordained medium you will connect to spirit and all its laws, wisdom and visions, to mention just a few aspects. In doing this you will see what is good in the evolution of spirit entities and what is bad about their deeds, which could be interpreted as the dark side of the lessons, but I prefer not to mention this in the same context. You know that all things spiritual are the essence of love and all its facets. Dark sides and evil are not within that realm. So how can darkness and evil be in any way part of spirituality? I will say to you that evil and darkness are in your minds only. There is no such thing as hell but I will not say that evil is perhaps in the same context, for man does evil things to man the world over. It is perhaps this which she chooses to like to be a part of. I will not let you, any of you, come to the same conclusions. If a person says to you that they feel darkness and gloom or evil, then tell them in return, that they have the choice to dwell in the house of darkness. Even though they stand at the door and welcome you in to join them, you need not be any part of it. You are in the essence of spirit and in that light and love you choose to develop and evolve. For them to like the dark side and all the visions they can muster is their choice and certainly will not result in any way in their progressing as is desired.

Why do we need to protect ourselves from others?

From whom are you asking for protection? I have told you many times that there are vibrations from people and individual persons which could affect your own karma if you are not aware of what is happening. In other words if you let others affect you with their own persona then they will. If you choose to not let this thing happen then it will not. In other words you ask for protection and you will receive it. But in fact what you are doing is saying that you are aware that the other person or persons are giving off this aura that you do not want and you see this thing. Know that it is good that you see this thing. For you are then aware which is the ultimate of all things of perception. You know it is there and you wish not to have it yourself. So you ask for protection from this thing only. You cannot meet a person who you perceive to be evil in your words and say that they can harm you. They cannot in fact harm your spirit unless you choose to let them do so. If you glue yourself to your beliefs and your protection from spirit then it will not happen. You are aware of spirit, that is all.

Can there be bad things that are sent through spirit to those people like us who put themselves open to this happening?

You ask about a virus that you have heard is in the very air around you and from some aspect of the spirit world. I would say to you that why do you think that this thing would happen? If God is love and so are all things spiritual why would we want to affect you with this for no reason? I have told you many times that for all things that happen in your life there is a reason. Either you have chosen to experience this thing, this aspect before you returned to your life on earth, or it is a result of your own cause and effect at the time. The second aspect can be changed, not the first. The effect of your cause cannot be anything sent from spirit as respect to a virus. You would not have all chosen a virus to strike you. I am presuming that you are referring to a virus which is to put you against spirituality. No this thing is a subject of someone's imagination that is all and it has spread. For the spread of the evil word is greater than the spread of the good word.

Is it true that people can be possessed by demons?

Your worldly concept of demons is nothing at all like the reality, for they are nothing more than what is in your mind and imagination. For all things that are good, you would expect there to be an opposite. Of course we should look at them that way. But if I said to you that your guides are purer in spirit than yourselves, which you know, then how could something spiritual be also bad? There is no bad force from which these things come with regard to a spiritual plane of existence. However I would say that there are demons which live in the minds of man. They are part of stories and games and films, but they are nothing to do with a spiritual existence. If you look at men who are perhaps in no way spiritually evolved to the level of the rest of mankind as a whole, the newer spirits, then you may say that they are different. They will act in a more inhumane way because they are not themselves spiritually aware or evolved. They may do horrors to mankind and as such will be classed as possessed with demons who make them do these things. That is all. Mentally sick people are often said to be with demons but it is the illness of their mind that makes their imagination and reasoning concoct these things. Self inflicted substances such as excess alcohol or drugs will produce hallucinations and strange demon like behaviour too.

Can a bad spirit entity that has passed over attach themselves to someone as a demon?

They can visit you, sometimes often in the early days, but to say they attach themselves to you would mean in a sinister way. That would not happen.

As a medium, channel or healer, how can we protect ourselves and why?

The action of curling a smoke screen of white light around you is symbolic in many ways. I will try and explain. Firstly it makes you believe that spirit is around you. For a thing that you envisage, you then make a reality. Spirit is with you purely because you made it encircle you. Next you must have the protection of spirit in this way. I am not saying that there are evil spirits out there which would harm you, but there are peoples' vibrations which you will not necessarily want to inhibit you whilst you are open to spirit. There are also lost souls which may be roaming and these must not influence you in any way either. So it is not spirit only that you need to be with you, or you need protection from, but you need to be in harmony with spirit too. This surrounding yourself with white light, which is in fact spirit, will help you with your meditation and make you more attuned with spirit too.

A person who sat in a development circle got frightened away because of the fear of being told she had to protect herself. Does this happen to many people?

I must say that the explanation that she was given at the time was frightening to her and this is the cause of her fear. If the emphasis had not been on the 'protection' she would have lightly taken it as not being harmful to her. She could of course have not protected herself with the white light and she would not have been harmed in any way. She may not have had a good session with her spiritual learning though, because the possibility, not the probability, may have happened that a lost soul may have been present. This is rare. It is like you buying an insurance policy for something that could happen but is unlikely. It is rare this will happen, but you do the white light thing all the same.

What is a lost soul?

All spirits are souls, it is just another name. When in a body the spirit is called the soul of the body. When a spirit leaves a body it returns home to this plane of existence. It is the choice of the spirit entity and in the majority of cases this will happen. However, when the spirit entity is not mature it may happen that the spirit will try and choose not to come home. To play with its freedom in roaming. Many times too it could be from a violent or unexpected death. The spirit is still aware that it has died but it tries to cling to the earth. In this case the spirit may try and interfere with the judgement of people on earth. It is very superficial and they do not do any danger, in most cases, but it is an irritant and frightening all the same to you people. So the lost souls as you call them, may see your group and want to participate in some way with the happenings. If you are an open channel then the soul may hinder (not harm) the proceedings. I say to you to protect yourselves from this hindrance by encircling yourself with a white light. This is spiritual protection. The lost soul will see the white light and be deterred. It will move away and try and have fun somewhere else.

Sometimes I get really strange and strong bodily feelings like being struck by lightning. These frighten me. Are they demons?

For your occurrence I will say this to you. Firstly I ask you not to be frightened when this happens. It is merely spirit trying to attract your attention. When you rest in bed, before you sleep this is the time when you are in fact most receptive. Another time is when you first wake in the morning. So let us look at you resting in bed and spirit will come to you by giving you as you say a bolt of electricity-like feeling that goes from the point of touch so to speak through your body and out at your feet, say. It is the same as a healing touch but in that instance spirit wishes to be recognized so let us say taps you hard to make you recognize that your guide is there. It happens when you are in need or progressing to need contact as has happened recently. What you must do is relax and get used to it. It is a great gift. Talk to your guide and say, for example, I am glad you are here please help me with this problem or tell me why this is happening or please be with me or whatever you wish. At other times pain or discomfort can be nothing more than a thought process of your mind.

The bible implies that when Satan, who was supposed to be the very highest angel, rebelled against God, he took a large number of the angels with him in rebellion. When their rebellion failed, they were cast out of heaven and they made

hell and I presume demons too. What are your thoughts on this one?

This is strange story or fiction. All spirits or souls as you may call them, were sent out from God in his own image to perfect themselves and return to their source, God. It is the instinct of all spirits therefore to be perfection. There is no mind game or one-upmanship in the spiritual world. No spirit wants to become other than like their own higher spirits. It is only in your worlds that you have the tests that this scenario would fall into. Who wants to be king? Is there a battle of supremacy? I think not. That is a manly thing. You must try and understand that if spirit is pure then demons are the opposite. Demon type spirits, if we can call them that, could return to earth or worlds many times to perfect their 'rebelliousness' but all the time God would love them as his naughty children. However, I would point out that it is the living of lives that they have the choice in how they behave. Once they return to the world of spirit they are encompassed with all the other spirits and with love. It just doesn't happen here.

I have read the theory from some religious people that many grossly perverted sexual practices, such as sadomasochism and pedophilia (a sexual preference for children), have demonic roots. Also schizophrenia can be a mental disease, but it can also be caused by demon possession. If it is not demonic possession what is it?

These are merely extreme tests. Man always has the knowledge of the truth in his own spiritual learning to date and has the choice whether to succumb to these actions resulting from temptation. If the action is said to take place as a mental disorder, then this is the same with other illnesses and may have been sent for an extreme lesson. For all illnesses there is help. The person has to recognise it and ask for help. If they don't then are they not agreeing to having it? When you return to your world you will be presented by many temptations and it is through your own spiritual learning that you know how to deal with them. In extreme cases as you mention it could be said that these are evil or with demon like behaviour patterns, and to this I agree they are depravity of the spirit. But always life is a choice. You choose how you behave. You know right from wrong in major things and in all those which you have already learnt as part of your lessons. These acts could be told to a very baby spirit and they would know they were against the laws of karma. But if it is man's choice to behave that way that is all it is. There is no demon taking over them and telling them it is a correct way to live out their fantasies. Because fantasies is all they are.

Chapter Sixteen

Suicide & Euthanasia

"Your time of death is pre-set and should never be changed"

I have decided to end my life. Tell me why you think this is wrong?
I will give you many words tonight with the teachings of spirituality and you must read them over and over again until you are quite clear as to my meanings. I will try and explain in simple terms. Not because you would not understand in another way, but merely because the whole aspect of spirituality is pure simplicity itself and does not need long words or incomprehensible data. Firstly you must see yourself as spirit and not a body. Spirituality is the energy, which fires your body to live. It is not your mind, your brain or your heart, it is something which is truly your very being and has seen you through many lives on earth and long existences on the next plane of existence which you call home. I will explain quickly the process so that you can be known to it again. Your spirit is just that, it has evolved over a long, long time. But we have no time so we need to talk more on that subject. If you can imagine you as a spirit only, and think that you have

292

progressed on this plane of existence from an ant to a human through many processes of evolution. I am not saying you were an ant, probably not, but the process is of learning and moving higher in your spiritual path. With each existence you learn. The whole purpose is to move higher and higher. As you achieve graduation in each lesson, you gain points so to speak when you return home to this level of consciousness. You then evaluate your progress and decide what you want to learn or experience next. So you see you map out your own lessons before you return to the world of matter. Let us look, then, at the people on your world as you suffer greatly and ask yourself why this is happening. You are all not terrible people and you do not want these things. Why is it that you suffer more than a rich healthy person who appears to have no worries in the world and has everything that they desire? The reason is merely this. For the suffering, you achieve the learning and its rewards. It doesn't matter whether you choose humiliation, frustration, ill health and pain or any other aspect, they all have to be experienced and learnt. Maybe you choose to have a large concentrated lot of misfortune this life so that you could move on more quickly. Why do you not think that say a child who is born with a severe disability, is in great pain and dies a year or so later. What is the purpose you ask yourself? Why should that tiny child suffer in that way for no reason? There is a reason, there has to be a reason. The spirit had chosen to be a child to experience the most terrible of lessons, hard, intense and quick so that it could return home the richer and with more mature spirituality so that it could move on. Now let us look at the progression of spirit through the various levels of consciousness. There are various levels and within each there are other segments or levels. There is no start and no end. The progression is continuous. But the ultimate is to move higher because that is supreme and what you have now is mere dust under your feet; it is of no importance. If you worry about today and its problems I will say to you, do not waste your time for it is nothing.

Please tell us your views on suicide?

What a difficult question that is to all of the people in your world. I must say to you that suicide is wrong in the eyes of spirit. The taking of your own life because you cannot face the lessons and tests which you had planned for your life on earth is not a solution which is acceptable to spirit. All of the horrors that you deal with on your earth have been planned and must be worked through. Spirit will choose when you die and this must be obeyed. If you choose to kill your body then you return to this world and the immediate punishment, if you are choosing to progress your spirit, is to return and not only face those problems again in another life and another place, but the problems will be worse because you have slipped back so to speak because you opted out. Do you understand? No one will kill themselves by suicide and then evolve higher in the spirit world without first having to rectify the wrong. It does depend a little on the circumstances. If the body is dying anyway in the very advanced stages, the punishment will not be so severe as someone who just did this thing for effect to see what harm it would do say on their family. The effect of suicide as a cause is generally very upsetting for all who are in the realms of experiencing the death of this person The people who have the effect may have chosen to experience this. It is very complex.

Please explain if a person committed suicide, would they have chosen that form of death?

No they would have chosen the situation and being given the choice in that situation to work through it or to die. They would not know that decision until they had worked through the test. I tell you that your death and the time of your death is ordained or decided before you return to earth. Yes with a person who commits suicide, the death is recorded the same, but remember that the person does not know that, so the test takes place anyway. The spirit will choose the lesson and understand the importance of the lesson, but when it becomes part of a body, it will not remember, so each hurdle in life is a test that the spirit does not know the answer. So I know you will ask, if the person has to make the choice whether to pre-empt death by taking his own life, or to choose to live through it, how can the time of death be pre-set? I say to you that this is so. Maybe, if they do not take their own life, then they will go on to die at another time later, but they may die the next week. If they make the decision, which changes the course of their life, then this will happen and death will occur. The time of death is not known so the time of death cannot be pre-empted. So you ask is a person then not pre-empting death if it is ordained to happen at that time? I will say to you that the time of death in this instance is the test. How will the person deal with their lesson, which brings them despair? That is the lesson. The time of death is not important to the lesson. It is the temptation to take the life and not live on to learn by the lesson that is important.

If a suicide was not ordained, then is it the same for the loved ones who are affected by the suicide? Is that affect also not planned?

Yes that person may have chosen to be in a particular place at a particular time to learn the lesson, of, let us describe it as deep emotional stress. Or maybe of losing a loved one, or being part of a help structure to help others who have lost a loved one. The person you ask about would have chosen the lesson and not necessarily the circumstances of the lesson. The lesson is what they wanted to experience, not the suicide.

You have explained how suicide is never pre-planned and that person's lessons will have to be re-learned. What about suicide bombers who kill others too? How does that affect their victims?

There are many ways to commit suicide. If you do so in a way that kills others too there is no difference. To kill other people by one at a time or many together, there is no difference. If you die with them, the act is the same. For the others to die, their time was right for that to happen for many reasons.

I have had one wrist-slash and three overdoses all in six months; I just feel it is only a matter of time till the next attempt.

Why are you presuming that this will happen again? By saying this you are admitting that there is no hope and the inevitable will happen. Why would this be the case? I do not understand why you would want to leave so much in your world undone. There are many who need you to be strong. Maybe there is a person, who you will not recognize as being in need of your love. I will say to you that love is the essence of all things spiritual. It will overcome all wrongs. For to face an enemy with love instead of hatred will unsteady them and they will not know how to act. They do not expect that kind of behavior and they cannot understand. For love in all things is the utmost of importance. For every living thing has a spirit no matter how low down the scale and at all times you should be aware of giving that thing respect as you would expect yourself from other people. You probably won't get that in today's world, but you should presume it all the same.

If suicide has not been successful, as in my case, who stopped them happening and who kept me alive?

You did.

Do the people who have the effect of a suicide not choose to be part of the effect?

Yes, they all learn.

Why can't I, who have reached rock bottom in this life and am still despairing, choose to kill myself and live further endless easy lives on earth? It is more appealing than anything else at the moment. Or when we die do we get a fleeting glance of something better?

Always the choice is yours. But you have no comprehension living on earth of what else there is in store for you. The other is a million times superior to where you are now. Anyway what's to say that you will have many lives that are peaceful, yet shallow, and you then crave to go on but have lost so much time? It is like a student who quit school and then wants to learn to read when they are old. Look what they have missed.

It is possible for suicide to be acceptable if it is part of a person's pre-ordained plan.

No because it is never pre-ordained. That just does not happen.

Why would we want to choose painful experiences? To learn they are painful? There is no lesson surely – we already know that pain hurts.

I have told you why you wish to experience unpleasant things, it is to learn. From pain you learn. You learn how to cope with it. Why does a baby learn to walk when it keeps falling over and hurting itself? Why doesn't it just sit for the rest of its life? If it doesn't take the step then it can't get hurt. But it must for to walk is to see many more wonderful things. You have to learn in order to move on. You know that physical pain of the body or the mind hurts, but we are talking only of the spiritual development, you will shed your body after only a blink of an eye. Your spirit goes on and on in time that is endless. Your life on earth is so minute in proportion that it is a mere grain of sand. Why not learn and move on?

Why is it that some of us suffer more than say a rich healthy person who has no worries? Why? Is it because they've learnt all their lessons?

No, not exactly. It may be that they decided to return to earth and not have lessons this time. They do not wish to move on. They have decided to rest for a few lives without having to experience and learn. They can do this many times but the end result is that they do not move on. Your world of matter is grey and dismal compared with the alternative to which you strive by learning your lessons. What you have in your world is of little consequence and you will see when you return that the alternative is supreme. You do not want to return to your world, it is a period in your evolvement that you wish to get behind you. But your spirit must mature and in doing so it has to experience bad before the good. But there are some spirits, like yourself, who choose a difficult life in concentrated doses of problems because they in themselves give you more points in one life to move on. The happy rich man gains nothing. His spirit was probably more in infancy and not so evolved.

With regard to a severely disabled baby, a baby is not aware of life, God, meanings etc. A baby can't be suffering the uncertainty of spirituality in its first year – it doesn't have the brain or knowledge. So why does it have to suffer?

Your spirit and its path is not physical. What the brain thinks or the intelligence tells you is not what makes your spirituality more mature. Understanding the concept by using your brain does. But a baby may have a spirituality that is old yet a body that is young. That spirit may have chosen a concentrated lesson on your world for a short space of time. The body and the brain of the baby are not the ones that are learning the lesson. It is the spirit of that body that is having to endure the frustration and the spiritual pain, not the physical pain. The baby will feel the physical pain and be in distress and the spirit will understand and learn. That is all.

Aren't doctors already prescribing medicine knowing that it will result in the death of the patient (e.g. cancer patients)? What is the difference between this and euthanasia?

Doctors will deny that they are prescribing anything other than things to make a terminal ill patient feel less bothered by the illness. Sometimes they have the false belief that they should prolong a life longer than is intended. If doctors left the patient without any help from drugs, then the person may be in a lot of pain and suffering. Whilst this may be their choice, it is also accepted that doctors need to help. So in answer to the question, no doctors should not and usually do not give drugs which by themselves result in a death. They may have to increase the medication as the patient requires pain relief, but that is not intentionally done to kill them before their time. Euthanasia on the other hand is intentional and will result in the person dying before the chosen time and that is why it is not permitted. If the choice of the person as one of their lessons in life was to die because of suffering, however that transpires, then it is wrong for any person to come in and alter that. For the patient to do so is equally as wrong.

What is the difference between withholding a treatment because it is futile and intentionally causing a death through act or omission? Are these not merely semantic differences?

If a person is dying and no drugs are given to prolong that life, then the person will be dying within the time frame that they had intended. If drugs are given to prolong the life, not to just give relief from the pain, then this could be considered to be wrong because it will alter the chosen time of death. But there is always the choice of knowing whether the drugs are given in the hope that the illness or disease will go away because of the treatment, and therefore does not fall into the category of uselessly prolonging the death. It's a fine line to know. To intentionally cause a death is a much more deliberate action and is always that it is pre-empting the chosen time of death.

Does the soul of someone who has committed suicide come back home to the next level by the same route and means as that of someone who has died a regular death?

Yes all spirits enter your world the same way. There is no difference in what they have been or where they are going. When a spirit returns to our plane of existence then the life it lived will be assessed and as a consequence, in this instance of suicide, then the spirit will see very clearly that its actions are not accepted. The penance, if that is a correct word, is that it must return to your world and live a life where it is in a similar circumstance of despair to see whether the lesson is learnt or whether it will take the same easy way out of ending the next life with suicide. It may be weak and inexperienced and it may take many lives before it learns the lesson. But always the choice of how to act is its alone.

Does the method of suicide make any difference to what happens when that person returns?

Unfortunately suicide is suicide there is no difference how it is done. It is still the taking of a life, which is not permitted. However if it is the taking of a life which is going to die anyway such as being in a fire and jumping from a window to escape being burned to death, then that could be seen to be a means to perhaps saving yourself. Every action of every person in every life will be analysed and critiqued so that the spirit entity can learn by what they have or have not done.

Other than being in pain (either emotional or physical), depression or insanity, are there any other reasons for suicide?

It is a choice. Always you have free will. Sometimes situations are presented to see how you will deal with them. Whether you will take the easy route which may be death. Maybe a person has killed others then kills themselves in order not to have to answer to other people for what they have done. But they do not see that the choice is bad because they can never escape a penance.

You have stated that there is never an excuse for suicide, and I once asked you what was the correct course of action if you had the chance to save a life but knew it would cost you your own. I think that you replied that it depended on the circumstances, but ultimately surely in that situation it is the right thing to do to save your own life?

Saving the life of another person and dying the process is not classed as suicide. This is because it is not an act done to purposely kill yourself. The main purpose is for the love or concern of the other person who you think you can help. Your spiritual existence on earth is to love and help people. If you die in the process and it can be seen to have not been premeditated as suicide then this is commendable. But how you interpret the action of saving a life may not be the same as it is seen from spirit if you use the situation to bring about your own death.

While it is back home, does the spirit of someone who has committed suicide stand out from others?

On this plane of existence all spirits are equal because there is no right and wrong and no spirit is in a position of being seen to be different. You may think I contradict myself by saying that our higher spirits will analyse and point out the non spiritual actions which took place in a life. That is only the teacher telling the pupil to see for themselves how differently they could have acted. Then the pupil is sent back into the classroom of earth to be presented with the same test to see if they learnt from their wise teachers and do not repeat the actions again.

If you have a terminal disease, are in a great deal of pain and it is certain that you will die shortly anyway, is it still considered suicide to 'pull the plug' on yourself?

I am afraid yes it is. If you have chosen to suffer before you die then suffer you must. So many of you bemoan your suffering but do not see that it was chosen in many cases to teach you something which is much needed in your spiritual development. You have merely forgotten that this is the case.

If suicide is the wrong thing to do every time, and spirit has the ability to do/be/create anything, why is it simply not so that suicide will never work?

It is the decision of how to act that is in itself free will. You all decide in all circumstances what you want to do. There are laws of Karma, your development, which must be realised and adhered to if you want to become more spiritually enriched. If you don't then you can do what you like and it doesn't matter at all. If you choose to do things, such as suicide, which are contrary to your development ideals then you will still have to face them again and again. Is it not better to see the test of your circumstances for what it is and then face it head on and get it over with in one life?

Chapter Seventeen

Vegetarianism

"Every living creature on your world has a spirit.
It is wrong to break the path of any spirit"

Would living more spiritually, for example, by giving up meat, making time to be closer to nature etc., help us work through our problems?

Of course. Being spiritually attuned is the answer to all things. You cannot ignore the things I say which are important to the laws of spirituality, and expect to still become more spiritually evolved. It just won't happen.

Why is it wrong to eat animals?

So you ask me again about the issue of eating or not eating meat. I will tell you again what I have said before, but perhaps in another way so that more people can understand my words. They are very simple. When there is nothing else to eat, you may eat what you will to stay alive, for that is nature, is it not? But when there are other foods in abundance, why would you kill to feed yourself? That would be taking a life when it is not necessary. There are other things to eat which do not have a spiritual progression. So what I am saying to you is more the being part of killing a creature in order to eat its flesh, more than the actual thing of eating the meat. So I know you will say to me well if the creature is dead anyway how am I doing the wrong thing in eating it? I did not kill the animal. Yes you are right in a way, but things have progressed so in your world that there is supply and demand. If there is no demand, there will be no supply, and directly there will be no breeding of animals for food, or killing them for the demand. It is a long route, but it is necessary that you all understand. There have been many times in years gone by that there was absolutely nothing else to eat to live and survive other than to eat animals. I agree with that, but when other crops and fruit became available, the killing of animals was not right. Not wrong or right, I would say, but without reason, which is perhaps more logical to you. The whole matter is that you now know what I say on the subject so therefore the decision is taken out of your querying when put in a situation where others want you to eat meat. If you did not know, then you could go ahead and spirit would not ask you why you did so. The decision is always yours.

Why should we not eat animals?

Animals have yet to be evolved souls and should be respected as much as man. You would not slaughter or abuse children just because they had not yet developed. Why should animals be treated this way then? They are the same.

What should we eat instead of meat?

I would ask you daily to observe all things. Observe nature and the marvellous bounty it provides not only to yourselves, but to all animals and birds and insects, giving them food for survival. Nature does this to you also. You have at your resources all the necessary elements to keep you healthy and alive. You need no more. Do not inflict suffering on any other spirit entity in any other form of body on your earth. Listen to the words of Ishamcvan and heed them. You will one day glory at the wisdom of what I have taught you.

Is it true that plants scream when they are cut or pulled out of the earth? If so, what is the difference between killing plants or animals?

Plants do not scream when they come out of the earth. That is a myth. Plants in any case are way down the spiritual ladder even from an organism like frog spawn. They are on a different dimension from say a cow. Way too different to be of consequence. But they do not feel or scream anyway.

Can you tell us more about not eating meat?

You have many questions in your mind and you are in conflict with yourself as to my words yesterday about eating the flesh of animals. I cannot always tell you what you want to hear and many times it will be against your former beliefs. It is not good from the view of spirit to eat animals. It is not wrong and it is not right in that you will not be punished for doing so. It is only wrong for your advancement because all lessons which you fail to learn in this life on earth must be experienced again for your reaction to be shown a second or a third or a fourth time or however long it takes. It is up to you. I can only tell you what is acceptable for your own karma, nothing else. These are not necessarily the opinions I would have given during my last life on earth, but they are very definite to the spirituality of my present being. If I tell you something there should be no doubt about my words. They cannot sometimes be right and sometimes be wrong, they are definite. I did say to you yesterday that eating animals was permissible under some special circumstances, but that is only in the case of eating them when you are in dire need of food and there is nothing else. Then it is a one time thing only. Natives of your earth in various parts of the world did this, but they only took what was required to sustain life, nothing more. They did not breed animals in paddocks or corals so that they always had meat. That is not acceptable. The decision is always yours.

**Next we have a quite different question for Ishamcvan
and that is again about killing animals. We need to know
more about your views on this subject please.**

Your group is still not wholly convinced by my teachings, are
they? I must admit that from your perspective it is a difficult pill to
swallow. Well, I will try and explain again. You ask about the fox
which killed twenty chickens and then was killed himself by man.
Was this death justified? In this case, was man permitted to do this
thing? Well I must say to you that I have said many times that you
should not kill animals to eat, but I did not say that you should not
kill animals. There are always exceptions to every rule and I have
already said that it is permitted to kill an animal in order to give you
food to keep you alive. To keep you from starving, that is all. To kill
an animal because it is killing other animals is quite another thing.
It is the natural law of the animal kingdom that animals hunt other
animals in order to survive. Animals only do this for survival. You
will not see an animal kill for any other reason. The fox probably
killed the chickens over a period of time; it did not just kill the
twenty chickens all in one go. The fox was hungry and his natural
instinct was to kill in order to survive. The same as I have told you
that you are permitted to kill to stay alive and eat. So let us look at
this scenario. The chickens were killed shall we say individually over
several days by a fox that was hungry. If the chickens were in their
natural habitat it would be of no consequence because that is the law
of the animal kingdom with regard to survival. Lots of animals eat
other animals in order to survive from the lizard and the ant, to the
alligator and the fish. It is of no consequence to the spirit world that
this happens. But for man, who has decided to farm the chickens to
give food to people who do not necessarily need to eat them, and
has failed to lock them up properly with this purpose in mind, it is
not permissible. The farmer is not letting the animals live by their
own natural laws and then doesn't like it when the fox acts in his
normal way by his normal instincts. So no, it is not permissible by
spirit to do this thing. The same thing would be for a bear that mauls
a person who strays into its territory whilst it is hungry. The bear will
act by instinct of survival so you should not kill that beast either

for using his own natural laws of the animal kingdom. If you are starving you may kill the bear. If you anger the bear you may not kill the bear. What, you ask, if the bear is behaving in a ferocious way for no apparent reason and is causing lots of harm to man by attacking for no reason? I will say to you that there is always a reason. Bears do not have mental breakdowns and act irrationally. That is a condition of man. There is never a reason to kill, other than if you are starving and that aspect is within the laws of karma.

Lots of animals kill for food. Why shouldn't we do so?

Because you are not an animal and can seek out other things to eat that is not a love of flesh. It is the breeding of vast numbers of animals that is wrong. If you eat the animals then you are part of this chain. If you mingle the flesh of an animal into your digestive system you will open yourselves up to lots of problems in your current time when hormones and other man made bacteria is put into the animals so that they are a good consumer product on the conveyor belt in the factory of gluttony.

Man has always eaten meat, probably before recorded time. Why now is it considered wrong?

Centuries ago man did not always have the choice on what to eat. Even now if you are starving and there is absolutely nothing else to eat you can kill and eat an animal. But you must eat every part of it and not be fussy over what you like and throw the rest away. In primitive times man did just this. They never ever stock piled the flesh of the animal. But I say to you this is only permitted and has always only been permitted if you have nothing else to keep you alive.

If animals hunt animals for food and this happens right across the animal kingdom, why cannot man hunt animal for food? What is the difference?

I will say to you that there is a big difference. I have taught you that spirit is on various levels of advancement within its spiritual journey. And those spirits which inhabit animals are not so old or as advanced as those spirits which are in a body such as your own. But at all times must you respect the spirituality of all other things, and you have the knowledge to do this. You are not at the same level as the spirituality of an animal. You have the power of vision if you choose to have it, of intelligence to uncover the secrets of spirituality and the knowledge to either absorb the laws of karma or discard them if you choose. You know that to ignore the laws of karma are not right or wrong. But to do so is not to advance in your spirituality which must be your ultimate goal in all things. But an animal does not have this reason. For an animal to hunt another animal is for this reason. Animals must do this in order to quell their numbers and to live by codes within their own animal kingdom. Spirits in creatures are only there for a short time in each life and the advancement of such spirits, being on a different plane of existence than yourselves, do so in a slightly different way. Now we get to your friend who wants to justify his love of hunting. All things can be justified by the person wanting to do this thing. We have talked about murders or madmen who do atrocities, they all have a justification at the time for their actions, it does not make them right in the laws of spirituality. All things that man does he has a reason or an argument. So for him to hunt and say that this is done within the animal kingdom is not a reason or excuse for the reason I have given. I have told you that the spirituality of all other living things must be respected and you should incur death on no other living thing. As for eating the flesh of the animal that has been killed or hunted, I would say to you that you may do so only if you are starving but for no other reason. If you have food to eat in any other way, then you must not kill. Food is plentiful, there is no need. Why would you choose to eat the meat of an animal if you have other food at your disposal? Why would you kill the spirit that motivates the body of the animal into life for your own gain, because of your love of the taste of his flesh and you like to chew his flesh in your mouth and gnarl his bloody bones with your teeth? I think you must see that this cannot be right. But the choice is yours and when you return to this plane of existence you will know with certainty the wise words of Ishamcvan and you will all remember how I told you that to kill is to not advance in your path of spirituality. You must return to learn your lesson again. You cannot cheat and you cannot make excuses for your greed to yourself. You have the choice.

People who hunt animals usually say it has been done for centuries, so how can it be wrong?

It would be a good day to see that all the lessons of Ishamcvan have been heeded and the world is a good and spiritual place. But I very much doubt this will ever happen in your world. The minority of spiritual people far outweigh those who have plausible explanations for their deeds and I know that if you listened carefully to these explanations, not having had the experience of spirit talking to you, you would probably see no wrong with reasons why man has hunted and destroyed animals in the name of sport or excess food for the tables of the gluttonous people. I know that this is a very controversial subject and we have talked briefly before when I told you that there is no right and wrong on the subject. I still say that.

If we all became vegetarian wouldn't we be overrun with animals?

Not at all. You are not merely eating animals which are plentiful you are doing so with those that have been purposely bred for that purpose. If your farmers had the knowledge that man was not going to eat meat again, ever, then they would not breed the animals in the first place. You do not see man eating animals such as stray dogs or cats which are in abundance and they are not over-running the earth as a result. They are not being bred to be eaten either. There will be a natural evening out of things as there would have been if man had never tampered with the generic production of animal goods.

If there was no more need for meat wouldn't certain animals die out?

No. Animals were not put on your earth for you to eat; they were put there for their spirit, which is on a lower level than yourselves, to experience life. There is a natural law of the animal kingdom which is ruled by their predators. Man should not interfere with that.

There would be no need for farmers if we stopped eating meat.

You would certainly not need so many. Maybe those masters of fattening cows and carving animal flesh into portions for your dinner table could learn another science that is much more beneficial to their fellow man.

Nowhere in the bible does it say that we must not eat meat. Christ ate meat and fish. When the prodigal son returned, it was celebrated by the killing and eating of the fatted calf. Please correct me if I'm wrong, but I don't believe any major religion advocates vegetarianism. Some never eat pork, others beef, but all eat some form of fish.

We must go back to my comments about the various churches and the way that they have manoeuvred spirituality to fit their needs, and not vice versa. You must not look at churches and their prophecies, only as a comparison to the word of spirit. It does not matter that one religion here doesn't eat pork and that one in India does. They are little clubs with their own little idiosyncrasies, that is all. You comment that Jesus ate meat. He did not. He ate fish, but not meat. The bible says that he did, but that is nothing more than something altered over the years. As for the fatted calf, that was a story not a fact. It was a parable of example. In that too there has been some alteration to the original. You say that no religion advocates vegetarianism. Probably not. But what does that tell you? Are you looking at the ways of the various religions in the world which are in fact man-made, or are you looking at spirituality and its laws which are not man-made? There is a vast difference. If the religion said you had to wear orange or blue to be spiritual, would you believe that too? No, of course you would question it. Your logic would tell you that there was no need. It is the same with various religions. Their differences are of no consequence. But with regard to them not being vegetarians, I would say to you that it is the same, for the members of the church in its original state may not have wanted to become vegetarians any more than you do, so invented a bylaw to overcome the word of spirit. It is that simple. To give up eating the spirituality of an animal is not an easy thing to do if you have that in your upbringing. With regard to your own spirituality, if you eat meat and you know that it will harm your progress, then it will do so. If you do not know that fact then it will not.

When this has been a way of life for thousands of years, it is a hard habit to break. I know many vegetarians, but usually they become this for moral or health reasons. I can never see a time when the world becomes vegetarian whilst religion is such an important part of their life. How is it possible that Christ, Buddha, Allah were wrong?

You are correct. Never will there be a time when man does not eat meat of some kind. Eventually when there are no more large animals it will be more difficult, but that will not be for a considerable time. But you say that for moral reasons many give up meat. What is moral if it is not being aware of the fact that you should not take the life of an animal for the pleasure of eating its flesh? Their morals as you call them are in fact spiritually based, are they not? For health reasons these are fewer for unless the animal is diseased it cannot usually harm them. But fortunately, the awareness of many teachings are making people think what is happening to make the actual meat come onto their table. As I have said many times, if you are starving and there is no other alternative, then you can eat meat. In biblical times the choice of food was very few. Many people would have starved if they had not eaten meat. It was probably in the most part the only available food. It is like a hunter in the hills many days away from a village, he has nothing to eat except to kill, say, a rabbit. That is different. Most people in the world choose to eat meat over any other thing, not because there is no alternative, but because they like to indulge in the taste and feel and smell of the cooked flesh of the animal who was killed and bred purely for that purpose. Whether religion has been going forever and does not say this is wrong does in no way mean that it is permissible. It is not.

Jesus fed on fish and gave them to the people?
The people were poor and food was scarce.

In the bible it tells of Jesus saying to the mother of a dead girl whom he had just brought back to life, to bring the child meat to feed on. Why would he say this if eating meat is not allowed by spirit? Was it because nothing else was available?

This is a variation of the truth as I have told you before which often happened with true meanings of incidents involving Jesus and the interpretation of them as was recorded. Firstly the child was not brought back to life, only that her spirit appeared to her family when summoned by Jesus. It would appear because everyone present saw her that she came back to life, but it was only her spirit which appeared in the guise of the child. The other piece of text, that Jesus told her family to bring her meat to sustain her, is not true. I know that you think that I am covering up facts which I do not know, but this is not the case. I am telling you the truth of the incident, nothing more.

Is it ok to eat fish?
Preferably not, because this is a living thing. But I must say to you that a fish is much lower down the scale of spirituality than a mammal. You must not eat animals because they are nearer to you, as are poultry and some birds. But fish are much lower down the scale and eating them is not so important. But you have the decision whether you want to eat these things or not. If you have strong feelings about the spirituality of any living thing, then you must not eat the fish. But if you study the levels of spiritual evolvement then you can see and make your own decision.

You have told us that to eat the meat of an animal when there is plenty of food to eat elsewhere is wrong. Do we not need the nourishment of some meat or fish?

I did not say to you that it was wrong. I said that you should avoid doing so unless you were starving. If you choose to eat the flesh of animals, then it is your decision. It is neither right nor wrong. But always you must respect the spirituality of other living things. To kill and eat an animal when you are not starving is doing this thing and you will have to learn the lesson at another time. Does their flesh give you necessary elements to sustain your body, no, not at a time when you may get these things from other food.

I am wondering about the spirits of animals with regard to killing them for food. You have told us about animals, but what about fish and shellfish? Is it permissible to eat these? Are the spirits in these of a lower advancement than that of animals?

I would say to you that a fish has a spirit entity, which is not so advanced as an animal or a mammal, but it has a spirit all the same. An insect is not so advanced as a fish. A fish is not quite so advanced as a bird, which is below an animal. It is difficult to be exact although what I have said is close. You could eat an insect better than you could eat an animal, but it is better not to eat any living creature unless you have dire need to keep you alive. In modern day living in your world it is unlikely that you will be without all other kinds of food, that you would need to eat animal flesh. You ask, or rather some of your group ask, that with the world population in poverty and dying is not generic farming necessary? Many, many nations do not eat meat at any time and many others live on a basic diet of crops and some have never eaten meat. To feed the dying nations then crops are essential, not meat. Meat is a rich mans food, not a food of the poor. Meat is bred for the tables of the more affluent societies of the world. For a poor man to eat meat would not be good for many reasons. Firstly, crops are cheaper and they are better for the growth of a body. Meat would not be good to digest by starving people.

312

Some of you put forward the argument that man has eaten meat since time began. Yes this is true. It was easy to hunt and meat has always been enjoyed. Some nations have hunted meat only for keeping themselves alive when crops were not growing in the winter. I have told you that if you are starving that it is permissible if there is absolutely nothing else. Then you ask me why is this so? Is it not better for us in a body to die rather than eat flesh which is forbidden? No it is not. Your soul is superior to that of an animal and although you must respect the soul of the animal at all times, if you are starving then it is permissible. This is the law of nature and survival. Survival is different to pleasurable eating.

Do we have your permission to eat shellfish?

You have this if this is what you wish. If you do not really need this then I withdraw my permission. The choice is yours. Shellfish is not a priority to give up. Red meat is a priority. Chicken is more important than shellfish and not as important as red meat. That is important because the soul of a large animal is so much more advanced than that of a chicken which is 100 times more advanced than a prawn. Do you understand? I think you do.

What are the consequences if fish or shellfish are caught for food?

I have never said to you that you should or should not do one thing, only that the laws of karma, your karma and my karma as laid down by higher spirits, say that all things have a perspective in life - some are good and can give you advancement and some do the reverse. It is up to you which you choose, but in the end all must be experienced and learnt, you cannot escape. So I say to you, what are the laws of karma and you make your own decision. In this case, I will say to you that the spirituality of a fish is not as advanced as the spirituality of a chicken who is not as advanced as a cow. A prawn is not as advanced as a fish, but both have a spiritual essence all the same. However, the lower down the scale of advancement the more is expected the failure rate so to speak. But I have told you only to eat a living thing if you are starving with no other alternative, have I not, as being the law. All that are living are with spirit. But you make the choice. The prawn is small, the cow is huge, with spirit, I mean.

How do you feel about eating fish? Is it as bad?

You know my rules. It is your choice. Are you starving? Can you find no other food? No you are not. The choice is always yours.

If I eat fish occasionally, what would you say?

I say, you know my words. You must learn another time if you do not wish to heed them now.

We would like to know about small farmers in poor countries who are self sufficient on the land and if the killing of a pig, or chickens, or other animals that they have raised is wrong in your eyes if they are eaten by the family.

In this question we will presume that the crops are grown for sale and eaten, and the animal that is killed is only for food. This is not quite the same thing as breeding and killing animals in large numbers so that there is a surplus always of meat for the cooking and feeding of people who are not hungry anyway. I am not saying that the killing of a single animal is right if it is eaten, more that it is different. You could say that that family too could eat crops and vegetables and fruit so why eat meat, but it is well known by country folk that this diet alone makes them ill, so they supplement by eating meat because they have no other means to do so. They eat meat to indirectly keep their family alive, but they do so in such minimalist dimensions that it is somehow permitted. To kill a pig and a few chickens every year is not the same as eating a pound of meat a day. Have I been clear?

What about the use of animal parts for shoes and wearing items. Is it correct if you are not allowed to eat meat?

I did not say that you are not allowed to eat meat, neither will I say that you must not wear the skins of animals, but I did say to you that if you ate an animal and knew that it was not the wish of spirit that you do this thing, then you would have to justify this action to yourself when you return home. No one will punish you. It is the development of your own karma that is affected, nothing else. So to wear the skins of animals is that wrong? I would say to you that mostly animals are killed for their flesh, not their skins, so that the skins and their by-products are a secondary item and not the reason that the animal is killed. Mostly the reason the animal is killed is for its flesh, for man to eat. So is it wrong to use the by-product? In fact it is wrong if the animal is killed for the skin or if the skin is used primarily. It is a fine line to say that you should not use this skin, but it is also fair to say that if the skin is thrown away then you did not crave for the skin in the first place. I must say to you it is your decision as with all things. If you think that the killing of an animal is wrong for any reason, then you must not use any part of it unless you are cold and need the warmth of the skin and there is no alternative. But to use the skin of an animal that is already dead for another reason is not so serious as using the flesh of the animal where this flesh also enters your body and your spirit is affected as the fleshes merge. You must be the judge. I can only give you guidelines, not the answers, otherwise you would return to this plane with most of your lessons having had the answers. You must trust your own conscious. I know that you are concerned that if you are asked this question from another person, as to what will you say? I will say to you that you must answer: the animal who gave this skin did not wish to die. Man killed this animal for his own purpose of greed when it was not necessary. It is your choice if you use the animal's skin for adornment of your body. If you need this skin to keep you warm because you are cold and have nothing else, then you are not adorning your body.

You said previously that if a person uses the skin of an animal, which is already dead for another reason, such as leather shoes, it is not as important as when the flesh enters your body and merges with yourself.

It is merely that if you eat the flesh of an animal you were directly responsible for its death because that is the reason it died.

The eating of the flesh does not harm your body, but it harms your spirituality because of the deed. You should not destroy spirit. If another man kills the animal for his food or the food of others, which is usually the prime reason for killing, then I said that to take the skin of that animal who is already dead and use it for making shoes or other item is not as bad. It is not good that this is done, but it is not as bad as being a contributory factor in the death of the animal. And as before, I say to you that any part of the body, and I repeat the body, of the animal or human used to help your doctors to prolong life is not going to affect the person. The spirit has left the body and the body is garbage. But to stop the spiritual path of a person or animal is so very wrong and this is what happens when any living thing is killed. Then you will ask me whether that animal chose to die at that time. Yes it did. It was part of the test of man to see if man would do so. So the dead animal was part of the failure of the lesson of man. If man looked at the animal and said no I understand the lesson and will not kill this thing then it is written that the animal will not die. Spirit does not predict the actions of man although of course it sees the same. There has to be paths and there has to be free will to man to make the choices.

Given that we induce pregnancy in cows to provide milk supply, is this allowed? And why are so many children and adults becoming allergic to milk?

For all forms of food, it is good to have them as a life force. By this I mean that to sustain life, the body must have food. Milk is a natural product of a mother for her baby. As being such, cow's milk was used as a substitute. Now it has gone beyond that. It is used as a delicacy that is not always required. I would say to you that you should drink coconut milk or the other things as substitute and not have so much milk. I would not say take it away altogether. But we are back to the topic of factory farming and harming the spirituality of the animal. But from that perspective, the producing of milk is not as harmful to the animal as killing it and eating its flesh. But the means of making the cow produce the milk are bad also. So although this is a complex question, I would say that you should only drink milk when you need to and not as an every day occurrence without considering from whence it came. As for the issue of people becoming allergic to the milk, I would say that this is the cause of the effect of the methods of farming used to produce the milk; from spirit and from the cow. Now I do not want you to think that spirit would send an allergy to a child because it drank the milk, more that I mean that the chemicals, injections and hormones needed to farm the cow to produce the milk is not approved and the body, spirit or whatever of the person drinking the milk retaliates. The body retaliates against the chemicals. The spirit retaliates against the method. The spirit of a baby can do so as well as an adult. The spirit may be mature and experienced, but in the body of a baby. That spirit knows the laws of karma and acts accordingly. It is not the body that is mature, but the spirit. It is cause and effect that is all.

Are some foods bad for us?

You know what you want to do, but you choose to play safe and go with the stream so to speak. It is not at all good for your body at this time to eat all things that you do. Go back to the more natural of foods and all will be well. Try and eat things that are grown on the land or that are harvested. It is not difficult for your world to grow and cultivate all that you need to survive. Much is said about eating many foods which are put before you by bad means and in hardship to living things and these need to be considered, as do all ways that man is spoiling his world. Think carefully on all these things, they are spiritually important for the development of all babies yet to be born. Think in one hundred years in your country how it has changed from when the natives fed from the land and harvested just what they needed from the seas. Now all is nearly lost in this way of living and it is sad.

The latest problem we have on our earth is about genetically modified crops. Scientists want to grow them, but the average person who understands what it entails does not

want them growing and contaminating other normal crops and destroying the environment. Last of all we do not want to eat them. Please can you tell me who is right? We know that we have to feed the starving, but at what expense? There must be another way.

Your world is a mess and that has been made by man over many generations. It is the effect to the starving people that is the cause of the people who neglected to take care of their environment, many years ago. I have told you many times that eventually the world will return to dust and then shoots of vegetation will come through and the world will be born again. Until then you all have a problem. But the main thing you are discussing here is purely the ego of the scientists in being able to create false fields of perfect crops. They have found the technology so they want to play with it. I would say to you that man should go back to basics with regard to farming crops and learn from their ancestors. The crops will be plentiful if they apply the means to grow them using natural fertilizers and other additives without having to go to using chemical warfare to the stomachs of the people. With regard to the starving countries, the same farming methods apply. They will spend many pounds to have chemically engineered crops, but not the same amount on irrigation and natural farming methods. No they will not because the profits will go to the scientists who invented the means to feed the starving, which is in fact costing the governments of these undernourished countries far more to pay the scientists than it would be to look in depth to the natural farming methods in their entirety. As to the poisoning of people by the methods of scientific engineering, then I would say to you that this is inevitable if this route were taken. Maybe not so immediately, but certainly as time goes by and the insides of the people who eat them become more acclimatized to the food.

My friend asks if by giving up those things which are abusing her body is she in fact more spiritual. Is the difference that easy?

I have told you all many times in my lessons that to abuse your body with any substance is not acceptable. Whilst I tell you that the spirit is more important than the body which you are using for your path through this life, it is also essential that you have the spirituality which is advanced enough not to succumb to any temptation which is harmful. For you to go against the laws of spirituality with the knowledge that this thing is wrong is in itself curbing your advancement. So if you look at these points, then by making herself more clean, so to speak, she is more spiritual. It proves that the karma needs this thing to happen. By being more spiritual she is better as a channel for healing. She cannot make this thing happen by wishing it to happen. But she has achieved this by listening to the words of Ishamcvan and proving that by doing as is requested, then she will be richer in body and spirit. So look for more, and try to overcome all that she knows is required.

I am not being strict and hard, I am saying these things for your own advancement, that is all.

Some people argue that our teeth and digestive systems are designed to deal with eating meat.
Are they? Not from our perspective.

I have read an article which claimed in one person's lifetime they eat an average of: 5 cattle; 20 pigs; 29 sheep and lambs; 780 chickens; 46 turkeys; 18 ducks; 7 rabbits; 1 geese and half a ton of fish. If this is an accurate assumption wouldn't becoming vegetarian mean a huge impact on the world's economy?
Yes, but that would be good. What about the impact on the spirits of all those animals, is that not worse?

Not eating meat must be the hardest test of faith.
There are many other subjects which we will discuss which will not please all of your group and this must be. You have different opinions to each other and that is not bad, so it is likely that you will disagree with your interpretation of Ishamcvan's teachings.

319

Chapter Eighteen

A Sanctuary of Learning

"You will get to a better place where you can work
totally with Ishamcvan. I cannot tell you where or
when. I can only say that this will happen."

Ishamcvan has talked lots on the concept of a spiritual
retreat type sanctuary where people can come and learn about
spirituality in a tranquil and beautifully peaceful setting. Many
people have expressed interest in hearing his words on this subject
so we are including some of his visions about the Sanctuary of
Learning in this book.

Ishamcvan's words to Aleisha about

THE SANCTUARY OF LEARNING

I would like to talk to you now about the aspect of all things
that are becoming and those things that are receding. I would
like to say to you that there is a new day with a new beginning
just around the corner. Imagine that you are in an open canoe

and you are drifting. Do not imagine the rapids ahead or the alligators in the water or the dark clouds overhead. Do not look in the rushes to see if you can see a gloomy form of a creature that may attack you, instead lie back and close your eyes and feel the warmth of the sun. Let the gentle current take the canoe and drift onwards with not a care in the world. Imagine that spirit has the paddles and is up front watching, observing, taking care on your behalf, so that when spirit sees a landing place it will stop and you can get off. Spirit will have chosen carefully the place. It will not be in a swamp to suck you down into a muddy dirty mire. It will not be in a encampment full of savages. It will not be on the edge of a waterfall in a position where you will plunge over into troubled waters. No it will be a sanctuary of a tranquil place, where you can run with bare feet across a pure field of green and smell the clear air and watch the unclouded blue sky. Then you can say you are home. The journey will be forgotten because you are there and that is all that matters. I will say to you that you must soon get into that canoe for the time is near when you must catch the tide and begin your journey.

But you will not be alone. For all those that you love will be there too and you need only to look or ask and they will appear. No it is not the world of spirit that I describe, but a world where there are the words of spirit to which you devote this journey and the outcome that must pursue. I will ask you to have strength to go and strength to arrive for it will need all of your countenance and the support of others. You need to drift. You need the solace and the sun. You need many things and these will come. I will say to you that you must give your life to spirit. I ask that you do this thing. When I say and how I say, it is important that you do. The choice is yours. But the way will be shown. I ask that you spread the words of Ishamcvan eventually so that you may help others with your words of wisdom as you have done before. Ishamcvan will speak through you. Ishamcvan is wise and will speak with forked tongue so that you have ancient wisdom with modern connotations speaking from your lips with the words of the wise spirit that is your very own.

Go in peace and reflect the purpose of all things. Never ask why me. For if you ask this thing then you are placing yourself away from the realms of spirituality and that is not a good thing. Always accept and learn, that is all that is asked of you.

THE CONCEPT

What should be done to prepare for the sanctuary for the teaching of your words?

You must plan all things as a project, not just the building. Your early planning will result in a quicker fruition when the time comes. You cannot develop, any of you, unless you are aware of your powers, your gifts and your inner sanctum of spirituality that can be shared with others. I have told you many times that a gift must not be used for profit. That is that you must never ask for money, no amount at all. To say, as you were told recently by another person, that you have to make a living to live, is not true. People will donate what they can afford. If they cannot afford then they will not have to pay. If you run things any other way, you are not working for spirit. You would be using spirit as a means to make money and doing so would exclude those who cannot necessarily afford it. The rules and laws of spirituality which were given to you as a gift from the spirit world were with no encumbrances or charges. Your welfare will be made available from spirit so that you will have all the necessities that you need.

THE BUILDING AND LOCATION

Could you describe the place as we will see it for the first time?

There is a house. It has a white roof and walls and it is

surrounded by trees to the rear and sides. It has a chimney with smoke. To the front there is some grass falling away to some water. There is a shed to the left. The shed is a fair size and has a loft. In the loft there is sleeping and below there are animal stalls. The house is old but well kept. There is a woman dressed in black in the house that welcomes you. She is kindly and reverend. She is to be your helper in your transition. For all things she is to be your guide on earth. Now let me tell you also that this house is in an area of pebbles and rocks. There is springy grass in-between the rocks, which are not in the water. The one tree, which stands near the water, has been used by Native Indians as a walk marker for so many generations. We will say that it has been touched by spirit many times. That is where you will be.

THE TEACHERS, HEALERS & HELPERS

What are we all doing in the sanctuary?

It will be a place of learning, healing and peace. I will say to you that all of you will do different things, but not all the time, you will come and go as required. Some days you will have classes and others one to one healing or helping people. It will progress as to necessity.

Do you have words about the actual spiritual teaching we will be doing?

There is one other point that we must get straight before we go any further and that is with respect to the time of understanding and the time of teaching. You must understand all things spiritual, all of you, before you attempt to teach. I want you to learn quickly and thoroughly, but this is not possible. You must re-read the lessons until you are all aware of each aspect thoroughly. Not lightly but thoroughly. You must never hesitate in answer to a question. You must be confident of the answer. Spirit will speak through you. If you are not conversant then you will fluster and stutter and get in a fuss and not listen to the words of spirit when we speak to you.

Those people in your world who are eager to learn the natural laws of the universe can be helped by you and this is the purpose of everything that we bring to you from the world of spirit. We bring you the laws and the time is now right for you to pass them on to others who are ready to listen.

Who will be at the sanctuary?

Most of the key people, who have been involved with my work with you to date, will in some way be involved with the sanctuary. It will be strange how they will all come and be part of everything.

Will you help us help people?

I will guide you. Where will you find sanctuary? I will show you. How will you cope? I will give you strength. How will you be able to converse? I will speak through you. How will the others of your group be able to do these things also? I will tell you. But they will not do as you and you will not do as any of them. They will all do different from each other. But the message will be the same. The meaning is the same and so is the simplicity of the message of Ishamcvan. But you will be the recorder - the scribe - and therefore the author indirect.

Do you want there to be other people helping at this building? Healers, therapists, people doing yoga, etc.

Yes. There will be facilities for them too. Providing they are spiritual believers, that is. There will not be room for people who do not understand amongst those who teach the words of Ishamcvan and practice his laws. If that is the case then those people must themselves be first in the role of pupil until they are enlightened enough to repeat all my words with ease and understanding. Then they can heal or talk or be of comfort. Until then they may not understand enough to react in the correct way even though they think they have the understanding. It will be, do not worry, for we will guide people too into their positions.

Do you think that the plan we have in place with other people helping in the healing centre is correct to your plans too?

Yes and no. It is important that the harmony be there for not only yourselves and your helpers, but for your 'patients' too for they are there to come to terms with the message of spirituality. If the harmony is not there between you all, then this will not happen. There must be no stress, no disbelief and no misunderstanding. The words of Ishamcvan, which are the words of spiritual existence, are the truth and are the light which all of you should follow.